Chaosmos

SUNY Series, The Margins of Literature
Mihai I. Spariosu, editor

Chaosmos

Literature, Science, and Theory

PHILIP KUBERSKI

State University of New York Press

Published by
State University of New York Press, Albany

©1994 State University of New York

All Rights Reserved

Printed in the United States of America

For information, address the State University of New York Press,
State University Plaza, Albany, NY 12246

Production by Bernadine Dawes
Marketing by Fran Keneston

Library of Congress Cataloging-in-Publication Data

Kuberski, Philip.
    Chaosmos : literature, science, and theory / Philip Kuberski.
        p.   cm. — (SUNY series, the margins of literature)
    Includes index.
    ISBN 0-7914-1913-4 (hc). — ISBN 0-7914-1914-2 (pb)
    1. Philosophy in literature. 2. Literature, Modern—20th century—
History and criticism. 3. Literature and science. I. Title.
II. Series.
PN49.K78   1994
809'.93384—dc20
                                                        93-44752
                                                           CIP

1 2 3 4 5 6 7 8 9 10

For Claudette Sartiliot

ᴕ—*Contents*

Acknowledgments

I would like to thank those who commented on earlier drafts of
this book: the anonymous readers at SUNY Press; Katherine
Hayles; and my teachers, friends, and colleagues Alexander
Gelley, Dennis Foster, Frederick Dolan, and James Hans. I owe
special thanks to Claudette Sartiliot for commentary and cor-
rections from the first draft to the last.

Grateful acknowledgment is given to Harcourt, Brace, and
Co. for permission to quote from the following copyrighted
works: excerpts from "The Waste Land" in *Collected Poems
1909–1962*, © 1936 by Harcourt, Brace, and Co, © 1954, 1963
by Harcourt, Brace, and Co, reprinted by permission of the
publisher. Excerpt from "Burnt Norton" in *Four Quartets*, ©
1943 by T. S. Eliot and renewed 1961 by Esme Valerie Eliot,
reprinted by permission of Harcourt, Brace, and Co. Grateful
acknowledgment is also given to Alfred A. Knopf for permission to quote from *The Collected Poems of Wallace Stevens* © 1954
and *The Changing Light at Sandover* by James Merrill © 1992.

∽—*Preface*

Despite the apparently pervasive critique of empirical and idealist attitudes that characterizes contemporary critical theory, we are still governed by the essentially reductive and divisive categories of the Cartesian heritage. We are still, despite the volumes of criticism devoted to postmodernity, enmeshed in the values of modernity. The axis of this commitment to modernity is the generally undisturbed faith, even among progressive social and aesthetic theorists, in the worldview constituted by scientific-capitalist culture: that the world is a vast, essentially meaningless machine, variously "constructed" by different "discourses" throughout history, or an array of resources whose only purpose is exploitation for human use. It is a worldview that equates short-sighted technical and social manipulation with knowledge and sometimes truth. This study is based on the premise that we should rethink our fundamentally suspicious attitudes about the natural world, and question whether it is in fact, as we have been assured for centuries, truly alien and merely the raw material for evolutionary change and human fictions.

Neither the historical nor the deconstructive strains of contemporary theory, however interwoven, have fully confronted the

1

revolutions in modern science and the implications they have for our understanding of human form-making in general. Both tend to accept the late modern, existentialist vision of a cosmos in which human fictions are fundamentally alien to natural processes. Given this ideological vision of the world, we supposedly can choose between the abyss revealed by deconstructive analysis and the determinate ground of history, as well as all the critical positions in between.[1]

Georg Lukács foreshadowed and prejudiced this argument when he posed the opposition between Franz Kafka, made to represent the ahistorical perspective on human existence (the Heideggerian "thrownness into-being"), and Thomas Mann, made to represent the historical perspective on human beings as socially constructed.[2] Yet it was Mann who began his novel sequence *Joseph and His Brothers* with these words: "Deep is the well of the past. Shall we not say it is bottomless?"[3] What if, Mann supposes, the abyss and history are coextensive? If this is so, then we cannot really choose between resolute historical analysis and a pursuit of weightless linguistic traces: we cannot step out of our own feet.

Indeed the play of determinacy and indeterminacy is everywhere, from the shifting patterns and molecules in our bodies to the circulation of signifiers that form the shifting patterns of human science, language, history, and criticism. Whether one turns to Werner Heisenberg, James Joyce, Jacques Derrida, or Lao Tsu, one sees this interpenetration of disorder and order, chance and necessity, improvisation and adherence, differentiation and relationship. The world is a continual coincidence of "quantum weirdness" and classical determinism. And the familiar phenomena of everyday life, like dripping faucets, cigarette smoke, rushing streams, the weather, have been found by the new sciences of chaos to behave unpredictably while describing, when graphed, stunningly beautiful and truly strange patterns that indicate an uncanny kind of order within disorder. With these insights recent scientists have begun to reconceive the relationship between chance or stochastic processes in biology and the appearance, formation, and evolution of life forms. Our own bodies, and other natural forms, may be understood someday in terms of "chaotic" patternings.

This study argues that certain works of literature, theory, and science forecast and confirm the shift from a modern to a truly postmodern culture. My objection to the conceptually amorphous, but tonally consistent, utterances taken to be "post-modern" or to describe "postmodernism" is that they are not sufficiently "after" or "other" to warrant the prefix. In this book I have attempted to describe elements in twentieth-century literature and science that are. In a few words, I have attempted to bring deconstructive and totalizing procedures and perspectives into a relationship that will be neither deconstructive per se nor totalized per se. Although I have drawn on a number of theorists in the course of this book, I have not attempted to construct a single and exclusionary model of the literary text or of the dynamic world and self from which it emerges.

The structural and thematic focus of the book is the paradoxical coincidence of order and disorder, cosmos and chaos, apparent within the atom but also within analogous nuclear sites such as the self, the word, and the world. The term I have chosen to describe and dramatize these coincidences is taken from *Finnegans Wake:* by "chaosmos" I mean a unitary and yet untotalized, a chiasmic concept of the world as a field of mutual and simultaneous interference and convergence, an interanimation of the subjective and objective, an endless realm of chance which nevertheless displays a persistent tendency toward pattern and order. Everything in the world can be seen as chaosmic: the subatomic microworld may not be susceptible to particular determinism but in the macroworld of large-scale objects Newton's laws remain in force; the conception of a human being involves the combination of two strands of DNA in which chance and law interact to initiate epigenesis along certain fixed lines while remaining conditioned by the environment; and poems are composed (and sometime seem to compose themselves) according to the play of chance and the emergent necessities of pattern, just as a reader never quite reads the "same" poem each time he returns to it.

In exploring and mapping this chaosmos, I have found it necessary to emphasize significant convergences between literary and philosophic, deconstructive and organistic, Eastern and Western, scientific and humanist points of views. Thus in order to facilitate the discussion and to maintain a workable intellectual context my treatment of literary works is intertextual, my use of Buddhist, Hindu, and ancient Egyptian perspectives illustrative, and my account of events in twentieth-century philosophy and science sometimes more conceptual and narrative than analytic and critical. I have only suggested the technical, philological context of Asian studies, and the institutional problematics, studied by historians and sociologists of science, involved in the legitimation of scientific truth.[5]

My purpose throughout has been to provide a new context in which to understand how a number of prominent twentieth-century literary texts form a coherent critique and alternative to a dualistic conception of reality. In doing so I have drawn on specific developments in twentieth-century science and philosophy precisely in order to undermine the ideology and worldview that science since the seventeenth century has engendered. Although the line is a fine one, and sometimes invisible, I hope it is clear that when I talk about Cartesianism or modernism or scientific dualism, I am primarily interested in the ideological extensions of scientific research into a worldview rather than the professional and technical activities of scientists.

Chapter I, "Towards Chaosmos," describes the central values of modernity (the material or mechanical universe, the isolated self, and the pure or unmediated sign) and then presents a critique of these values through the work of Werner Heisenberg, Gregory Bateson, Michel Foucault, Ilya Prigogine, and other scientific and intellectual pioneers of recent decades. These scientists and philosophers indicate that the ideological assumptions of scientific materialism and determinism have persisted even after the weakening of their foundations in Newtonian physics by the advent of quantum mechanics and the theory of relativity. In postulating a poetics of chaosmos, this chapter draws on a wide range of sources, from cybernetics to chaos theory, but centers on this paradoxical coincidence of order and disorder that I am calling, after Joyce, "chaosmos."

Chapter II, "Joycean Chaosmos and the Self-Organizing World," explores *Finnegans Wake* and the shift away from the modern perspective, from a Eurocentric to a global context, through the analysis of a "dream text" that presents a planetary economy of realities, subjectivities, and languages. Joyce's book assimilates the philosophic consequences of twentieth-century physics and prognosticates several postmodern scientific hypotheses that seek to transcend the objectivist categories of Cartesian thought. Joyce thus employs a technique of verbal fission to dismantle the material universe of European scientific culture and a method of fusion that reconstitutes what he calls a "chaosmos." This chapter draws on a number of contemporary theorists in physics and biology—Murray Gell-Man, David Bohm, John Bell, and James Lovelock—to illustrate the relationships between these scientific and literary attempts to reimagine reality.

Chapter III, "The Chaosmic Self," examines the intertext ual relations between Indian and Western critiques of the philosophic subject and the individual ego. Tracing the reverberations of the syllable "Da" in the *Upanishads*, Freud, Eliot, Lacan, and others, this chapter demonstrates the ways in which words and subjects are articulated in an endless series of relations. Beginning and ending on a consideration of the words from the *Bhagavad Gita* that came to Robert Oppenheimer's mind following the first atomic explosion ("I am become Death, the shatterer of worlds"), this chapter extends the nuclear themes of chapter I and shows how isolated subjectivity is constituted by splitting and alienation. Through analyses of *The Waste Land*, the *Brihad-aranyaka Upanishad*, Lacan's *Ecrits*, and Forster's *A Passage to India*, one sees the eclipse of the authoritative subjectivity attributed to scientific rationalism and the appearance, at least conceptually, of *Brahman*, the Hindu principle of undifferentiated identity.

Chapter IV, "Chaosmoi," examines the meaning and the possibilities of death in the philosophies of Martin Heidegger and Jacques Derrida as a necessary aspect of any imagination of a world. For Heidegger and Derrida, death is intimately related to representation, just as "reality" and the "subject" are. Consequently, they conceptualize, imagine, and thematize death in order to introduce a gap into the general sense of what we think we know. Indeed, modern thought has tended to exclude death from serious reflections or inquiry because it represents such an obvious and crucial blind spot in its researches, one which in effect threatens all modernist certitude. For Heidegger, death is a "possibility" on the horizon of every subject which cannot be presumed or denied; it is necessarily a "part" of each subject's life. For Derrida, death is implicit in the ordinary play of language and our own daily existence is punctuated by a series of deaths and passings that are memorialized in speech and writing. Through an analysis of Norman Mailer's *Ancient Evenings* (1983), James Merrill's *The Changing Light at Sandover* (1982), and Doris Lessing's *Canopus in Argos* novels (1979–1983) this chapter explores other worlds, alternate worlds, that derive from our own but present explicit "chaosmoi" wherein the deconstructive and totalizing activities are clearly in play. Mailer's ancient Egypt, Merrill's occult worlds, and Lessing's evolutionary universe of galactic colonization are presented in what would ordinarily be regarded as less than serious, if not debased genres: the historical novel, the occult or New Age revelation channeled from the beyond, and science fiction. The fact that esteemed writers like these have used such genres is in itself indicative of the resistance of contemporary realist and expressive genres to new and sometimes stunning worldviews.

ᐱ—Towards Chaosmos

Nothing distinguishes me ontologically from a crystal, a plant, an animal, or the order of the world; we are drifting together toward the noise and the black depths of the universe, and our diverse systemic complexions are flowing up the entropic stream, toward the solar origin, itself adrift. Knowledge is at most the reversal of drifting, that strange conversion of times, always paid for by additional drift; but this is complexity itself, which was once called being. Virtually stable turbulence within the flow. To be or to know from now on will be translated by: see the islands, rare or fortunate, the work of chance or necessity.

—Michel Serres

The Situation

In 1919 Paul Valéry claimed, in an essay entitled "The Crisis of the Mind," that the civilization produced by modernity had reached its limits:

> The illusion of European culture has been lost, and knowledge has been proved impotent to save anything whatever; science is mortally wounded in its moral ambitions and, as it were, put to shame by the cruelty of its applications; idealism is barely surviving, deeply stricken, and called to account for its dreams.[1]

Modern civilization, by Valéry's account, was neither dead nor alive. It had instead entered a shadowy period of uncertainty and suspense, a period between historical epochs: "No one can say what will be dead or alive tomorrow, in literature, philosophy, aesthetics" (97). Likening the ancient names of Elam, Nineveh, and Babylon to those of France, England, and Russia, Valéry saw modernity as if already in the half-tones of antiquity, yet another ruin in a history of ruins.

7

Despite the different ways this "crisis" has been described since 1919, we can probably recognize this posthumous or uncanny era as still our own. Within the last decade the term "postmodern" has absorbed and routinized these ambivalences while also assuming an aura of novelty. The term promises a break with the values of modernity, but it maintains a reassuring relationship with it; it promises a departure, but remains bound to modernity—if by nothing more substantial than a prefix.

Jean-François Lyotard claims that the word "postmodern" is "probably a very bad term, because it conveys the idea of a historical periodization. 'Periodizing,' however is still a 'classic' or 'modern' ideal."[2] It is a "bad term," however, only if one wishes to suggest that it does indeed signify something unique, and of this Lyotard's banal description makes one increasingly dubious: "Postmodern' simply indicates a mood or better, a state of mind. . . . [It is] a change in people's relationship to the problem of meaning: simplifying a great deal, I would say that the postmodern is the sense of the absence of value in activities" (209). Compare Lyotard's description of postmodernism in 1986 with Nietzsche's definition of nihilism in 1886: "The end of the moral interpretation of the world, which no longer has any sanction after it has tried to escape into some beyond, leads to nihilism. 'Everything lacks meaning.'"[3] Like nihilism one hundred years earlier, it would appear that postmodernism is less an attempt to conceptualize a new (or different) cultural order than yet another symptom of the modern malaise described by Valéry. It is less a "post" modernism than an attenuation of modernism, a hypermodernism, characterized by a highly ironized, parodic, nearly weightless relationship to the philosophical and scientific assumptions of European modernity established by Descartes and Newton. It is for this reason that the movement has become older and older as theorists have attempted to give it intellectual definition. Jürgen Habermas, one of its major critics, thus locates the "entry into postmodernity" with Nietzsche.[4]

If philosophers like Lyotard and Habermas have shown that postmodernism, despite its recent appearance in critical discourse, is deeply involved with what used to be known as modernism,

Stochastic - random
determinism - event determined by unbroken
chain of prior occurances
Towards Chaosmos —◦ 9

perhaps the key to understanding the value of the term lies in less abstruse realms. The sociologist Todd Gitlin describes the popular meanings of postmodernism with reference to an inventory of journalistic clichés from the late seventies and eighties. Punk and new wave music and dress, for example, are an ironized form of fifties and sixties "modernity." Postmodernity, as Gitlin sees it, is counter to the romantic and utopian visions of the sixties: where the sixties exulted in LSD and the ideal of expanding vision and consciousness, the postmodern eighties' drug of choice was cocaine which, instead of giving visions, chills the brain and dries the throat. Gitlin's description of postmodernism uncovers what I believe is its basic quality: the desperate attempt to claim that parody, attenuated self-consciousness, and skepticism about meaning represent a genuine historical transformation, a new "sensibility."[5] Whether one adheres to Lyotard, Habermas, or Gitlin's definitions, one realizes that postmodernism is really a *symptom* of modernity, another symbolic rebellion—like romanticism, orientalism, nihilism, dada, beatism, and the sixties' counterculture—against the crushing power of scientific and bureaucratic modernity.

These artistic and cultural revolts against modernity failed to alter the bleaker forms of modernization, from the gradual destruction of the environment in the name of industrialization to the infantilization of public discourse and the commercialization of spiritual, aesthetic, and folk experience. Explanations for these failures, from the romantic revolt of the early nineteenth century, through utopian and socialist projects of the nineteenth and twentieth centuries, to the apparent failures of the recent counterculture to renew the ways of life available even to the fortunate few in the advanced industrial countries, seem to center on a single dilemma: modern life can offer either practical but dispiriting compromises, which simply preserve the status quo, or ideal but dangerous reorganizations of culture, which probably endanger more than they can deliver. We can decay slowly and comfortably or quickly and with style.

For Habermas, modernity remains the only viable and rational enterprise of democratic institutions and industries. It is not a depleted idea but an "unfinished project" that carries the traditional ambitions of liberal culture. To implement these values and projects, Habermas attempts to establish the protocols of a "communicative rationality" toward which modernism has been moving for centuries. Postmodernism, by contrast, is an "irrational" movement has abandoned liberal values by its commitment to a retrograde "philosophy of the subject." As a defender of the modern project, Habermas appears to picture himself as a virtuous parliamentarian resisting the advances of charismatic forces, here represented by Martin Heidegger and Jacques Der-rida, who evoke the irrational authority of nostalgia and mysticism. In this attack Habermas is ready to see Heidegger's complicity with fascism as an effect of his philosophic critique of modernity while also maintaining that Derrida's deconstruction of metaphysics is allied to "Jewish mysticism." Habermas thus implies that any critique of reason and modernity must invoke "mystical" or, again in Habermas's phrasing, "pseudo-sacral powers." Since he associates these powers with fascism, all critiques of rationality are not only irrational, ipso facto, they are also reactionary.[6] The fact that philosophers and scientists (one thinks of Whitehead and Heisenberg immediately) demonstrated the internal contradictions and paradoxes (the usual earmarks of "irrational" or "sacral" discourses) of scientific reason goes unnoticed. We are presented with the choice between the liberal consensus achieved by the merger of scientific and technical values and the dangerous prospect of fascist-mystical authorities. Habermas's argument demonstrates how modernism can always reinforce the deficiencies of "reason" with the rhetoric of coercion.

The crises of modernity, whether described by Nietzsche in 1886, Valéry in 1919, or Lyotard in 1986 have all more or less been in protest against the application of instrumental, technical reasoning to human beings and the products of their imagination. And each of these protests, and those that precede them in the romantic era, has revealed the persistent, if not always cumulative, disenchantment with the ideologies of progress and advancement promoted by those who have most to benefit from the real conditions of self-aggrandizement and exploitation that they conceal.

The project of modernization and, more importantly, the ideologies which naturalized and advanced their interests, have been breaking down for over a century. Postmodernism, as it is popularly imagined, is an impotent form of revolt because it accepts the modernist assumptions of the dilemma that Habermas presents and only simulates a response. Academic research has produced in response what could be called the political and philosophic poles of postmodernism. The political pole maintains that "history" is the sole determinant of human values and thus the analytic solvent for all reified and constituted "metaphysical" values that block the liberation of the masses. The major task of this postmodernism has been to expand the Western canon to include the discourses and perspectives of women and non-European peoples and to denaturalize and exhibit the historical determinations of humanist values. Philosophic postmodernism has focused its attention on the logic of European culture and tried to show the ways that Western idealism, from Plato through Heidegger, has privileged voice, masculinity, presence, and the center at the expense of writing, femininity absence, and the margins. Philosophic postmodernism has concentrated on deconstructing the exclusionary logic of Western metaphysics in the hopes of establishing a "different" way of thinking.[7]

The ironies of this admittedly simplistic sketch are obvious: political postmodernists see philosophic postmodernists as elite or aesthetic formalists, and philosophic postmodernists see the politicians as unreconstructed modernists still thinking in logocentric terms. Both of these positions reveal their own basically conservative, modernist, Eurocentric tendencies, but in different ways. The political postmodernists may critique modern capitalist society but can only imagine a society where everyone has fair and equal access to its material benefits. Only the poverty maintained in the Third World by First World economies prevents their enjoying the benefits of a denatured global society. The philosophic postmodernists, on the other hand, are involved in an interminable critique of Western logocentricism, but nonetheless remain hypnotized by a handful of German and French philosophers and the tradition of European classics. Nietzsche,

Heidegger, Lacan, and Derrida may point elewhere—to Buddhism, or Taoism, or Vedanta, or Kabbalism, or hieroglyphic and ideogrammatic writing—but their readers and critics, for the most part, prefer to stay on the safer ground of critique rather than plunge into the dangerous currents of non-Western metaphysics and modes of thought. Despite their own suspicions about Western metaphysics, they remain strangely loyal to the narrowest line of Greco-Germanic philosophers.

Both poles of academic theory seem unable to dissociate their critiques of modern values from their commitment to the intellectual assumptions of modernist intellectual labor that remain disciplinary and critical rather than interdisciplinary and synthetic. Any movement beyond this stalemate of deconstructive complacence and political impotence will require a differentially integrated worldview that could inspire more than half-hearted or ironic intellectual work.

The ambivalence of both positions, which should not be confused with the many ways in which they are blended and balanced when articulated, derives from a certain disregard for the challenges to the ideologies of objectivity by philosophers of science and philosophizing scientists alike since the earlier decades of the century. For it is their implicit acceptance of the fundamental premises of mechanistic science, so evident in Marxian and Freudian thought, that confine critical theorists to their largely impotent position as critics of modernism. According to William Paulson, "One major reason why students of literature and society need to study cybernetics, emergence, order from fluctuation, and self-organization from noise is the potential pertinence of new kinds or concepts of causality."[8] Working only with the classical causality derived from Newtonian physics and the mechanistic presumptions of Cartesian science, intellectuals devoted to the philosophic and artistic imagination are limited in their ability to appreciate literary form and dynamics. Fixed, spatial, structural, mechanistic, and architectural models have dominated critical thinking in the twentieth century, while romantic theories, drawing on organic models and processes for aesthetics, have often been considered either naïve or simply "metaphorical."

In order to sketch the coordinates of a culture and art truly beyond the confines of modernity, this book develops a concept of organicism and self-organization which draws on often widely separated and yet intimately related realms of thought: those areas of contemporary science attempting to break with the dualistic and mechanistic vision of nature, the traditions of Hinduism, Buddhism, and Taoism which anticipated the contemporary critique of the "subject" by thousands of years, poststructuralist and deconstructive analysis which undermines the textual ground for various idealisms, and the literary text as a complex formalization of possible worlds. This book has developed as an intertextual and interdisciplinary linkage of these various challenges to modernity. More than isolated challenges, however, they also form an alternative perspective, a countermodernism, which centers on the idea of a self-organizing world. Scientists such as Ilya Prigogine, Gregory Bateson, David Bohm, Erich Jantsch, Humberto Maturana, and Francisco Varela have questioned and moved beyond the assumptions of mechanization and objectivity that guide modern science and technology. Rather than working strictly in the traditions of Judeo-Christian and Cartesian dualism, these scientists conceive the world in fluid, self-organizing terms that suggest Taoist process at least as much as Newtonian mechanics. In moving towards this self-organizing view of the universe, these scientists break with a pronounced Western perspective that views nature as essentially brute matter, stuff, objectivity awaiting the formative intelligence of a God, a set of laws, a language, or a technology.

According to the historian of science Joseph Needham, Western science was insufficiently detached from its own religous and philosophical traditions to ever achieve its ideal of a purely rational and objective perspective on nature: "Europeans suffered from schizophrenia of the soul, oscillating for ever unhappily between the heavenly host on one side and the 'atom and the void' on the other."[9] By contrast, Needham writes, "The Chinese world-view depended upon an entirely different line of thought. The harmonious cooperation of all beings arose, not from the order of a superior authority external to themselves, but from the fact that they were all parts in a hierarchy of wholes forming a cosmic and organic pattern" (36). Indeed Needham has argued that organicism is quite alien to the Judeo-Christian and Greek origins of Western thinking. As it manifested itself in Western philosophy and science, as well as the romantic movement, organicism required a different source and Needham claims that it is directly attributable to Leibniz's studies in the Chinese nature philosophy of neo-Confucianism.[10]

Until the nineteenth century, natural science in the West was confined largely to the placing of fixed, created "natural" artifacts into fixed categories.[11] It was Darwin's great philosophical and scientific achievement to make the evolution or self-fashioning of nature acceptable to Western science by postulating a "natural selection" that had the effect of an organicist process without discarding the traditional Western idea that nature and matter were "fallen," inert, and in need of external or divine intervention in order to achieve form. Darwin could do this only by accepting a dualistic world in which individual species were understood strictly in terms of their opposition to an environment that was alien to them. The mechanics of natural selection, as developed later by the neo-Darwinians, was based on accident, chance mutations in the replication of genes, that could lead to competitive and coherent evolutionary change.

Thus the orthodox evolutionary biologist, for example, must consider the efficient cause of the symmetrical placement and structure of the eyes, together with the stereoscopic vision they make possible, to be the result of chance mutations governed by the invisible hand of evolutionary mechanics. Even Darwin was worried by the challenge that vision presented to natural selection and sought to break up the process into stages.[12] The fact that two eyes can produce the illusion of depth and thus a third dimension cannot, from an orthodox perspective, be related to the symmetrical appearance of two eyes and the simultaneous evolution and refinement of two optic nerves which take their electric impulses to the brain. To do so would be to introduce teleological considerations of a final cause into the biological world. Instead the evolutionary development of stereoscopic vision must be understood strictly in terms of the greater chances of survival that such vision confers. But only a consideration of a final cause can help one to understand the efficient cause here. How else can one understand the gradual evolution of parallel structures in two eyes that give the brain, not two confusing and contradictory visual fields, but the necessary input to form a "third" vision that deepens the seen world with a third dimension?

The natural world, according to the central dogma of neo-Darwinism, could be "self-organizing" only if the engine of organization was somehow alien to the intrinsic genetic code of an organism. Like a creating god, the agent of organization—chance—had to be extrinsic to the order of nature which could still be understood in traditional terms as brute stuff. According to the perspective of self-organization, the separation of intrinsic order and extrinsic chance is misleading: the "nature" of an organism could be seen as having or being certain "chaotic" functions which contribute to self-organization. Robert Wesson writes, "Evolution is infused with deterministic chaos, which converts stochastic molecular events into evolutionary change. Under natural selection, this implies something that may be reasonably called progress" (156).

If some contemporary scientists, artists, and philosophers have begun to see the world as a concidence of processes *and* artifacts, of self-organization *and* mechanics, of the nameless Tao of nature and the exacting Logos of mind, perhaps this indicates something more than exoticism or wish fulfillment (as is so often claimed). It is possible that the development of a post-dualistic science of chaos and complexity, of an autopoetic chaosmos, will demand such hybrid models and languages made available by the appearance, confrontation, and creative interference of once-alien cultures.

Literature and Science

Descartes' philosophic and scientific works established the primary and emblematic act of modern thought: the division between physical and spiritual forms of significance. In doing this

Descartes was merely repeating and "modernizing" the split between human beings and the world that characterizes Judeo-Christian and Platonic sources. The second of Descartes' "rules" in *Discourse on Method* is "to divide each of the difficulties that I was examining into as many parts as might be possible and necessary in order best to solve it."[13] The primary "difficulty" that Descartes confronted was the world's resistance to adequate and certain representation. Having decided that everything he had imagined knowing was not ultimately secure, Descartes set out to "divide the difficulties": "I thereby concluded that I was a substance, of which the whole essence or nature consists in thinking, and which, in order to exist, needs no place and depends on no material thing; so that this I, that is to say, the mind, by which I am what I am, is entirely distinct from the body, and even that it is easier to know than the body, and moreover, that even if the body were not, it would not cease to be all that it is" (54).

Werner Heisenberg, the physicist whose work most conspicuously returned science to a consideration of the "uncertainty" that Descartes tried to expel, describes Cartesian methodology this way: "While ancient Greek philosophy had tried to find order in the infinite variety of things and events by looking for some fundamental unifying principle, Descartes tries to establish order through some fundamental division."[14] Descartes offers his methodology in a modest fashion as a simple solution to the difficulties besetting philosophers and scientists: "I hope it will be useful for some without being harmful to any, and that my frankness will be very well received by all" (P&P 29). But this was certainly not the case, for as Heisenberg writes, "This partition has penetrated deeply into the human mind during the three centuries following Descartes and it will take a long time for it to be replaced by a really different attitude toward the problem of reality" (P&P 81). Boileau registered the immediate effects when he said that Descartes had "cut poetry's throat."

In *Madness and Civilization* (1961) Michel Foucault describes the origins of neoclassicism figuratively as the "great confinement" of the mad in asylums. More than madness was involved, however, in this rounding up of suspects: poetry, language, mind, and thought had all to be examined and disciplined by a rigorous rationalism.[15] Indeed, seventeenth-century scholars and scientists undertook a thorough examination of Renaissance, medieval, and classical traditions and enforced their decisions according to a series of divisions and categorizations—from Descartes' bifurcation of man and his world to the decapitation of Charles I, men had learned to reason with the blade of a knife. Foucault writes in *The Order of Things* (1966), "the seventeenth century marks the disappearance of the old superstitions or magic beliefs and the entry of nature, at long last, into the scientific order . . . the whole domain of the sign is divided between the certain and the probable, that is to say, there can be no longer an unknown sign, a mute mark."[16] The mass of forms and phenomena within the natural realm are thus either placed in the grid of a scientific order or banished from intellectual consideration and curiosity.

Language was the first among these troublesome elements which thrived within and without the boundaries of reason. Mathematics, although it had yet to conserve anything like moral law, seemed a preferable form of discourse. "Above all I enjoyed mathematics," Descartes writes in the *Discourse on Method*, "because of the certainty and self-evidence of its reasoning, but I did not yet see its true use and, thinking that it was useful only for the mechanical arts, I was astonished that on such firm and solid foundations nothing more exalted had been built, while on the other hand I compared the moral writings of the ancient pagans to the most proud and magnificent palaces built on nothing but sand and mud" (31). Christian theology could bolster such linguistic foundations only through "special grace from heaven." Given this situation, two things likely to happen happened: mathematics assumed a certain divine prestige, and language was subject to a severe reformation. While Descartes sought to define God through geometric formalism, natural languages were confined and reorganized. Foucault describes the development this way: "From the seventeenth century, it is this massive and intriguing existence of language that is eliminated. It no longer appears hidden in the enigma of the mark; it has not yet appeared in the theory of signification. From an extreme point of view, one might say that language in the Classical era does not exist" (79). Literature in the seventeenth and eighteenth century developed within such constraints. Poetry and drama assumed neoclassical regulations and featured chastened abstractions and allegorical plots. When the novel appeared it was guided by the rules of empirical description and linear cause and effect. Novelistic characters, like the billiard balls of Newtonian physics, were subject to the laws of action and reaction.

Imaginative writers represented a world guided by the two central values of science: abstraction and linearity. Inspired by the triumphs of mathematics and physics and influenced by the arguments of both continental rationalists and their supposed antagonists, British empiricists, European poets and, later, novelists turned from the richly complex linguistic textures of Renaissance poetry and narrative to what they supposed were neo-classical virtues. Here certainly were poetic constitutions of reality no less imaginative and bold than those of Wordsworth and Coleridge. Yet there was a difference: seventeenth- and eighteenth-century literature seemed agreeable, more or less, to the rational genius of the age. It was utterly modern in that regard.

From the seventeenth to the nineteenth century, literary language was constrained by a "neoclassical decorum" that had as much to do with mathematical abstraction and linear description as the "classical" qualities of Greek and Latin literature. According to Foucault, the romantic, symbolist, and modern movements had to begin, then, by finding their way back to a "raw being forgotten since the sixteenth century" and within such work "the being of language shines once more on the frontiers of Western culture" (44). "From the romantic revolt against a discourse frozen in its own ritual pomp, to the Mallarméan discovery of the word in its impotent power, it becomes clear what the function of literature was, in the nineteenth century, in relation to the modern mode of the being of language. . . . Literature . . . leads language back from grammar to the naked power of speech, and there it encounters the untamed, imperious being of words" (300).

By severing physical from metaphysical values, Descartes had established the terms of a persistent modern tactic, followed by Kant and others, which was to preserve the integrity of the physical sciences and metaphysical (or aesthetic) speculation by detaching one from the other. As the physical sciences, from Newton through Boltzmann and Maxwell, gained more and more prestige, precisely by ignoring the role of consciousness and life in the scheme of their laws, the metaphysical traditions were neglected and decayed. Christianity receded from serious intellectual discussion and its totalizing myths were replaced by the anti-aesthetic, atomized myths of material progress and bourgeois competition.

Since Kant and the English romantics, literary thinkers have thus tended to view the claims of literature as different in kind from those of science. Coleridge could thus write in chapter 14 of the *Biographia Literaria,* "A poem is that species of composition, which is opposed to works of science, by proposing for its *immediate* object pleasure, not truth; and from all other species (having *this* object in common with it) it is discriminated by proposing to itself such delight from the *whole,* as is compatible with a distinct gratification from each component part."[17] The most telling inference to be drawn from this celebrated passage is that "truth," having been assigned to the "work of science," is no longer understood as the relationship of the whole to its constituent parts. The New Critics, having accepted the premise that modern science was "rational" and "actual," could only "defend" or "apologize" for poetry by distinguishing its claims on us from those made by science. John Crowe Ransom made the distinction quite clear: "Science gratifies a rational or practical impulse and exhibits the minimum of perception. Art gratifies a perceptual impulse and exhibits the minimum of reason."[18] Separated from pleasure, truth is also separated from the very idea of a whole and from the "delight" which an apprehension of wholes prompts. The truth of literature has thus to be viewed in symbolic, archetypal, or hortatory terms, while the truth of science is seen as literal and actual but, as a consequence, divorced from delight and pleasure. The Platonic coupling of the beautiful and the true having been broken, modernists must choose between pleasure and truth, fictive wholes or sundered facts. The philosophical and social category of the "aesthetic" thus served to substantiate an opposing perceptual category which in the modern world has come to be called the "real," the focus and preserve of scientists. "Literature" in its familiar modern sense was thus born the moment poetry renounced claims to any but "fictive" truth.

Modernist literary historians tend to put the best face on the segregation and trivialization of art by claiming that Kant, by establishing the constituitive powers of the individual mind, had empowered the poet. With this epistemological authority, the poetic imagination could breathe significance into the world while the metaphysical fictions of Christianity were yielding to the emergent culture of industrial and consumer capitalism. Ironically, literary historians, like Douglas Bush and Basil Willey, who sought to maintain the virtues of poetry in the face of modern scientific claims, often accepted the idea that science was inimical to poetry.[19] Since the principles of modern science were not in doubt, this interpretation had the effect of marginalizing the poetic or aesthetic project of dramatizing the relationship of parts to wholes, of subjectivity and objectivity.

Science is of course not inimical to poetry (as I hope to show), but science has changed the way critics have described the value and purpose of art. Thus in the sixties Frank Kermode, following Wallace Stevens, proposed that we view literature as "fictions" of totalization that we enjoy even as we understand their fictiveness.[20] The world rendered according to the various discourses of scientific "truth" appeared to be utterly chaotic, insignificant, perhaps absurd: "fictions" were required to discern any coherent meaning in it—which is to say any sense, however partial, of totality. When Thomas Pynchon's novels appeared in the sixties this tradition achieved its reductio ad absurdum: in *V.*, *The Crying of Lot 49*, and *Gravity's Rainbow* the "world" outside and beyond individual consciousness was revealed to be so filled with random but irrefutable facts, so complex and yet so real, that any attempt to perform an aesthetic reduction or a holistic construction of it was either a form of paranoia or the unlikely discovery of a vast and complex historical conspiracy.[21]

Indeed, New Critical formalism and the theory of "fictions" were the last attempts to equate the aesthetic with the hypothetical and the unreal: in a sense they were the most recent platonism. The poststructuralist critiques insist that philosophy, science, history, and literary formalism are all discursive in varying degrees and thus characterized by aesthetic and rhetorical premises and practices. All knowledge is seen, according to the strongest of these critiques, to be aesthetic in the sense that it has an irreducible metaphorical and paradigmatic center.[22] Although defenders of formalism and the humanist tradition in letters, like Murray Krieger, tended to see poststructuralism as a threat to poetry's supposedly unique function among all human discourses, poststructuralists were actually providing a general aesthetics which could establish links between the sciences and the arts and provide the intellectual tools for a chaosmic analysis.[23]

Even as the New Critics and humanists in general maintained the modernist valuation of science the better to establish the values and uses of poetry, the psychological and physical sciences had begun to register the limits of scientific representation. The separation of aesthetic and scientific representation established by Descartes became increasingly difficult to maintain. Physics, the fundamental science and the inspiration to the others, went through a series of crises and revolutions which have radically challenged the division between mental and physical experience, while psychoanalysis claimed that consciousness and reason are features of a wider psychic economy which includes the unconscious. Physics was in the forefront of this growing awareness of the aesthetic dimension of scientific reasoning precisely because it confronted both the most basic and the most abstract of phenomena: the nature of space, time, matter, and movement.

The blurring of the distinctions between the scientific and the aesthetic, objectivity and perspective, as well as the meaningful and the real, first revealed in the theories of relativity and quantum mechanics, indicated a gradual movement away from the modern assumption that nature could and ought to be representable in a single code or register. This weakening of the fundamentally abstract and linear ambitions of modern science led to current theoretical views describing the multiple temporalities, spaces, and laws observable simultaneously in the world. After Newtonian physics replaced Aristotelian physics, the general enlightened view was that all movement should be subject to a single set of laws. In principle, according to Laplace, a thorough knowledge of present conditions would lead to a knowledge of all future movements and developments. But as Newtonian principles have been supplemented by thermodynamics, the theory of relativity, quantum mechanics, and chaos theory it seems— despite efforts to postulate a Grand Unified Theory—that physics can no longer be conceived as a fundamental science, if by that one means a singular and inviolable set of uniform principles.

It is this very emergence of *complexity* and *plurality* in science, William Paulson argues, that reopens the dialogue with literature cut off, as Foucault reminds us, precisely because of the complexity, density, and texture of literary language: "In an apparent paradox, the current literature-science dialogue . . . is made possible by the very properties of literature that long made it seem the antithesis of a scientific object."[24] In *Finnegans Wake* especially one sees the triumphant emergence of the "imperious being of words," complexity, interdisciplinarity, just as one sees it in the deconstructive projects of Jacques Derrida. No longer kicked upstairs into the transcendental attic, literature can be seen as both theory and example of the chaosmic, plural, and self-organizing world.

New Reckonings

Gregory Bateson's most comprehensive exposition of conclusions drawn from fifty years of research in anthropology, psychology, communications, and cybernetics appears in *Mind and Nature: A Necessary Unity* (1979). The title indicates how closely Bateson's analysis and speculations on the nature of mind is a direct response to Cartesianism. For Bateson, the advent of scientific culture and the sequestration of philosophy and literature within humanism was a fundamental error. "I hold to the presupposition that our loss of the sense of aesthetic unity was, quite simply, an epistemological mistake. I believe that that mistake may be more serious than all the minor insanities that characterize those older epistemologies which agreed upon the fundamental unity."[25] Bateson summarizes this mistake in these terms:

> a. the Cartesian dualism separating "mind" and "matter."
> b. the strange physicalism of the metaphors which we use to describe and explain mental phenomena—"power," "tension," "energy," "social force," etc.
> c. our anti-aesthetic assumption borrowed from the emphasis which Bacon, Locke, and Newton long ago gave to the sciences, viz. that all phenomena (including mental) can and shall be studied and evaluated in quantitative terms. (240)

These traits of science led to the modern view that mankind exists as an inexplicable superfluity in an otherwise ordered universe, a kind of passenger upon or within material and mechanical vehicles—the earth and the body. Through excluding mind from the arena of scientific thought, and considering undisciplined perception as a contaminant of truth, reality and objective experience were produced, and so too the "underlying notion of a dividing line between the world of living . . . and the world of non-living billiard balls and galaxies" (7). Although this division led to the industrial and technical transformation of the world which we all find so convenient and necessary, it also effectively assigned the "pleasure" which comes from understanding the relationship of parts and wholes to the aesthetic or false discourses of religion, philosophy, and art.

In their places Western industrial capital eventually erected a massive consumer culture, which imbues language, dress, identity, and purpose with the discourses of "products," but which has also provided security, convenience, and the creation and temporary satisfaction of desires—at least for those able to purchase them. Although these desires are spiritual or subjective in nature, the satisfactions offered are invariably material and objective.

Thus the fundamental argument of consumer culture, which is the usual expression of modern liberal values (or the lack of them), is that the desire for wholeness can only be satisfied by more and newer products, works of art, and critical trends. Modernity thrives on this endlessness of production, guided by demands for novelty and originality, values which are still largely unquestioned, however much critical theory in the last several decades has cast doubt on them.

This confusion between quantitative and qualitative conceptions of wholeness is characteristic of the schizoid reasoning engendered by Cartesianism. Bateson claims that this legacy has cost us every myth, indeed every conception and possibility of aesthetic unity: "We have lost the core of Christianity. We have lost Shiva, the dancer of Hinduism whose dance at the trivial level is both creation and destruction but in the whole is beauty" (19). In the place of myths of unity, modernists and "postmodernists" thrive on plans, projects, and programs which begin by offering valid critiques of past regimes of value but must defer offering one themselves as long as they can, knowing as they do that it is at that moment that the market of ideas will demand new criticism and plans. For it is as a critique that intellectual work earns its reputation, just as it is by originality that works of art achieve theirs.

There are of course good precedents for this skepticism: the "aesthetic unities" proposed by Pound and Eliot or attempted by Hitler and Mussolini have innoculated most intellectuals against the infection of aestheticized politics. Even so, what Bateson proposes is much less and potentially much more than these totalitarian solutions. He is proposing that we re-evaluate what we mean by our minds and what we mean by nature, and determine how wise we are in rejecting the very possibility of thinking in terms of wholes. Although we have all been conditioned to view the "loss" of Christ or Shiva as nostalgia for imaginary Edens and urged to agree to consensual realities which preserve the concert hall, the museum, and the theatre for our aesthetic requirements, we should not ignore Bateson's calm assertion that modern culture is not the result of a mythic fall—simply the history of an error.

The ideologies engendered by the scientific revolution can be seen within the tradition of artificial dualisms forced upon the continuum of humanity and world which give rise to powerfully repressive or aesthetically impoverished cultural epochs. Like Judaism, Platonism, and Christianity, all of which divided mind from matter in order to constitute an external, immaterial, and eternal realm of pure significance far from human praxis, modern science sought to decipher the eternal laws hidden within the workings of nature and represent them in the atemporal discourse of mathematics. These cultural discourses all presuppose "falls" into contingency and chaos, into the physical realm of unending transience, in order to explain the gap between the significance they seek and the existence they represent. The fall is a fall outside of a privileged discourse which has been abstracted and placed within a sacred or eternal dimension in order to maintain its purpose as the source of human significance. Scientific laws, however, represented an advance beyond the Judeo-Christian scheme: unlike the will of God, they could never be violated. By legislating truly immutable laws within nature, scientific culture seemed to require a kind of agent of order or an ontological tendency within matter toward order which it consistently denied in practice.

Bateson believes that a reconciliation between human beings and their world can occur only through an epistemological revolution, one that would necessarily nullify what I have described as the modernist dilemma. Instead of privileging one of the traditional poles of modern epistemology, whether it be subjective or objective, or imagining their ideal fusion or transcendence, Bateson claims instead that neither of them are in the slightest sense real. For Bateson, the world is not a duel between fictitious mental orders and blind material processes, for the simple reason that they are aspects of one another. Bateson's entire argument is based on the premise that "mental function is immanent in the interaction of differentiated 'parts.' 'Wholes' are constituted by such combined interactions" (104). When computer scientists claim that a computer is "intelligent" or that it is "conscious," they are working from a similar premise, although somehow when the idea that mind is an interaction of parts and wholes is applied to a machine it seems hardheaded and antihumanist and when it is applied to an ecology it seems softheaded and irrational. This is probably because we tend to see natural organizations as chance constructs of evolution which sustain us and give us pleasure and machines as expressions of the human mind which work for us and solve problems. For Bateson, however, mind and nature are aspects of the same patterning: "the pattern which connects is a metapattern. It is a pattern of patterns. It is that metapattern which defines the vast generalization, that indeed, it is patterns which connect" (12).

Cartesianism has so imbued our thought with the conviction of its own immateriality, its own difference from the "outside," that Bateson's proposition seems nonsensical. Kantian epistemology holds that such patternings are projections of the Understanding, and that whatever noumenal truth there may be in them will remain a mystery to mortals. But for Bateson, the world is not held together by a physical framework of reality which must perforce exclude the image-making or spiritual dimension of mind. The world, from atoms to people, from people to planet, is held together because of the logic of its patterning, just as planets, people, and atoms form a world. The mind that perceives and is composed of patterns is necessarily natural, just as nature is essentially mental in the sense that it is holistic. The "laws" which describe/guide the movement of the planets in their orbits, no less than the laws which describe/guide the beating of our hearts, could just as well, and with as little or much anthropomorphism, be called "narratives." Bateson writes:

> The fact of thinking in terms of stories does not isolate human beings as something separate from the starfish and the sea anemones, the coconut palms and the primroses. Rather, if the world be connected, if I am at all fundamentally right in what I am saying, then thinking in terms of stories must be shared by all minds, whether ours or those of redwood forests and sea anemones. (14)

In place of the antagonistic opponents of modern epistemology, which derive from Judeo-Christian conflicts between human will and divine law, Bateson sees a self-regulation or cybernetic system of mind. For subjectivity and objectivity, then, Bateson substitutes his conception of mind, "an aggregate of interacting parts or components" (102). The logic of these interacting parts is narrative itself, "a little knot or complex of the species of connectedness which we call relevance" (14). Narrative is not, then, syn- ony-mous with "fiction" but with the logic of relationship, of chance and order, evident in the conception of a thought or a fetus, the development of a story or an embryo, the evolution of a genre or a species. The boundaries between these instances of form making are not as secure as modern aesthetics would assure us, especially when we begin to doubt the reality of individual subjectivities, styles, and thoughts. "The boundaries of the individual, if real at all," Bateson writes, "will be, not spatial boundaries, but something more like the sacks that represent *sets* in set theoretical diagrams" (146).

Where contemporary narrative theorists typically emphasize the ways in which human texts reduce and tint the text of the world, Bateson sees human texts as instances of the larger narratives in which our bodies and minds, the cells of crustaceans and our cells form a continuous, however, intertextual, story about our relatedness to everything else. The modernist strategy, of which such narrative theories are a part, consisted primarily in alienating the self (as well as myths and stories) in order to construct a vast illustration of its destructive desire for objectivity. It is this worldview that produced existentialist notions of a universe isolated from the contaminating significance of any narratives but those featuring entropy and absurdity.

According to Stephen Toulmin, Bateson's work "gives us a tantalizing glimpse of what, in the new era of 'postmodern science,' an overall vision of what humanity's place in nature will have to become."[26] This new era, Toulmin believes, will be characterized by the

death of the spectator. . . . Within our own "postmodern" world, the pure scientist's traditional posture as *theoros*, or spectator, can no longer be maintained: we are always—and inescapably—participants or agents as well. Meanwhile, the expansion of scientific inquiry into the human realm is compelling us to abandon the Cartesian dichotomies and look for ways of "reinserting" humanity into the world of nature. (255)

Toulmin explains how the "death of the subject" insisted upon by structuralist and poststructuralist theorists and deplored by defenders of humanism will necessarily lead to a more profound and integrated role of subjectivity within the natural world. Conceived as a "spectator," the subject is an artificial band of the spectrum which joins human beings via the world to other human beings. Nostalgia for the tragic or existentialist mask of the Cartesian ego should not distract us from recognizing that the death of the subject is overdue, and presents us with an opportunity to break with the logic of objectivity and alienation.

Neither Bateson nor Toulmin directly explains the historical and political reasons that allowed science to secure its exclusive position of authority. Ilya Prigogine, the Russian-born physicist whose work on thermodynamics won the Nobel Prize for Chemistry in 1977, and Isabelle Stengers, the French philosopher, explain in so many words: Cartesianism triumphed because it was an instrument of power. In their book *Order out of Chaos* (*La Nouvelle alliance*, 1979) Prigogine and Stengers demonstrate, through scientific and historical analyses, that modern science described a world that resembled the artifacts and automatons of human invention rather than the developing, organic world of nature. "The world of classical physics is an atemporal world which, if created, must have been created in one fell swoop, somewhat as an engineer creates a robot before letting it function alone."[27] The achievements of classical physics are inseparable, Prigogine and Stengers claim, from the "debasement of nature" "parallel to the glorification of all that eludes it, God and man" (51). The fact that Newtonian law could describe the movement of celestial bodies and earthly ones urged scientists to denature, to domesticate, and to colonize the universe with the most banal human concerns and desires: schedules, constancy, reliability. Thus "God," like a decapitated monarch, was replaced by a system of laws, and honored as an icon of a discarded universe.

Modern technology set itself the task of taking dominion over nature, as if following God's injunction to Adam, through trickery directed both against humanity and nature. Modern people could allow themselves the benefits of seizing what control they could over nature only if they imagined that their technologies of mastery served the cause of reason. In this way, transforming nature and understanding it became synonymous: rationality became defined by an acceptance of technology. Prigogine and Stengers write, "The words we still use today— machine, mechanical, engineer—have a similar meaning. They do not refer to rational knowledge but to cunning and expediency. The idea was not to learn about natural processes in order to utilize them more effectively, but to deceive nature, to 'machinate' against it—that is, to work wonders and create effects extraneous to the natural order of things" (39). This view was openly and memorably expressed in 1802 by Sir Humphry Davy in the course of a distinction between primitive and civilized man. Primitive man, Davy concludes, is "submissive to the mercy of nature and the elements," while civilized man is "informed by science and the arts, and in control of powers which may almost be called creative; which have enabled him to modify and change the beings surrounding him, and by his experiments to interrogate nature with power, not simply as a scholar . . . but as a master."[28] The equation of knowledge and domination thus becomes the irrevocable axiom of modern thinking, the irrational heart of rationality which ensures that only knowledge which contributes to the interrogation of nature deserves the name of knowledge. The rest is considered either to be proto- or pseudoscience.

While the significant was divided from the true, and consciousness separated from reality, so "life" was separated from the elements which constitute it. Classical physics contributed to modern ideology the idea that the universe was best likened to a mechanical operation from which life had unaccountably emerged, because in a sense it was superfluous. The physical universe and organic nature were constituted by the same atomic fabric, but they inhabited, so to speak, different kinds of time. The universal nature of classical physics is outside of historical time, which is to say that all dynamic relations exist in terms of lawfulness, determinism, and reversibility, not in terms of historical, one-directional time. Astronomical events could, in other words, be described in reverse by the very same means. The movements of planets, like billiard balls, can be reliably plotted whether they move forward or backward, here or there, now or a million years from now. But living things are a different matter. Contrary to the eternal reversibility of things, organisms develop historically, both as individuals and species. While the universe supposedly moves toward greater and greater disorder (or entropy), the living world has moved from simplicity toward greater and greater organization. The rise of organic systems may not violate the second law of thermodynamics, but it does contradict the ideological assumptions which it has inspired.

Modernism as an ideology was largely constituted by setting aside, segregating, confining, and repressing the less orderly, which is to say the less "predictable" aspects of physical, organic, and human behavior. This strategy was largely successful because it was found that society could function quite well, for the time being at least, according to mechanical reality. For the timeless universe of Newtonian law did not require the intervention of a God, but neither could it admit the actions of a living physicist, a thinking organism still unregulated by the laws he observed in the world around him. Prigogine and Stengers explain that the very universality of this view excluded humanity itself as a knowing subject, for behind the Newtonian world machine was Isaac Newton, an acting, desiring subject who spent a good deal of his time, we now recognize, involved in alchemical research because he considered physics too narrow to describe the wonder of God's creation. "Manipulation and measurement are essentially irreversible. *Active* science is thus, by definition, extraneous to the idealized, reversible world it is describing" (61). In this way classical physics established the exemplary version of what Theodore

Roszak calls the "strange interplay of objectivity and alienation," the way in which modernism satisfied a desire for certainty by accepting a position outside the world itself. The certainty of modern physical sciences absolutely required a metaphysical position for the physicist himself. Alexander Pope inadvertently revealed this relationship in his proposed epitaph for Newton: "Nature and Nature's laws lay hid in night:/God said, let Newton be! and all was light." Newton's authority derives from God, and thus his "revelations" are in effect metaphysical in their origins, however physical in their reference. The modern spectator, exemplified by the scientist, is not, however, able to escape the consequences of the pact. Prigogine and Stengers imply that the apparently bright prospects of Cartesian and Newtonian science darkened when it excluded humanity from its scope or constituted it by means of mechanical reality. "To deny time—that is, to reduce it to a mere deployment of a reversible law—is to abandon the possibility of defining a conception of nature coherent with the hypothesis that nature produced living beings, particularly man. It dooms us to choosing between an antiscientific philosophy or an alienating science" (96).

This is the philosophical and scientific dilemma that has become increasingly clear in the West since the romantic revolution and the formulation of the laws of thermodynamics. These cultural and scientific phenomena of the nineteenth century shared a distrust of the timeless world of neoclassical art and science. Where Leibniz and Pope, for instance, offered explanations of how universal and local cultural values were joined in this "best of all possible worlds," Blake, Hölderlin, Hegel, Darwin, and Boltzmann describe the world as historical process. Prigogine and Stengers describe this historical change as a change in metaphors: "For classical mechanics the symbol of nature was the clock; for the Industrial age, it became a reservoir of energy that is always threatened with exhaustion. The world is burning like a furnace; energy, although being conserved, also is being dissipated" (111). The clock-universe reflected the advances of mathematics and civil organization in the seventeenth century, just as the world-furnace reflected the age of steam engines and revolution: in both cases natural orders are quite unconsciously modeled on the most recent human inventions. As physics changes so do metaphors, and with their use the universe begins to appear differently: the cold, galactic order of the Newtonian world ignites. The fire spreads to the aesthetic realm with Blake's fiery Orc, just as it burns through neoclassical decorum in the paintings of Turner and Goya. Hegel's *Phenomenology of Spirit* (1806) discards the clock-work mechanics of Kant for the historical engine of dialectic progression, just as the revolutions in France will spread throughout Europe. Looking over the bourgeois revolution propelled by similar forces, Marx and Engels could write in 1848: "All that is solid melts into air, all that is holy is profaned, and man is at last compelled to face with sober senses his real conditions of life and relations with his kind."[29] All of these events, representing either one movement or several, dramatize the general weakening of the simple idea of order derived from Euclidean geometry and Platonic abstraction. From this point forward disorder would necessarily be seen as a part of order.

Thermodynamics became what Prigogine and Stengers call a "science of complexity" because it demonstrates the way in which equally valid, mathematical descriptions of the world could, counter to classical logic, contradict without conflicting with one another: "A physical theory had been created that was every bit as mathematically rigorous as the mathematical laws of motion but that remained completely alien to the Newtonian world. From this time on, mathematics, physics, and Newtonian science ceased to be synonymous" (104). Thermodynamics, in other words, did not invalidate Newtonian law, but it offered a perfectly scientific description of heat which contradicted the Newtonian world picture. Physics thus became more and more scholastic in the sense that its validity was limited to certain artificial categories: Newton could account for earthly and celestial mechanics, thermodynamics could describe the dynamics of heat while neither of them could begin to account for the physics of life. Life contradicted both Newtonian reversibility and the second law of thermodynamics, which calls for the maximization of entropy or disorder (although this disorder should not be confused with simple randomness: heat death, the projected outcome of entropy, would be characterized by a final and perfect distribution of energy). As opposed to Newtonian bodies or thermodynamic heat, "life" seemed to elude physics entirely and was left to the natural sciences until Darwin and Mendel uncovered the evolutionary and genetic aspects of organisms. From that point in the nineteenth century to the present, the appearance of life could not be accounted for by physical theory and became the province of biochemistry which, since the discovery of DNA, has tried to convert life into the material implementation of a natural code. Prigogine and Stengers, after reviewing these developments, wonder: "What significance does the evolution of a living being have in the world described by thermodynamics, a world of ever-increasing disorder? What is the relationship between thermodynamic time, a time headed toward equilibrium, and the time in which evolution toward increasing complexity is occuring?" (129) In advance of a major scientific breakthrough, one can only assume, like Serres (after Einstein), that universal time is a delusion, and the world is characterized by incommensurate temporalities.

Measurement first established and then undermined the universal claims of modern physics. It was science's own aspirations toward a fundamental knowledge of matter which exploded Newtonian law and pointed toward an era where subject and object were joined. In 1926 Alfred North Whitehead claimed that the advances of quantum physics required a thorough revision of scientific terms and values: "The progress of science has now reached a turning point. The stable foundations of physics have broken up: also for the first time physiology is asserting itself as an effective body of knowledge, as distinct from a scrapheap. The old foundations of scientific thought are becoming unintelligible. Time, space, matter, material, ether, electricity, mechanism, organism, configuration, structure, pattern, function all require reinterpretation."[30] Moreover, Whitehead claimed that such terms had never been secure or properly defined, because science began as and continued to be "an antirational movement, based upon naïve faith" in "the ultimate fact of an irreducible brute matter, or material, spread throughout space in a flux of configurations" (16–17).

Prigogine and Stengers reiterate Whitehead's views some fifty years later: "We subscribe to the view that classical science has now reached its limit" (54), but they are also ready to outline the requirements of a postclassical science, a science reconciled with the dimension of time, aware of the limited nature of so-called "universal" laws, and oriented toward historical becoming instead of eternal being. Indeed the task of *Order out of Chaos* is to sketch the framework for the new alliance between physical and organic forms, between natural process and intellectual process. Within such a new arrangement, knowledge can no longer be construed strictly within the lexicon of technology that has legitimated scientific truths in the modern era. No longer would dominion over certain features of natural process be equated with understanding or knowledge, any more than the medium of a particular measurement could be equated with reality. For Prigogine and Stengers, "the wealth of reality. . . overflows any single language, any single logical structure. Each language can express only part of reality" (225). At the same time, if human beings and their subjectivity are at all real or natural, then they must not only be a part of, but essential to the structure of the world. "We believe that [these findings show] the important role intellectual constructions play in the conception of reality" (292).

But still our Cartesian presumptions are not satisfied by this conclusion. We "know" that our individual death and the extinction of humanity would not affect the movement of the earth around the sun, and the movement of the solar system within our galaxy, and our galaxy within the universe. And yet it is precisely this universe—the one we conceive as existing before or after our existences—that we feel is real. So strong is our sense of the irreality of our own lives and minds.

Bateson believes that thinking, whether conscious or unconscious, voluntary or autonomic, is not only a necessary part, it is an inevitable part of the world of process. Conception, reproduction, and maturation are not by chance terms taken from both biological and aesthetic description. Spinning a yarn, spinning a web, spinning a cocoon: these are both narrative and natural activities, although our self-consciousness about art makes us consider that aesthetic acts are only metaphoric forms of the literal activities of spiders and caterpillars. Describing the writing of *Mind and Nature* as an analogue for conception, development, and maturation, Bateson writes:

> as I was writing, mind became, for me, a reflection of large parts and many parts of the natural world outside the thinker. . . . On the whole, it was not the crudest, the simplest, the most animalistic and primitive aspects of the human species that were reflected in the natural phenomena. It was, rather, the more complex, the aesthetic, the intricate, and the elegant aspects of people that reflected nature. (5)

We are not used to considering natural form as either the transformation of a code or of formal thought, and neither are we used to considering our own thoughts as the expression of the very same transformation of a code. Our thinking is supposedly the linguistic expression of an anatomical expression of a species' expression, and so on. Scientific modernity has taught us to consider both natural language and individual thought to be unreal for the simple reason that they are all more or less different depending upon who is speaking or thinking. Through discipline and a purified formalism, however, we can all be taught to see the same vision. Only then, the modernist project insists, will we know the real.

Modern reality was constituted in response to the uncanny principle of difference. Human beings confront difference through the cognitive act which Bateson calls "abduction," the "lateral extension of abstract components of description" (157– 58). Abduction is necessary because our lives are an unending confrontation with difference, nothing but difference. "Perception operates only upon difference. All receipt of information is necessarily the receipt of *difference*" (31–32). Given this endless receipt of difference, modern science has instituted convenient but merely conventional laws of measurement which, because they can be confirmed by other measurers, give us an objective—that is to say a communal, form of knowledge. While Bateson, a practicing scientist, would certainly endorse the necessity of established forms of measurement, he does not endorse the rough translation of scientific objectivity into a cultural ideology that aligns the world as process and complexity with the clean terms of measurement. For to do away with difference also does away with relationship. Because difference, far from introducing a gap or discrepancy between real entities, is precisely the bond of relatedness that mind supplies in the form of metaphor via abduction. Thus even Derridean concepts such as *supplementarity* and *différance*, which have come to play a role in Francisco Varela's theory of autopoeisis, can be seen in this context as postulations of the interplay between deviation and convergence.[31] Modern attempts to eradicate difference are attempts, then, to eradicate the relatedness which mind supplies.

The views of Whitehead, T. S. Kuhn, Bateson, and Prigogine and Stengers are not, of course, widely or generously received by research scientists. Focused on the specific issues of their own research, they are suspicious of generalist proclamations and paradigm shifts. And there can be no doubt that conceptual arguments about science as a whole tend at times toward metaphysical or unverifiable claims. Philosophizing scientists are sometimes regarded by other scientists as past their prime, exhausted by the demands of research and anxious to reach some personal and professional conclusions unwarranted by the evidence. There is a good deal of truth to such views, but they conceal philosophical premises of their own that, because they are widely held, appear nonexistent. Anyone reading an issue of *Scientific American*, for instance, sees the interplay between mechanistic metaphors in the articles and the gee-whiz advertisements for technical and mechanical products on the intervening pages: in such a context machines begin to appear more natural and inevitable than bodies, parts more prevalent than wholes.

But the whole, that Hegel identified with the true *(Das Wahre ist das Ganze)* and that Theodor Adorno identified with the false *(Das Ganze ist das Unwahre)* is neither: it is the inevitable relationship that minds have with themselves in the world of percepts.[32] In *Holism and Evolution* (1926) Jan Christian Smuts refers to the mind as "an organ of wholes": "Mind here appears as the great creative artist. But it is more than that; for its work is no mere picture of reality, but is reality itself. It is the great archetype of the artist, and it has this pure creative power because it is but a form, a phase of the supreme activity of the universe."[33] Some fifty years later, Bateson sees the same interplay between matter and meaning: "We are discussing a world of meaning, a world some of whose details and differences, big and small, in some part of that world get *represented* in relations between other parts of that total world" (210). Any intellectual and cultural movement beyond modernism will have to recognize that the opposition between difference and identity produces relationship. But such a passage beyond modern epistemology cannot be achieved through complacent nostalgia, cynical parodism, apocalyptic quietism, aesthetic indifference, or revolutionary flourishes. "We must pass through the threat of that chaos where thought becomes impossible," Bateson warns.

Chaosmos

The Greek etymologies of "cosmos" and "chaos" alert us to certain revealing complicities. *Kosmos* primarily signifies "order," then "ornament," and finally "world " or "universe." *Chaos* signifies an "infinite space," and then by association a chasm or gulf; personified by Hesiod, it is the original condition of everything. If *kosmos* signifies both "order" and "ornament," then its order must also be compromised by the notions of superfluity, decoration, and aesthetic illustration, even pleasure: the semantic distance between "cosmos" and "cosmetic" is radically abridged by their etymologies. Signifying "infinite space," chaos must also be compromised by the fearful pleasures of the abyss and the sublime. What is explicit and yet missing in these terms are not only the reactions they provoke—the cosmos is a pleasing ornament, a cosmetic, while chaos suggests the swallowing up of all such pleasures—but also the birth of a different pleasure that comes with the extinction of the self and its comfortable sense of definition, its nagging sense of limitation.

The confusion arises from the attempt we make to deny our own methods of observation and the way we represent those observations. This in itself is an attempt to repress the ineffable nature of the world, the way it always slides away from the embrace of concepts, the perspectives of vision, and the outlines of words. Creation myths, whether one consults *Genesis*, Hesiod, or Ovid, usually begin by offering some glimpse of chaos, that yawning abyss of formlessness from which all escaped. In the telling, however, the chaos of precreation seems, if anything, more ordered than what follows. Ovid provides this paradoxical description: "Before ocean was, or earth, or heaven,/ Nature was all alike, a shapelessness,/ Chaos. . . ."[34] Such chaos seems indistinguishable from uniformity or equilibrium, the most fundamental and persistent kind of order, in which neither differentiation, shaping, nor position intrudes. Ovid describes creation as the coming of difference, distinction, position, and relationship that transforms the One into the Many. In this way order, allied with difference and relationship, is brought out of chaos, which if anything represents the unsatisfactory nature of a complete, homogeneous order or uniformity. While all this is implicit in a work like Ovid's *Metamorphoses*, Taoist texts actively affirm the interpenetration of the two. In *Myth and Meaning in Early Taoism: The Theme of Chaos*, N. J. Girardot writes, "The Taoists affirmed that the silent, hidden, or real order of the Tao embraced both chaos and cosmos, non-being and being, nature and culture."[35] Where creation myths rely on the intervention of an act of divine speech which orders the separation of cosmos from chaos and the active construction of the world as an artifact, the process myths of ancient China describe the emergence and reflexive governance of the Tao. "The secret of life," Girardot writes, "the mystical secret of salvation, is to return to the primitive chaos-order or 'chaosmos' of the Tao. In early Taoism chaos, cosmos, becoming, time, and Tao are synonymous for that which is without an Orderer but is the 'sum of all orders'" (3).

The cosmos per se is thus seen in creation myths as a material artifact, the invention of an external or divine force, the effect of speech, whereas in process myths the cosmos and chaos form a single unfolding of "chaotic" possibilities. The "fiat lux" of *Genesis* and the creating "word" *(logos)* of the John Gospel indicate a common commitment to the creative/divisive powers of speech, while the Tao spoken at the beginning of the *Tao Te Ching* is used as a polyseme meant to cancel out its own pretensions to naming the origin and "way" of the living world. Zhang Longxi translates the famous opening of the *Tao Te Ching* this way: "The *tao* that can be *tao*-ed ["spoken of"]/ Is not the constant tao;/ The name that can be named/ Is not the constant name." Thus the Tao, Longxi claims, did not need to wait until the twentieth century to be deconstructed.[36]

The meanings of entropy and its opposite, negentropy, display an analogous interpenetration of opposites. Although entropy means the increasing "disorder" in a system, this disorder comes about by an incremental diffusion and balancing of energy which finally results in "heat death," a perfect distribution of energy so that no further interactions can occur. Entropy, rather than a principle of chaos, could be considered the means of a perfect harmony or equilibrium. Negentropy, on the other hand, is the contradictory movement toward greater and greater order in a system—"order" here defined as an increasing imbalance or disorder in the distribution of energy. It is this imbalance which allows for the actions and reactions characteristic of any organic or mechanical system. People live by contributing to the entropy of everything they consume and yet they also engineer negentropic systems which increase their supply of consumable energy. Used in this way, these words, no less than "cosmos" and "chaos," "order" and "disorder," become difficult to define because they are not properly scaled to time and perspective. Our experience of the world, like our effects on the world, takes place in different times, with respect to what Michel Serres calls "multitemporality": "Perhaps it [is] difficult to intuit a multitemporality. We willingly accept, however, the fact that the things around us do not all share the same temporality: negentropic islands on or in the entropic sea, or distinct universes as Boltzmann described them, pockets of local order in rising entropy, crystal depositories sunk in ashes. . ."[37] Our unreflected belief in universal time blinds us to these contrapuntal relations between order and disorder and would lead us to consider the distinction itself untenable—but even that reveals our desire to impose a single temporal and spatial scale on the world around and within us.

Only when one enters explicitly into the experience of what the modern world calls "art" are these demands, if not set aside, undermined by the contradiction between literary and nonliterary, explicitly fictional and implicitly fictional, demands for credibility. When one is involved in a work of literature, one is "lost," removed from the determinations of a single temporal and spatial scale. That we often feel pleasure in this doubling of scale and dimension should not be surprising, for in a sense our pleasure expresses our appreciation, as Coleridge explains it, of the relationship of parts to wholes, of the dissolution of our own socially constructed ego into the general context of signs. One could say then that pleasure exists only off the scale of a single perspective, and is thus allied with ecstasy and self-forgetting. Pleasure as an aesthetic response is thus similar to a sublime enjoyment of the loss of ground, an appreciation of the infinity bound in the covers of a book. Our habitual Euclidean interpretations lead us to equate the space of the book with the space of the work, the author with its source, and the reader (us) with its receiver. But the space of the work is, as we know when we are lost in it, finite but unbounded—for the simple reason that as self-conscious subjects we have temporarily ceased to exist, just as the author has by entering into language. The work of literature focuses the complicity of naming and un-naming, order and disorder, cosmos and chaos, definition and infinity, fiction and reality. Thus we tend to consider great those works that are able to reconcile the greatest complexity with the greatest order.

Poetry, fiction, and critical theory in the twentieth century have established this simultaneous presence of order and disorder through a number of radical forms, all of which break with modern norms of representation relying on linearity and abstraction.

And yet this disruptive aspect was always an attempt to undo the written forms allied with Euclidean and Newtonian assumptions about idealized forms and atemporal relations. Literary fragmentation, presented theoretically by Friedrich Schlegel and anecdotally by Coleridge and often practiced by later poets and novelists, is both a critique of wholes and an approach to a more comprehensive whole which would transform the reader from spectator into an active and necessary participant in his own dissolution and pleasure. It is this complementary relationship between deconstructive and imaginative projects that best describes the literature studied in this book.

A powerfully dramatic emblem and authority for fragmentation and integration can be found in the development of atomic theory and practice during the twentieth century. Atomic theory had begun with Leucippus and Democritus as the supposition that all matter was composed of irreducible atoms (*a-tomos,* i.e., uncuttable) moving within a void. This atomistic, dualistic conception of reality was maintained, according to either mathematical or positivist definition, despite the fact that physicists believed that light was a continuous wavelike phenomenon. Throughout the nineteenth century, Lancelot Law Whyte writes, "the particle theory of matter and the wave theory of light coexisted without provoking physicists to discover some physical relation between these contrasted ideas, as though they had coexisted in independence or pre-established harmony from some original act of creation."[38] By the twentieth century these and other contradictions in physical theory had become only too obvious and troublesome. Not only had Max Planck determined the discrete—as opposed to the wavelike or continuous—nature of radiation and Albert Einstein discovered that light could be described as a particle, but the atom was discovered, contrary to definition, to be composed of a nucleus of protons and neutrons and orbiting shells of electrons. When Louis Victor de Broglie and Erwin Schrödinger demonstrated that "wave-particles" alternated between field and quantized states, the formalistic aspects of physical theory became impossible to ignore. "Atomism" had been transformed from a classical example of a metaphysical dualism (being and nothingness, presence and absence, ground and abyss) into a discipline of formal relations that could be statistically calculated but not definitively predicted.

Seeing into an atom was more than technical experimentation into a certain "problem" in physics. In a sense quantum physics provided an analogy for (and interpreted the insights of) psychoanalysis, which like quantum physics could be said to date from 1900. Whyte's remarks on this link deserve to be quoted at length:

> We hear of unstable particle in physics and of unconscious mind in psychology. Is this a mere chance, or a sign of a parallel between the two sciences? Is there some common factor which leads both to name a basic idea in this back-handed manner? I believe that there is and that it throws light on the position of both sciences. . . . Physics and psychology are each using the negative prefix un- to announce a transformation of ideas which is still incomplete. Because they have not yet reached clarity about the new ideas which are necessary, they can so far describe the change only by the denial of the old idea. . . . More precisely, what has happened is that these sciences are rejecting ancient views about the nature of things: the Democritean view that stable atoms are the basis of phenomena; and the equally old view, sharpened by Descartes, that *conscious* mind is a second, independent mode of existence. These are being discarded because they no longer fit the facts, or do not seem to. . . . [T]his two-letter bomb [un-] is allowed to get away with its dirty work at the crossroads where an old method and a new one intersect. (4–5)

Implicit within these parallel revolutions is the recognition that the languages humans use to interpret and express their minds and even the mathematical expressions of their minds have serious limitations when they approach the uncanny realm of the *un-*. "If so deep a transformation is in progress," Whyte writes, "it is not surprising that particle physicists are reaching the conclusion that a new physical language is needed" (7). For different but analogous reasons writers, poets, and psychoanalysts in the early twentieth century came to similar conclusions.

As physicists began to see more and more of their research bound up with the nature of mind and language and the act of representation, they became philosophers. It should be said, of course, that Heisenberg and his fellow physicists and philosophic colleagues were not *seeking* to overturn the Cartesian worldview out of some philosophic assumption that "wholeness" was superior to "dualism." Heisenberg's philosophical narratives of the quantum revolution emphasize the disappointments that their research caused. The philosophic interpretation of quantum physics, rather than the actual research, by Heisenberg and Bohr should be seen as a self-conscious attempt to rethink the conceptual basis of modern science in direct response to the anomalies that they encountered experimentally.

Many physicists and philosophers of science have insisted that the uncertainty principle has no real consequences for large-scale predictability, let alone for philosophy and that Heisenberg was wrong to assign it any discursive significance outside the world of quanta. In his lectures on quantum electrodynamics, for instance, Richard Feynman argues humorously but with intent that by using diagrams to explain the physics of light "uncertainty" can be avoided: "If you get rid of all old-fashioned ideas and use the ideas that I'm explaining in these lectures—adding *arrows* for all the ways an event can happen—there is no need for an 'uncertainty principle!'"[39]

Feynman's remarks seem transparent enough: we can ignore the "philosophical" consequences of quantum mechanics best by avoiding the language of philosophical reflection. But even though "quantum weirdness" can be confined to arrows and diagrams, and even though it has no impact on the behavior of large-scale objects, the fact that it lies at the actual and material basis of all large-scale physical determinism remains a fundamental philosophical issue that should make us *think*, in an active way, the plurality of determinisms at work in the "same" world and even the "same" objects. Newtonian, thermodynamic, quantum, and chaotic determinisms can all be relevant to a human body, not to mention hormonal, genetic, social, cultural, economic, linguistic, psychoanalytic, and literary determinisms. One can claim that some are more relevant than others, but such decisions—such as claiming that quantum physics cannot lead to a generalized philosophical "uncertainty principle"—would themselves be determined. Whenever someone privileges a supposedly "fundamental" determinism he is trying to privilege not only its relevant reality but his own authority.

Resolutely rational as the particular mathematical expressions of "quantum weirdness" are, the inevitable attempts to understand by representing the worldview implied led to logical paradoxes and oxymorons. Niels Bohr illustrated the uncanny and unpredictable nature of subatomic reactions through allusions to the Taoist principles of Yin and Yang, the complementary nature of opposites. He went so far as to adapt the *t'ai chi* symbol as his own coat of arms with the legend *Contraria sunt complementa*. Werner Heisenberg saw in quantum physics the basis for a fundamental critique of the western notion of objectivity and scientific observation and wrote that precedents for the logic of quantum thinking could be found "in the philosophical ideas in the traditions of the Far East."[40]

These hints have led some to equate the Hindu conception of *Brahman* (the World-Soul), the Buddhist principle of *Sunyata* (Emptiness), and the Taoist "Way" (Tao) with the universe of subatomic particles revealed by quantum physics, claiming that the relationship between fluid energy and quantized particles is analogous to the relationship between the individual self and the world of process, individual particles and the field of particles. This interpretation makes an intentional category error by associating such terms as *Brahman, Sunyata,* and Tao, which are neither "physical" nor "metaphysical," with the physical field of sub atomic particles. Precisely because of this "error" it provides an extremely powerful metaphor (another name for a category error) for the relationship between wholes and parts, the necessarily permeable or communicative nature of categories or levels of reality. One should not ignore the fact that the parallel between quantum physics and Eastern thought, so irksome to science journalists like Jeremy Bernstein, who are intent on defending the objective and rational nature of physics against kooks, was made by founders like Bohr and Heisenberg, who, even if they were making "category errors" by doing so, used their research as a stimulus to rethink the Cartesian legacy.[41]

Whyte draws out the epistemological consequences nicely: "The twenty or thirty 'elementary particles' of deep physics are no longer the permanent *res extensa* (space-occupying substance), nor is the extended 'mind' of deep psychology the *res cogitans* (conscious substance) of Cartesian doctrine. . . . The sciences are manifestly converging; atom, man, and universe are, in an objective and inescapable sense, deeply related" (6–8). This convergence is not only evident in the parallels between Indian and Chinese thought and quantum physics, but in twentieth-century works of literature that discard the linear or exclusive frameworks of "realist" literature, for the organistic synthesis of order and disorder within a thriving chaos of interfering and yet complementary causal orders.

The new scientific theories of "chaos" and "complexity" demonstrate that quotidian physical phenomena are, despite their familiarity, no less weird than the world unveiled by quantum physicists. The French mathematician Benoit Mandelbrot has shown how finite forms contain within them the elements of infinity.[42] All that is required is an ability to understand that the observing and measuring mind has within it a permanent access to infinity through the reiteration of a finite procedure. A simple ball of twine resembles a point at thirty feet; at ten feet it becomes a sphere; at twelve inches it acquires grooves; under a magnifying glass, filaments spring from the landscape; and under a microscope the filaments explode with detail. Each observation of the ball of twine is scaled by a different point of reference. All of them are correct and all of them are incorrect. If one were asked to determine the circumference of this ball, one could thus choose between a brisk eight inches and a number approaching infinity. It would depend upon the standard of measurement used and the standard of measurement would depend upon what uses you had in mind for the twine.

Mandelbrot thus demonstrates with disarming simplicity that measuring an object always requires a certain degree of short-cutting: to measure means to apply one idealized standard against things in the world. With the exception of ideal Euclidean constructions such as lines, circles, and triangles—which, because they are imaginary, are always equivalent to their measurements—nothing in the sublunary realm can be measured without a certain violence or approximation that reveals our own position. We think of the world with reference to unreal entities such as circles and spheres, lines and planes, but the world we live in, the world of dust, trees, and smoke is relentlessly different, and similar only to itself. Measuring an object, we measure our measurements and ourselves. Seeing the chaos in the simplest thing, we lose our sense of locatedness and stability.

When Prigogine presented the theory of how material entropy could lead to organic negentropy, how in other words, a dead or dying chaos of matter could lead to a cosmos of beautifully varied life-forms, he was seeing an analogous form of difference-in-identity. He coined the phrase "dissipative structures" to describe such "far-from-equilibrium" conditions as occur in a rushing stream when a rapid fluctuation of patterns will suddenly produce an apparent "form" such as a vortex. John P. Briggs and F. David Peat explain that such a form is paradoxical: "it can survive only by remaining open to a flowing matter and energy exchange with the environment. In fact, matter and energy literally flow through it and form it. . . . This means that resistance to change must itself be a kind of flowing. The structure is stabilized by its flowing."[43] From such paradoxical forms, Prigogine believes, the structural possibility of organisms is born.

Literary works can be understood as "dissipative structures," focused expressions of the fluctuating orders which reach from the atom to the expanding universe. Within such a progression of patternings, ideas of mind, organism, machine, and text appear more like variations on the theme of difference-as-relationship than as actual and distinct entities. This is essentially the argument that Erich Jantsch makes in *The Self-Organizing Universe* (1980). Developing Prigogine's conception of dissipative structures, Jantsch presents a general theory of "autopoiesis" that would include the formation of life, social forms, works of art, and "open science." "The self-organization of the creative work—its mind— and human self-organization dynamics—the human mind—are two sides of one and the same evolutionary process; they form a complementarity."[44] For David Porush, the literary text as dissipative structure is "best viewed as the result of the intersection of the author's mind with a very peculiar technology (a sort of antimechanistic technology) designed in its most advanced forms to capture the evanescent movements and fluctuations of the mind itself."[45] The complementarity of art and science is possible because both genres of human intellectual activity evolve from the same context of dissipative structures. A literary work is not a "solid-state" artifact but an ongoing and self-transforming activity, similar to a vortex which thrives by drawing upon its environment to sustain its own immaterial form. Texts such as *Finnegans Wake* and *The Waste Land*, which abandon the linear and abstracting tendencies of modern literature, show how chaos and cosmos can be reconciled and yet appreciated distinctly within the dynamics of a multileveled, multitemporal, plurivocal language whose surplus of meaning begins to resemble the "noisy" but engendering status of chaos. As genetic information becomes creative potentially insofar as it does not achieve a perfect univocality and replication of information, insofar as it allows noise into its channels of communication, so literary language—as Porush recognizes—functions as a truly *creative* medium. Paulson explains that "insofar as literary texts are both communicative and ambiguous, they are noisy channels. . . . The qualities of a literary text, in this view, are emergent."[46] In other words, the deterministic and the noisy aspects of literary texts enact the cosmic and chaotic functions of the living world and lived experience.

The myth of the muses, romantic inspiration, psychoanalytic descriptions of the spontaneous appearance of unconscious material, and the contemporary view that literature arises from the structure of language: all these ideas attempt to explain the mysterious and sometimes spontaneous origin of the work of art. But whether one invokes the muses, inspiration, the unconscious, or language, one is still trying to explain how art is the expression of more than individual will and intention. Joyce thus claimed that *Finnegans Wake* was writing itself, and that after a certain point he could leave it to his friend James Stephens to finish. *The Waste Land* was drafted by an emotionally exhausted man taking a cure in Switzerland and revised by another poet. And *The Changing Light at Sandover* derives in large part from the transcripts of Merrill's and his friend David Jackson's experiences at the Ouija board.[47] Whether one cites Homer, Shelley, Freud, Roland Barthes, or Erich Jantsch, one gets the sense that art is less the product of the laboring ego than of a larger context achieving expression through an ego.

Like quantum physics, relativity theory, psychoanalysis, and the critiques of metaphysics and language achieved by Nietzsche and Heidegger, literature in the early twentieth century began to conceive of time, space, and reference in a fragmented and yet newly integrated way. Thus the tradition of cosmological, dream allegories is quantized and reformulated by *Finnegans Wake, The Changing Light at Sandover, Ancient Evenings,* and *Canopus in Argos* so that the whole world of myth and religion and literature have a place. And the traditions of quest literature and meditation are fragmented, fused, and renewed in *The Waste Land, A Passage to India,* and Lacan's *Ecrits,* each of which shows how European subjectivity is radically challenged and yet complemented by non-European thought and myth.

The deconstructive and reconstitutive aspects of quantum physics, the transformations of mind in Prigogine, Stengers, and Bateson, the aesthetics of chaos in Mandelbrot's geometries of nonideal forms, and the nonlinear works of twentieth-century literature are kinds of dissipative structures, neither stable nor unstable, neither ordered nor disordered, neither cosmic nor chaotic: in Joyce's coinage, they present us with a "chaosmos."

ᴑ—Joycean Chaosmos and the Self-Organizing World

> Intelligence and material process have thus a single origin, which is ultimately the unknown totality of the universal flux. In a certain sense, this implies that what we have commonly called mind and matter are abstractions from the universal flux, and that both are to be regarded as different and relatively autonomous orders within the one whole movement.
>
> —David Bohm

Joyce's Critique of Enlightenment

In 1900, with impeccable timing, Max Planck discovered something that would finally destroy the model of physical reality which physical scientists had inherited from the nineteenth century. While investigating the nature of blackbody radiation, Planck realized that the energy emitted in this gradual radioactive decay did not occur in a continuous, constant, and linear fashion. It occurred in discrete, self-contained packets which he called "quanta"—because they were mathematically quantifiable. "The hypothesis of quanta has led," Planck wrote, "to the idea that there are changes in Nature which do not occur continuously but in an explosive manner."[1]

Twentieth-century physics, in accommodating itself to the theory of relativity and quantum mechanics, gradually had to accept the apparent fact that the world could not be equated with the continous, incremental nature of measurement. The world was potentially too explosive to be amenable to standardized and universal forms of measurement. Both relativity theory and quantum theory, developing Planck's findings in macro- and microscopic contexts, postulated that observation and measurement

49

could no longer be safely distinguished from the discrete object and context of their attentions. Science, in effect, constituted the world according to its own highly precise but premised means of apprehension and representation. In the broadest sense of the word, representation—as a potentially ideal, technical faculty—could no longer be understood in terms of an ultimate goal of perfection: a factor of indeterminacy, relativity, and uncertainty had entered into physical representation. The fixed and certain gap between the philosophical subject and the material world, so central to the Cartesian tradition, had closed.

Planck's discovery provided an emblem and a scientific analogy for the works of contemporary writers such as Stéphane Mallarmé, Henry James, and Joseph Conrad. In these writers one sees how the increasing complexity of poetic and novelistic languages does not begin to resolve the difficulties of representing a state of consciousness or a particular narrative of conflicting points of view: the more sophistication and detail brought to bear on a subject, the more the gap between particulars and generalities, perceiving mind and perceived world, appears to widen.[2] The gap between life and language, consciousness and expression begins to appear irresolvable, an essential feature of a universe characterized by discontinuity between modes of representation and levels of detail. Discontinuity could no longer be ascribed to a fault in the methods of representation: the world was apparently both continuous and discontinuous, composed both of constant patterns and intermittent eruptions. Lancelot Whyte explains this paradox rather neatly:

> "Discontinuity" is then evident in the existence of discrete point-centres localizing and terminating the spatial relations, and "continuity" in the uninterrupted variation, in course of time, of these relations.[3]

Any attempt to translate the activity of the world into the code or language of a scientific or aesthetic discourse would have to assume the limitations of its premise and bear the exponent, so to speak, of its value. As the technical faculties of representation develop in the twentieth century the elusiveness of an absolute or final representation is both discovered and brought about. By the end of the twentieth century uncertainty has become not only a theoretical cliché but a central aesthetic theme.

For some thinkers in the early years of the century, such as Edmund Husserl, this turn of events was nothing less than a crisis of European culture brought about by an excessive reliance on the findings of empirical science and its literary correlaries. Husserl believed that what he considered to be the unique nature, the superiority of European culture, was in danger of being lost. "Philosophy," as Husserl understood it, is a particularly Greek and European faculty which had been destined "to exercise through European man its role of leadership for the whole of mankind."[4] "Therein lies something unique," Husserl claims, "which all other human groups, too, feel with regard to us, something that, apart from all considerations of expediency, becomes a motivation for them—despite their determination to retain their spiritual autonomy—constantly to Europeanize themselves, whereas we, if we understand ourselves properly, will never, for example, Indianize ourselves" (157). Idealism and cultural imperialism have rarely been so blandly equated. For Husserl, it would appear, an ideal and purely "logical" apprehension of the world was closely bound with the European mission of colonizing and transforming the world. The philosophical and historical consequences of the late modern critique of the idea of mimesis included nothing less than the fate of the world, at least as it was imagined by one of Europe's great thinkers.

Husserl's student, Martin Heidegger, believed that philosophical, scientific, social, or aesthetic discourses could easily enough describe the degraded entities of modern life, but were unable to represent or express the "Being of beings," the ideal origin of all that is. It was this state of affairs that forced Heidegger to devise his own modes of writing a philosophy of being. In his introduction to *Being and Time* (1927) he provided what amounts to a manifesto for a new kind of philosophical representation: "With regard to the awkwardness and 'inelegance' of expression in the analysis to come, we may remark that it is one thing to give a report in which we tell about entities, but another to grasp entities in their *Being*. For the latter task we lack not only most of the words but, above all, the 'grammar.'"[5] In essence, Heidegger is announcing the philosophical consequences of the widening gap between the being of the world in its deepest sense and the corrupted modes of representation: he is calling for a new language.

When Heidegger wrote these words in the 1920s, James Joyce had already begun writing *Finnegans Wake,* a work that forges a new vocabulary and a new grammar while dissolving the languages and myths of Europe into the languages and myths of the world. Joyce's last work forms a single planetary text that provides a visionary version of the aesthetic whole that Bateson describes and the cultural melange Husserl feared. Joyce disassembles the vocabulary of modern realism and in its place constructs a linguistic dream in which verbal alchemy and natural process are aligned with one another in order to approximate a world where mind and matter, subjects and objects, exist only as mutual influences and transformations. Yet the Joycean text does observe "rules," although they are certainly alien to the order of modernist reality and alien to most of the traditions of literary representation. In doing so, it breaks with formalist and humanist traditions which, since Kant, have more or less accepted the Newtonian world machine and sought to authorize the microcosms of subjectivity and the work of art in compensation for the restricted scope of reality that scientific culture brought about. By inventing a new vocabulary and devising a new grammar, Joyce stages a wake for the death of one kind of language and the rebirth of another. This other language rejects the entities of modern discourse in order to speak, in several registers and several languages, of a Joycean "beingtime."[6]

It would be a mistake, then, to assume that *Finnegans Wake,* because of its canonical status, has really been assimilated into modernist culture. But it would also be mistaken to assume that it is a literary curiosity, a monument to an elitist and priestly modernism which sought to transcend history and mass culture. In order properly to appreciate the magnitude of the *Wake,* one needs to read it as a critique of the fundamental humanist values which come down to us from the Enlightenment. Three principles are central to this legacy:

1) the self as an enclosed, rational entity defined by the Cartesian *res cogitans*. Delimited by Descartes specifically in order to vanquish doubt, this self or subject exists strictly as an interior principle, isolated from and yet trapped within the world and the body;

2) the world as a material and mechanical construct—in Cartesian terms, the *res extensa* outside the *res cogitans;* for Locke, the origin of sensory experience; for Newton, the lawful, determinate and reversible system of dynamic relations described by mathematics;

3) the word as "neutral" sign; ideally motivated by its equivalence to the subject and the word; such a word must be disciplined by its masters in order to represent a predeterminate reference.

The novel, the dominant literary form of modernity, developed the premises of an alienated subject, an empirically generated world, and an efficiently factual or historical word. Ian Watt explains that "the previous stylistic tradition for fiction was not primarily concerned with the correspondence of words to things, but rather with the extrinsic beauties which could be bestowed upon description and action by the use of rhetoric. . . . It would appear, then, that the function of language is much more largely referential in the novel than in other literary forms."[7] Watt shares Foucault's later view that the seventeenth and eighteenth centuries attempted to neutralize language the better to represent the real world of objects and subjects. Specifically this neutralization meant the reduction of the ternary sign (significant, signified, and their conjuncture) to a "binary" arrangement which seemed to "link" human concepts and fictions to things.[8] The novel further familiarizes and naturalizes this reality by pretending to offer histories instead of fictions, real (common) people instead of heroes (nobles). This change leads, according to Watt, to an integration

of the newly individuated character into the temporal-spatial
dimensions of social reality:

> The "principle of individuation" accepted by Locke was that
> of existence at a particular locus in space and time; since, as
> he writes, "ideas become general by separating from them
> the circumstances of time and space," so they become partic-
> ular only when both these circumstances are specified. In the
> same way the characters of the novel can only be individual-
> ized if they are set in a background of particularized time
> and space. (21)

Watt thus describes the way in which the idea of particular or
individual subjectivity is strangely linked with the historical and
material qualities of empirical reality: by equating such condi-
tional existence with reality, the novel begins the process of natu-
ralizing modern life, transforming social arrangements into the
same order of reality as rocks and stones and trees. Thus when the
middle class began to gain power, literary ideology seized as its
authority—neither the ancients, the church, nor tradition in general—the apparently inarguable reality aligned with the structures
of early capitalism. However critical of those conditions, the
genre itself was in complete accord with the philosophical and
political premises of this reality.

Robinson Crusoe (1719) illustrates the modern worldview by
presenting a solitary subject in an alien world which is gradually
subdued by the exercise of reason and common sense. It is also
obvious that Defoe's novel represents the imperialist side of
empirical modernism and reflects the foundations of Great
Britain as an imperial power. Indeed European colonialism in
general reveals the obverse of the supposedly civilized values that
distinguish scientific culture from the superstition, dogma, and
social repression of the middle ages. Thus the Cartesian subject,
like Adam or Crusoe, is a political master who seeks to dominate
the outside world—especially in regions, like Asia, Africa, and
the Americas, where subjectivity and reality await construction.
The non-European lands are viewed strictly as a single revelation
of a civilizing mission, since individuality is an exclusively

European faculty, associated with power and technology. The "world," like Crusoe's island, moves from nature to natural resources, an array of possessions, data, and experience. Having rid themselves of the metaphysical legacy of premodernity, the English map and regulate new worlds the way Galileo and Newton did the solar system. Like the heavens themselves, the future colonies "lay hid in night" and awaited the coming of European logic and law.

The political and metaphysical significance of *Finnegans Wake* might be better appreciated as a critique not only of empiricism but of imperialism. The subject, the world, the word, and the novel are shattered and reformed in the chaosmos of the Joycean night according to an economy and an order that recovers premodern mythologies and foretells a postmodern worldview. But it is significant indeed that Joyce chose to work specifically within the modern medium of prose and the novel— not, like Pound, in the noble medium of poetry. By working through modern values and forms in *Dubliners* and *A Portrait of the Artist as a Young Man* and then moving into the complex textuality of *Ulysses* and *Finnegans Wake,* Joyce demonstrated, from within, the logical erosion of modern representation, insofar as it is allied with imperial and empirical culture. Like Bohr and Heisenberg, Joyce showed that realist or material explanations become weakened and qualified as one focuses closely on the atoms of experience. If modern epistemology is bound to the modern project of subduing nature, then Joyce's critique of enlightenment is inevitably political. As Philippe Sollers has written, *Finnegans Wake,* far from being a nonpolitical work, "is an active transnationalism, disarticulating, rearticulating and at the same time annulling the maximum number of traces—linguistic, historical, mythological, religious. . . . [It] is the most formidably anti-fascist book produced between the wars."[9]

Joyce's transmutation of European modernism from within depends on his own marginal status as a colonial subject of Great Britain and on his own complex relationship to the English language. Only by being both expert in and alien to both language and the novel as a genre could Joyce perceive and then dismantle them. A passage from *A Portrait,* reporting Stephen's response to the dean of studies, conveys this ambivalence:

> The language in which we are speaking is his before it is mine. How different are the words *home, Christ, ale, master* on his lips and on mine. His language, so familiar and so foreign, will always be for me an acquired speech. I have not made or accepted its words. My voice holds them at bay. My soul frets in the shadow of language.[10]

What Joyce recognized about language by being a colonial subject, Heidegger, Lacan, and Louis Althusser would see functioning in all language, especially one's "own": the way it precedes us and recruits us into its rutted attitudes and allegiances. Joyce chose neither to reject English nor to accept, like Samuel Beckett, another language, but to make his own language out of it from within and without. If to imagine a language is to imagine a world, in *Finnegans Wake* Joyce had not only imagined a world, he had brought it into existence.

Joyce's lecture on Defoe to an Italian audience in 1912 reveals the nature of this linguistic ambivalence and how it leads to the transformation of English that he brings about in the *Wake*. Joyce expresses admiration for the author of *Robinson Crusoe* for having invented realism and prophesying the British Empire. "The story of the shipwrecked sailor who lived on a desert island for four years reveals, as perhaps no other book throughout the long history of English literature does, the wary and heroic instinct of the rational animal and the prophecy of empire."[11] As a prophecy emerging from the secular language of modern realism, *Robinson Crusoe* presents an ideal that it was Joyce's destiny to emulate and transform. Only through rewriting and thus transforming this realist tradition in *Dubliners* could Joyce cast, like Defoe, "a prophetic spell" which would reverse the "prophecy of empire" in a vision of a decolonialized, derealized world.

Modernist and technical prejudices have led some to regard the formal changes in Joyce's prose from *Dubliners* to *Finnegans*

Wake as a series of "experiments" or "innovations." This may be true with regard to the formal qualities alone. But it would be more accurate to see *Finnegans Wake* as a dismantling, word by word, of the modern house of fiction that reached its perfection in *Madame Bovary* and *The Portrait of a Lady.* Joyce's technical achievements are directed against the progressive, linear, and instrumental values of the enlightenment which sought to disguise the rhetoric of language within the discourse of realism and rationalism. The ideal of the invisible Flaubertian artist does not represent the extinction of the self or subject, as some have supposed: it represents its final, Cartesian ascent to complete, divine autonomy. *Finnegans Wake* is the monumental example of Foucault's conception of the compensation that modern literature offered for the impoverishment of language by the demands of objectivity. In an even more dramatic gesture, Joyce simply reverses the terms of modern enlightenment: where the basic imperial contract was to seize native sources of wealth in exchange for the English language, law, engineering, administration, and culture, Joyce's prophetic contract insists that English be shot through with the languages, myths, religions, and tropes of planetary culture.

Jacques Derrida sees in this project the reverse of Husserl's attempt to critique modernity through a renewed idealism. Joyce, Derrida writes, is willing "to repeat and take responsibility for all equivocation itself, utilizing a language that could equalize the greatest possible synchrony with the greatest potential for buried, accumulated, and interwoven intentions within each linguistic atom."[12] By the eighties, critics inspired by Derrida, Lacan, and others had interpreted the *Wake* in terms of this intitial Joycean mode of decentering and splitting words and worlds. Margot Norris relied essentially on the psychoanalytic and deconstructive notions that the fall of the father (Finnegan, H.C.E., etc.) and the "fall" of language are aspects of the same action: "The Wakean vision of a universe hurtling toward chaos is based on the theme of the fallen father. . . . The task confronting Joyce in letting the language reflect a universe whose structure is determined by substitutions and free-play, is to deconstruct the language itself."[13]

Colin MacCabe emphasized the political and historical consequences of Joycean practice as it relates to Joyce's own situation as
a former imperial subject: "What is subverted is a political event
of central importance. For with the loss of the punctual subject, it
is no longer possible to indicate discrete areas in which the punctual subject is represented."[14]

Joyce thus transforms modern Eurocentric culture and
exemplifies the first event of planetary culture, no longer ready or
able to enforce the "borderline," to protect the frontiers between
countries, cultures, languages, myths, and subjects. The porousness of languages and myths is demonstrated in *Finnegans Wake,*
Eliot's *The Waste Land,* and Pound's *Cantos,* texts written by exiles
who pioneered worldviews characterized by homologies of narratives, myths, and languages. In his introduction to Husserl's *The
Origin of Geometry,* Derrida describes the Joycean project as a circulation of buried and equivocal linkages: "this endeavor would
try to make the structural unity of all empirical culture appear in
the generalized equivocation of a writing that, no longer translating one language into another on the basis of their common cores
of sense, circulates throughout all languages at once, accumulates
their energies, actualizes their most secret consonances, discloses
their furthermost common horizons, cultivates their associative
syntheses instead of avoiding them, and rediscovers the poetic
value of passivity" (102).

The prophetic core of this critique and creation can be located, like the exploding galaxies of signifiers, at the center of
Finnegans Wake. One of the countless versions of the fall of the
father, the shooting of the Russian general by the Irish soldier
Buckley, is dramatized by the rival sons Butt and Taff in the third
chapter of book two. The significance of this shot is registered in
these remarkable stage directions:

> [The abnihilisation of the etym by the grisning of the
> grosning of the grinder of the grunder of the first lord
> of Hurtreford expolodotonates through Parsuralia with
> an ivanmorinthorrorumble fragoromboassity amidwhiches
> general uttermosts confussion are perceivable moletons skap-

ing with mulicules while coventry plumpkins fairlygosmoth-
erthemselves in the Landaunelegants of Pinka-dindy.
Similar scenatas are projectilised from Hullulullu, Bawl-
awayo, empyreal Raum and mordern Atems. They were precisely the twelves of clocks, noon minutes, none seconds. At
someseat of Oldanelang's Konguerrig, by dawnybreak in
Aira.] (353.22–32)

The "abnihilisation of the etym" includes precisely those values
that I have associated with the appearance of modernity: the ety-
mon, or the true word, Adam, or the authorizing subjectivity; and
the atom, or the fundamental component of material reality. In
one moment, Joyce explodes these atomic values and allows their
effects to be felt throughout the book and across the scope of
human history. But just as these modern values explode and scatter, another kind of context begins to develop: the Cartesian subject, the true word, and the point of irreducible reality form a
single fabric, a system of reference, a dream, which joins men and
mountains, women and rivers, words and voids, death and
rebirth, fiction and prophecy. In this way, Joyce literalizes the
meanings of apocalypse: both destruction and revelation, annihilation and creation (*ab nihil, ex nihilo*) are parts of each other.
More importantly, and following this "logic," one may conclude
that the "dream" of *Finnegans Wake* is also an attempt to reveal the
being of the world, to allow the earth itself to speak in its many
voices.

Joyce not only wove myths, literatures, and languages into a
single verbal fabric, he also used the advances in science evident
to an interested layman in the first four decades of the century,
from Einstein and Rutherford to Freud and Jung, to supply range
and depth to his condensation of world culture. One of his constant concerns when working in such material was to blend the
abstruse with the banal, the scientific with the mythic, and the
most advanced insights into the oldest wisdom. It is difficult to
say exactly how much Joyce understood of twentieth-century
physics in any strict sense since in the *Wake* he is more interested
in imbricating and elaborating on such themes than in displaying

erudition. Throughout *Finnegans Wake* Joyce tried to work as much from contemporary science as was relevant to his themes, in the same way that he worked in esoteric principles, political trivia, Malaysian rivers, and autobiographical minutiae. Despite his characteristic use of source material, it is clear that the science was not merely ornamental: he apparently saw a deep convergence between his own work and that of physicists and psychoanalysts—his fellow explorers of the "etym." Strother Purdy makes what I think is a persuasive case when he argues that *"Finnegans Wake* remains our century's greatest artistic expression of the sense of the changed world science has given us."[15]

The scientific career of Ernest Rutherford, later Lord Rutherford, was a long and productive one and Joyce seemed to take interest in it because of parallels with his own. Several themes in Rutherford's work are relevant to the *Wake:* the "disintegration hypothesis," the discovery that radiation is spontaneous atomic disintegration; that "alchemical" reactions and recombinations (to cite Rutherford's amusedly ironic description) are always going on in nature; and that such natural and spontaneous radiation can also be achieved artificially. In 1915 Rutherford described how "it is possible that the nucleus of an atom may be altered by direct collision of the nucleus with very swift electrons or atoms."[16] His discovery of the systemic, rather than the elemental, nature of the atom, which so interested Joyce, came about as a result of his laboratory's "scatter experiments." Physicist Heinz Pagels describes them this way:

> A radioactive source of alpha particles is placed near a metal foil (Marsden [Rutherford's assistant] used gold foil). The alpha particles are projectiles, like little bullets being fired at the foil. Most of the alpha particles go straight through the foil and are detected on the screen. However, on a hunch, Rutherford asked Marsden to look for alpha particles that were strongly scattered by the foil and widely deflected. By placing the detecting screen away from the line of sight to the alpha source, Marsden found a few deflected alphas.
>
> He observed that some even scattered back toward the alpha source. It would be like firing some bullets at a piece of

tissue paper only to find that some bullets bounced backward. . . . By carefully studying these deflections, Rutherford
determined the major features of atomic structure.[17]

Pagels explains the significance of these findings this way: "The
idea of atoms, held by many people, was that they were without
parts, completely elementary, the end of all material structure—
the building block for the rest of matter. . . . Rutherford's simple
scattering experiment gave human kind its first glimpse into the
structure of the atom" (52).

The "abnihilisation of the etym" passage describes and
exemplifies Joyce's literary method by blending his own verbal
theories and techniques with Rutherford's atomic "disintegra-
tions" and the subsequent "alchemical transmutation of elements." Like Rutherford, Joyce (and Buckley the Irish soldier)
would fire one verbal element against another in order not only
to distintegrate but also to transmute and so reveal the structure
of the word: its systemic rather than its atomic character, its field
of relations rather than its punctual significance. Joycean writing
in the *Wake* demonstrates that the "ground" of everything is
"annihilated" when the "etym" is. And yet, if the classical conceptions of the etym and atom fly apart, they also fly into each
other to reform new combinations, transmutations of the sort
that alchemists dreamed of and which psychoanalysts revealed in
our dreams. Seeing the consequences of this creative destruction,
Joyce shows how the annihilation of the reified world of modernity is simultaneously the reconstitution or creation of a more
comprehensive world of connectedness. Thus the "grisning of
the grosning of the grinder of the grunder of the first lord of
Hurtreford expolodotonates through Parsuralia"—the experiments of Rutherford (himself scattered and recombined as
"Hurtreford" [from *heurter*, French, "knock or crack"] in order to
suggest H.C.E., as well as Dublin, or Hurdleford) actually initiate an implosion of the world which spans both space and time,
demonstrating that singularity, separateness, and discreteness
are simply aspects or features of plurality, relationship, and connectedness.

In order to probe the atom Rutherford and his students J.D. Cockcroft (who is commemorated along with Rutherford as "cockshock" and linked with one "J.P. Cockshott" [56.4–5; 524.14–34]) and E.T.S. Walton invented the first atomic accelerator in 1932. A.S. Eve describes this achievement, which was widely covered by the popular press of the time: "[They] hurled protons, with a voltage exceeding 600,000, at lithium, and the lithium . . . split violently into two fragments, each helium."[18] Pagels describes how Cockroft thus "succeeded in inducing nuclear transmutations with his beam of protons—a sure sign that the nucleus had indeed been penetrated. Humanity had touched the nuclear core of atoms" (172). Joycean practice similarly bombards or shoots the "etym" with signifers, often from many directions, in order to break the shield or aura of the "word" to reveal its systemic or parasystemic relations with other words. *Finnegans Wake* can be seen as a kind of verbal accelerator or cyclotron involved in a destructive and synthetic intervention within the languages of the world.

Bohr, who elaborated on Rutherford's first experiments, commented on this link between physics and poetry to Heisenberg: "We must be clear that, when it comes to atoms, language can be used only as in poetry. The poet, too, is not nearly so concerned with describing facts as with creating images and establishing mental connections."[19] Perhaps it is a statement like this, where wildly different disciplines are linked and related, that has made Karl Popper, for instance, call Bohr, although one of the greatest of all physicists, a "miserable philosopher."[20] It seems, however, that Bohr is involved in something a good deal more primordial than philosophy here: one could call it wonder or amazement. Bohr, Heisenberg, and Joyce share a marked tendency toward such "category errors" or metaphors of connectivity. They see that "language," whether poetic or scientific, cannot be objectified and that more is lost than gained in the attempt to fortify the relationship between signifiers and signifieds. Bohr told Heisenberg in this regard: "Of course, language has this strange, fluid character. We never know what a word means exactly . . . other meanings arise in its darker recesses, link up with different concepts and spread into the unconscious" (PB, 134–35). The "strange, fluid character" of the *Wake* demonstrates the truth of this claim by tracing the drifting of atomic particles and etyms in the dark recesses of language and the unconscious—recesses similar to the atomic flux which Bohr despaired of representing in language.

A number of the *Wake*'s critics (William York Tindall, Clive Hart, and Lazlo Moholy-Nagy among them) have drawn attention to Joyce's acquaintance with and implementation of quantum and relativity physics.[21] David Overstreet has examined in detail the relations between Joyce's technical developments in the *Wake* and quantum physics. The key to this linkage, Overstreet believes, is the oxymoronic nature of atoms and etyms, a linkage which Joyce does his utmost to demonstrate. Drawing attention to the fact that "oxymoron" ("pointedly foolish") is itself oxymoronic and that matter is similarly embraced by its anti-matter opposite, Overstreet reads the *Wake* as a self-interfering pattern of oppositions. The lineage of this procedure, as he indicates, is a prestigious one, including Aristotle's "unmoved mover" and Lao Tsu's *Tao* which, as we have seen, is a self-canceling term. "All sub-atomic particles," Overstreet writes, "have their own oxymoronic anti-particles. . . . Whenever a particle and its anti-particle meet, they annihilate each other and become two photons, i.e., two puffs of light."[22] This activity is one of the inspirations for the circulation, collision, fission, and fusion of etyms in the *Wake*. Words like "phall" and "woid" indicate how Joycean verbal technique resembles both the metaphysical paradoxes of Aristotle and Lao Tsu and the scatter experiments performed by physicists. Overstreet shows how such oxymorons "create singular effects like sparks jumping across diodes. Paradoxes are puzzles in logic. Oxymorons are aesthetic experiences wherein the perceiver creates out of the polar elements the third element, synthesis, in which a trinity of elements are imaginatively perceived as one 'true sense.' Oxymorons either intuitively happen or they don't" (55). Joyce's central oxymoron is presented in his book's title(s): *Finnegans Wake* means both the funeral and the resurrection of Finnegan—and Finnegans in general.

Joyce's composition of *Finnegans Wake* has often been regarded as a search for and assimilation of trivial parallels, analogies, and devices that would contribute to the universality of reference. We ought to recognize, however, that the apparently mad desire to include, for example, as many river names as possible in the text is entirely rational: Joyce sought to show how particular and yet how repetitious the fabric of the world was. He remarked: "I made [*Ulysses*] out of next to nothing. *Work in Progress* I am making out of nothing. But there are thunderbolts in it."[23] Like Rutherford, Joyce was interested in both disintegration and recombination, annihilation and transmutation—and the "thunderbolts" of Vico's *New Science* and the atomic blasts of Oppenheimer's Manhattan Project are told, retold, and foretold in Joyce's telling. Joyce's "etymic" physics explores the voids within the real and the way the real seems to reside on a void. Like the general male principle in the *Wake*, H.C.E., Joyce may well have been "mentally strained from reading work on German physics," while, like Professor Jones, "working out a quantum theory" to explain the meaning of words (543.24; 149.34). However amateur his reflections on the topic, Joyce clearly saw the *connection* of science to art as crucial to his encyclopedic work.

Joyce thus orients atomic physics to psychoanalysis in a general sense by aligning the destabilization of the atom with the destabilization of the Cartesian subject which Freud's work achieved. Like Adam, Descartes was authorized by God (the idea which he could not have invented) to establish a language for the world: Adam named the beasts and Descartes established the philosophical basis for a mathematical discourse of reality. Cartesian and Newtonian science provided the basic modern terms for objectivity but they could do so only for a fixed subject which does not recognize that its own will to reality is inevitably subjective. It is in this sense that Wallace Stevens saw Cartesian thought as a return to Adam's naïve naming of the physical world: "Adam/ In Eden was the father of Descartes/ And Eve made air the mirror of herself,/ Of her sons and her daughters."[24] Joyce saw the correctness of Cartesian skepticism (his annihilation of the normative world), but he seemed to believe that Descartes had not actually carried his skepticism far enough: "Sink deep or touch not the Cartesian spring!" (301.25). Only by piercing matter, language, and consciousness and exposing their systems, associations, and unconsciousness can the spring of the muses flow. Modifying Pope's advice ("Drink deep or taste not the Pierian spring"), Joyce suggests that Cartesian art which doubts the reality of appearance but not the reality of the perceiving subject is deluded. In this context, one may appreciate Joyce's claim that his work was "a deliberate break from a certain Cartesianism."[25]

Like Adam, Descartes fell when he demanded that knowledge be determinate and certain; to do so he divided the world in half—divided man (and his subjectivity) from God (or the whole world). Joyce makes this association explicit with regard to Newton, whose intuition of a mechanical, regulated "world" was popularly associated with the fall of an apple: "[Finn MacCool] thought he weighed a new ton when there felled his first lapapple" (126.28–29). Joycean redemption requires a dismantling of the very idea of an "individual," an "atom," an "etym," and "Adam"—it requires that Joyce demontrate how the appearance of isolated subjectivity is itself the fall. However focused on the fall, the *Wake* demonstrates this redemption by taking the subject apart and showing how it is indistinguishable from a word or complex of words—which his text scatters like seed from a fallen apple.

The "abnihilisation of the etym" is consequently felt in the fall of Adam, which is also the fall of any discrete origin in the book. Adam is "consistently blown to Adams" since any "birthright pang" "would split an atam" (313.12; 333.25). Just as an "atom" was never split in actuality (since it was never "one"), so Adam is never unfallen. Joycean writing thus does not maintain the orthodox value of etymology, based on the idea of true, originary roots, but creates in its place "a very fairworded instance of falsemeaning adamelegy" (77.26). The Joycean "science" of words is a wake or elegy for adam, atoms, and etymons practiced by "adamologists" (113.04) (as opposed to etymologists) who recognize that words, like humans and apples, are always falling. Like Anna Livia's letter, Joyce's text is not meant to "dizzledazzle with

a graith uncouthrement of postmantuam glasseries from the lap-
ins and the grigs" (113.01–02), but to provide for "the hardily
curiosing entomophilust" (107. 13) who has a "good smetterling
of entymology" (417.04) the "intimologies" (101.17) of humanity
and its language. In these instances Joyce fuses "etumon" (true
word) with "entomon" (something cut in segments, an insect) to
demonstrate the simultaneity of wholeness and fragmentation in
his literary practice of creation and destruction. The splitting of
the etym is, Joyce suggests, implicit in the "entym" or earwig
which, like words, pierce the ear. The sin of Earwicker is thus
conveyed in the secret lives of words, the "intimologies" which
"adamologists" read. Etumons, entymons, and atoms, swarm, fly,
and buzz everywhere in *Finnegans Wake* with an electrical intensity.

Despite this haze of electrical discharges, the *Wake* is not
simply a cloud of indeterminate shapes: certain well-defined
patterns characterize the general system of interactions. Joyce's
fundamental debt to the novelistic tradition is his attention to a
single middle-class family. In a letter to Harriet Shaw Weaver,
Joyce explained how he combined this traditional novelistic
focus with his own revolutionary form of writing: "In making
notes I use signs for the chief characters. It may amuse you to see
them . . ."

ᴨ	(Earwicker, H C E by moving letter round)
Δ	Anna Livia
Ⲋ	Shem-Cain
Λ	Shaun
Z	Snake
S	S. Patrick
T	Tristan
⊥	Isolde
X	Mamalujo
☐	This stands for the title but I do not wish to say it yet

until the book has written more of itself.[26]

These working notes are partially presented in a footnote in the so-called study chapter as the "Doodles family ⋔, △, ⊣, X, □, ∧, ⊏," (299.06). The five members of Joyce's nuclear family are thus represented in schematic fashion in order to indicate that they are more like patterns of energy and kinds of syntax (as we shall see) than intrinsic and unified subjectivities.[27]

Roland McHugh explains that such "personages as ⋔, △, ⊏, and ⊥ are fluid composites, involving an unconfined blur of historical, mythical and fictitious characters, as well as non-human elements. Joyce's technique of personality condensation is ultimately inseparable from his linguistic condensation."[28] Precise as this description is, it misses the point that such "condensation" of character is also, and perhaps more importantly, an explosion of characters, governed by the kinds of energies noted by Joyce's sigla. Whenever an acronymic attractor like the letters h,c,e emerge in the course of a noisy Wakean sentence, it begins to exert an influence on the neighboring signifiers, assembling phrases like "here comes everybody," "hircus civis eblanensis," "home, colonies, and empire," or "Howth Castle and Environs." So that as Joyce reduces "subjectivity" to a core of letters or sigla he also allows an unprecedented expansiveness and circulation, as well as an organizing influence on local conditions.

Jacques Lacan and M. M. Bakhtin provide clues to how this relationship between language and character (or subjectivity) is established. Lacan explains that what we usually refer to as subjectivity, voice, speech are all effects of a syntax, a complex style of self-representation, situated in the unconscious: "Syntax, of course, is preconscious. But what eludes the subject is the fact that his syntax is in relation with the unconscious reserve. When the subject tells his story, something acts, in a latent way, that governs his syntax and makes it more and more condensed. . . . In relation to what Freud, at the beginning of his description of psychical resistance, calls a nucleus. . . . To say that this nucleus refers to something traumatic is no more than an approximation."[29] Bakhtin writes of "intonational quotation marks" in novels which suggest the speech or consciousness of different characters, even when they do not speak: "The language of the novel [*Eugene*

Onegin] is a *system* of languages that mutually and ideologically interanimate each other. It is impossible to describe and analyze it as a single unitary language."[30] In such novels, the various idiolects or syntaxes, function as images of subjectivity, and thus the dramatic encounters between characters are also carried on between highly formalized languages. Together, Lacan's and Bakhtin's remarks explain how characters in *Finnegans Wake* are both empty and full, condensed and expanded, local and universal. Since subjectivity and novelistic character are the result of repression or the shaping of unconscious verbal energies, Joycean syntax is presented in miniature in each of the "characters" of *Finnegans Wake*.

At the origin of this family one finds, in effect, a particle/wave duality: the atomistic father and the relational mother, the nucleus of repressive energy and the fluid energy of release, the mountain of the giant Finn and the river of Anna Livia. Earwicker is immanent within periodic, highly subordinated, and confused "sintalks," just as Anna Livia is immanent within peritactic, coordinate, and fluent syntax. Their children reflect the decay of this original but elusive wholeness through parodistic syntaxes. Since the sons Shem and Shaun are like split particles of the old Atom, their syntaxes reflect the decay of an original integrity. Shaun's convoluted presence is indicated by an inflated and unconvincing imitation of his father's repression, while Shem reflects the feminine aspect of his father by an ironic but fluent parody of his mother. The daughter Izzy is an illusory, shallow reflection of her mother, and her language is a kind of palindromic and narcissistic baby talk. Joyce's nuclear family is indeed an atom or an etym whose splitting releases a torrent of energetic combinations and collisions which become articulated through an epic or encyclopedic population of human history, from Adam to Lord Hurtreford, from atoms to Lord Rutherford.

These textual operations depend upon Joyce's punning, a literary device that violates the purported integrity of words, splits them, but at the same time integrates them within a wider field of relations. The pun was especially condemned by modern and neoclassical critics who saw in it a lapse in decorum, a fall from

classical grace and modern scientific clarity. Dr. Johnson was dis-
mayed by Shakespeare's eagerness to play with words and make
puns: "A quibble is the golden apple for which he will always turn
aside from his career or step from his elevation. A quibble, poor
and barren as it is, gave him such delight that he was content to
purchase it by the sacrifice of reason, propriety, and truth."[31]
"Reason, propriety, and truth," lofty as they are, are nevertheless
susceptible to the "poor and barren" quibble, the toy which poets
like Shakespeare and Joyce could not resist. In the *Wake*, the reader is asked to join the poets: "(Stoop) if you are abcedminded, to
this claybook, what curios of signs (please stoop), in this
allaphbed! Can you rede (since We and Thou had it out already)
its world? It is the same told of all. Many. Miscegenations on miscegenations" (18.17ff). The syntax becomes rudimentary and
undeflected by the customary "flotsam," as if the "wholemole
millwheeling vicociclometer" (614.17) slowed to reveal, for a
moment, its jewelled bearings and an image of itself. The passage
assumes that the reader is "abecedminded," satisfied with the
logic of linear syntax and modern discourse, and thus "absent-
minded." To be "abcedminded" is to surrender the plenitude of
the world to the arbitrary logic of the alphabet and the book. It is
thus toward a different "logic" that the reader stoops when he is
confronted with the Joycean "claybook" and begins to see the clay
of his own origins and the *clef* (key) of his own world in the
"curios of signs." When signs themselves become the object of
curiosity they cease to be transparent figures of thought: they
enter the world of process, along with mind and nature.

A kind of etymic "cyclotron," Joyce's "wholemole millwheeling vicociclometer" was devised "for the verypetpurpose of subsequent recombination so that the heroticisms, catastrophes and
eccentricities transmitted by the ancient legacy of the past
. . . may be there for you" (614.34–615.08). Invented by Ernest O.
Lawrence not long after Rutherford's accelerator, the cyclotron is
a "device that accelerates ions in a spiral path by the influence of
electrical and magnetic fields until they emerge at a great speed,
at which point the ions can then bombard other elements for
the creation of other atoms."[32] Joyce's "vicociclometer" combines

Vico's theory of historical cycles (Divine, Heroic, Human, and then a recycling, or ricorso) with a cyclometer, which of course simply counts cycles or repetitions in a rotary device, in order to suggest an analogy for *Finnegans Wake*, whose endless cycling accelerates and energizes etyms in order both to discover the interior world of language and to create new words and a new language.

Joyce claimed that he had come to the end of English *(Je suis au bout de l'anglais)* not through an excess of arrogance but because he had begun to see ordinary language as a conceptual prison. "I'd like a language which is above all languages, a language to which all will do service. I cannot express myself in English without enclosing myself in a tradition."[33] The "abnihilisation of the etym" shatters the verbal bricks of this prison and releases the tropes, dreams, follies, and puns *confined*—to recall Foucault's powerful figure—or at least disciplined since the advent of modernity. Early critical responses to the *Wake* appropriately mentioned madness, pride, and blindness as explanations for its excesses. These are more helpful responses than one might have thought, for Joyce had intentionally let loose every kind of mythic and verbal folly he could within the empirical and prosaic world of the English novel and language only to discipline them according to a chaosmic logic all his own. Like a huge mass of "anti-matter," as Hugh Kenner has called it, "counterpoising" his earlier fiction, or like the "dark matter" undiscovered by astronomers but insisted upon by the calculations of mass that must have been generated by the big bang, *Finnegans Wake* is an affront to the ongoing modern quest for Cartesian certitude and objectification.[34] Joyce's book was thus not only a "book of the dark" and a "book of dreams," it was an admission and exploration of the vast scope of the world unrecognized and ignored by empiricism and rationality: play, madness, indeterminacy, sleep, dreams, darkness, night. *Finnegans Wake* is a massive joke at the expense of the *enlightenment* inspired by Bacon, Descartes, and Newton, perpetrated by one of its most rigorous students: an encyclopedic compendium of world history, human sciences, and art—all consigned to darkness.

Joycean Holography

Joyce set himself two fundamental and opposing tasks in *Finnegans Wake:* to demonstrate the complex unreality of absolutes, abstractions, and universals ("metaphysics" in the pejorative sense) and to reveal the pervasive, endless inter-connectedness of the universe within the sleeping mind and macrocosmic body of humankind as represented by H.C.E. and A.L.P. It was inevitable that Joyce would express this contradictory synthesis in a "word" which is not "one": *chaosmos.* For this word is more a collision of etyms and a crossing of concepts than a denotative signifier. One could understand this word structurally as the Greek letter *chi* (X) which is itself an image of a crossroads, the trope of chiasmus and, prophetically enough, the shape of the chromosome that forms the most complex of living languages. The "X" is a "knot" of relevance, a "story" in Bateson's sense, about how chance and order, chaos and cosmos, penetrate the core of atoms, cells, and words to form and unform the ground of life. Joycean chaosmos preserves the mystery of human existence, but it opens the network that would inform us, in Bateson's words, "*of stories* . . . shared by all minds, whether ours or those of redwood forests and sea anemones."[35]

The Joycean pun, indispensable to this demonstration, derives its "authority," as Joyce admitted, from Christ: "the Holy Roman Catholic Apostolic Church was built on a pun. It ought to be good enough for me."[36] Christ was a punster, then, when he founded his church: "You are Peter *(Petrus)* and upon this rock *(petrus)* I will build my church." By renaming Simon, Peter, Christ repeated in verbal terms his own incarnation and thus sanctified his vicar on earth through a simulacrum of divine birth. Joyce commemorates this episode on the opening page of *Finnegans Wake* by punning on Moses' and St. Patrick's divine callings: "nor avoice from afire bellowsed mishe mishe to tauftauf thuartpeatrick" (3.09-10). The pun in both cases represents the calling, naming, and transforming of subjectivity through an apparently superficial play on words. Indeed, Christ's own name is part of this process: "Christ" (significantly linked with "home," "ale," and "master" in the litany of alien words Stephen cites) derives from the Greek *chriein* (to signify, to annoint with oil). When Jesus (Hebrew *Yeshna*) is "christened" his name is "name," the Jew-Greek Jesus Christ: the figure of Christ's incarnation (both in intellectual history and within the narrative of Christianity) can be found in the *chi* which crosses the Greek and the Hebrew, the divine and the human. A letter which can be reversed and inverted, the *chi*, however it is positioned, remains the same. In *Finnegans Wake* "Xristos" (342.18), besides being the central cultural expression of the mythic principle that life comes out of death, is associated with the fish *(ichthos)* which repeats the transformation of spirit into flesh, the communication and communion of God with carnality: "now pass the fish for Christ sake, Amen" (384.15); "pass the loaf for Christ sake" (393.02); "pass the Kish for crawsake" (7.08). Christ's incarnation, his miracle of the fishes and the loaves, his naming of Peter, his last supper, and his crucifixion are characterized by the "X" of crossing and canceling. *Finnegans Wake* as a whole repeats this figure of crossing at every level: sub-atomic, linguistic, religous, mythic, philosophic, political, historical, and cosmic. Every "word" in *Finnegans Wake* is "under erasure" in order to shift our attention from its logocentric substitution to the multivalent world that is always escaping it.

If Christ's story can be found in a Greek letter, then perhaps Christ is an example of other chiastic relations: the appearance of order out of chaos, the birth of the cosmos from chaos, and the collapse of order into chaos. The Joycean chaosmos superimposes these abstractions lying at the center of the incarnation and the sacraments by destroying and fusing the etyms of planetary culture in each "woid." This "woid" thus "contains" the multitemporality that Serres describes within life and matter: orders are rising towards greater complexity, while others are inevitably dissipating. Joyce forges (creates/counterfeits) a language in which these opposing and yet synthesizing forces within matter enter into the realm of meaning. Serres proposes a "theorem" to describe the impact of thermodynamics, steam engines, and the foundry on Turner's paintings which could, by analogy, describe the Joycean "smeltingworks" (614.31): "beneath the forms of matter, stochastic disorder reigns supreme. To smelt is to rediscover chance as fundamental. The furnace is the engine for going back toward chaos. The foundry is where creation starts over at zero."[37] Joyce reveals this coincidence of order and disorder in each word and so describes "this furnaced planet" and "blazing urbanorb" according to a logic which Serres discovers in the heart of matter (412.17, 589.06).

The familiar illustration by Leonardo of "Vitruvian man" (with the arms and legs extended into two patterns touching the circumference of a circle and the sides of a square) suggests the premodern assumption that the human form was a microscosmos.[38] The assumption is that the human form is proportioned so as to square the circle but also that the human form defines the boundaries of square and circle. Such a figure both constructs and deconstructs the representation which it offers of the cosmos because it illustrates the fact that the world—our world—is necessarily a human world. Serres describes, as a complement to multitemporality, the very detailed ways in which the body cannot be said to exist in a simple space: "My body . . . is not plunged into a single, specified space. It works in Euclidean space, but it only works there. It sees in a projective space; it suffers in another; hears and communicates in a third; and so forth, as far as one wishes to go" (44). When one talks about the physical and mental existence or identity of a human being, it is only by the crudest corporeal fictions that one can locate this being in a given "Euclidean" space: subjectivity and physicality do not have the ideal outlines of classical geometric forms.

It is according to such presumptions that Joyce superimposes Ireland upon the cosmos ("Oh Kosmos! Ah Ireland!" [456.07]) and reads the cosmos into Ireland. Continuing this process, he superimposes Dublin upon Ireland, and H.C.E. and A.L.P. upon Dublin: all elements are related to one another according to the order of a reflexive patterning, not according to the insistence of extended matter and fixed subjectivity. The body of Christ is one with the cosmos according to this practice, insofar as it is the form of divinity cast into the world. Shaun, who imagines himself to be Christlike, explains this superimposition in parodic terms:

"I can easily believe heartily in my own spacious immensity as my ownhouse and microbemost *cosm* when I am reassured by ratio that the cube of my volume is to the surface of their subjects as the sphericity of these globes . . . is to the ferocity of Fairnelly's vacuum" (150.35ff., my emphasis). The individual "cosm" is also and simultaneously a chaos, as Shem's "own individual person life unlivable, transaccidentated through the slow fires of consciousness into a dividual *chaos*, perilous, potent, common to allflesh, human only, mortal" (186.03ff., my emphasis). The two brothers, who are but the halves of their father form the chaos of cosmos and the cosmos of chaos. Joyce avoids the trap of purely metaphysical speculation by reforming language to permit the expression of such contradictions and inclusion of opposites: "Ab chaos lex, neat wehr" (518.31). Translated into linear, noncontradictory discourse, this reads: "From chaos comes law, *nicht wahr?*" (not true?, right?). But also, "From chaos comes law, a neat weapon."

Joyce's technical innovations are serial demonstrations of chaosmos, not the means for its expression or representation. Traditionally, epic or mythic representation supposes a certain cosmic integrity which resembles the form of the book. The Bible, for instance, begins with creation and ends with apocalypse. The doubling of word and world occurs without many consequences and appears authorized by the *fiat lux* of the Creator and the appearance of Christ as the Word in the New Testament. The cosmos has been imagined as indistinguishable from a certain linear syntax that informs the book as a representational instrument. Although eternity (both before and after the created universe and history) is admittedly the broader frame of this narrative, its major characteristic is its resistance to representation. Joycean chaosmos breaks with this Western identification of cosmos and the book, primarily by demonstrating a discrepancy between its own beginning and the unimaginable beginning of the cosmos. Indeed, Joyce's own beginning ("riverrun") overflows the inaugural and authorizing position and spreads out into timelessness. Joyce thus superimposes time and timelessness, cosmos and chaos, when he uses words to represent neither things nor ideas, but to demonstrate the formation and disappearance of things and ideas. In doing so, his book becomes an "untitled mamafesta" or letter dictated by the river Anna Livia and destined to redeem or dissolve the sins of historical existence. The *Wake* is fused, then, not only with a certain kind of reality but also with that letter which supposedly explains the history of the fall into sin and time. An analysis of the letter by a Wakean critic details these qualities:

> Because, Soferim Bebel, if it goes to that, (and dormerwindow gossip will cry it from the housetops no surelier than the writing on the wall will hue it to the mod of men that mote in the main street) every person, place and thing in the chaosmos of Alle anyway connected with the gobblydumped turkery was moving and changing every part of the time: the travelling inkhorn (possibly pot), the hare and the turtle pen and paper, the continually more and less intermisunderstanding minds of the anticollaborators, the as time went on as it will variously inflected, differently pronounced, otherwise spelled, changeably meaning scriptsigns. (118.18–23)

The letter and the "chaosmos of Alle" resist objectification, literalization, and temporalization: in both the chaosmos and the letter all elements were "moving and changing every part of the time." Time is spatialized and space is temporalized, just as "everything" (Alle) and God (Allah) are involved in the crossing of cosmos and chaos—to create a double focus of order and disorder, creation and destruction, what Joyce refers to elsewhere as "Thisorder" (540.19). The order of the *chi* is associated, apparently, with chaosmic events which the chiliasm portends. The allusion to Allah and Islam suggests as well the world destruction described in the Koran: "when the sky is rent asunder; when the stars scatter and the oceans roll together; when the graves are hurled about; each soul shall know what it has done and what it has failed to do. . . . On that day mankind will come in broken bands to be shown their labours. Whoever has done an atom's weight of good shall see it, and whoever has done an atom's weight of evil shall see it also."[39] We read of H.C.E. "whaling away the whole of the while *(hypnos chilio eonion!)* lethelulled between explosion and reexplosion (Donnaurwatteur! Hunder-thunder!) from grosskopp to megapod, embalmed, of grand age, rich in death anticipated" (78.03–06). The *chilio eonion* (from *chilius*, one thousand) marks the thousand year reign of the resurrected Christ and remarks Joyce's interests in this crossed letter, this *chi*, so evident in Christ, his cross, his reign, and his name.

One can see in this Greek letter a figure of the *coincidentia oppositorum* which Joyce adapted from Nicholas of Cusa and Giordano Bruno and established as the central "logic" of *Finnegans Wake*, which then associates these Renaissance conceptions with their contemporary reincarnations in psychoanalysis and physics. Jung explains Christ's place in this tradition: "Christ, as a hero and god-man, signifies psychologically the self; that is, he represents the projection of this most important and most central of archetypes. The archetype of the self has, functionally, the significance of a ruler of the inner world, i.e., of the collective unconscious. The self, as a symbol of wholeness, is a *coincidentia oppositorum*, and therefore contains light and darkness simultaneously."[40] The self, according to these terms, is whole but also dual, an effect of *chiaroscuro*: "under the closed eyes of the inspectors the traits featuring the *chiaroscuro* coalesce, their contrarieties eliminated, in one stable somebody" (107.28–30).

While Jung presented a psychoanalytic explanation for the coincidence of opposites evident in all the fallen but redeemable children of Adam, Bohr presented his own physical version of the esoteric principle evident in the Christian and Jungian self: the famous wave/particle duality of light. In the nineteenth century it had been "proven" that light was a wave frequency, but by the twentieth century that it was "also" supposed to be, following Einstein's work, corpuscular. Following this and other apparent absurdities that his own research uncovered in subatomic dynamics, Bohr formalized the principle of "complementarity" which describes "a situation in which it is possible to grasp one and the same event by two distinct modes of interpretation. These modes are mutually exclusive, but they also complement each other, and it is only through their juxtaposition that the perceptual content of a phenomenon is fully brought out."[41] In other words, the composition of light—that central emblem of rationality illuminating the concept of enlightenment—can only be known through the coincidence, crossing, complementing of opposites. Although complementarity as a concept in physical science was proposed to account for such instances where single perspective descriptions could be displaced by other single perspective descriptions, Bohr seemed ready to give the concept more general application, invoking as he did the Taoist emblem of the interanimation of Yin and Yang, darkness and light. The world itself, it could be said, following Bohr's Taoist extension of complementarity, is never adequately described by the logic of noncontradiction. As Bohr told Heisenberg, "The opposite of a correct statement is a false statement. But the opposite of a profound truth may well be another profound truth" (102).

Joyce may have seen in the work of Bohr and Jung an analogy for his own practices in the *Wake*, for he would appear to "collide" Bruno's thesis with Bohr's: "And let every crisscouple be so cross complementary, little eggons, youlk and meelk, in a farbiger pancosmos" (613.11–12). Every couple or opposition in the *Wake* is "complementary" in the way that the liquid and solid aspects of an egg are both one and two, just as the world-egg and the Fabergé egg represent the macro- and microcosmic forms of this wholeness whose fracture begins historical time.

It must be obvious, then, that one cannot speak of a Joycean chaosmos according to the modernist terms of a world-picture, a structure, or an interpretation. Instead one might recall the Hindu God Shiva, who represents, who "is," both creation and destruction. It is precisely this ability to think in terms of collapsing and emerging opposites that Bateson believes we have lost in the culture of Cartesianism. In order to redress this loss, we could start thinking *within* the words that Joyce wrote: "abnihilisation," "thisorder," "chaosmos." The chiasmus of Joycean writing operates consistently through frustrating the conceptual categories that modernism, following logocentric procedures, organized in order to exclude the mysterious, the unknowable, or the paradoxical. In this sense, the words of *Finnegans Wake* resemble riddles or koans, knots in discursive logic which cannot be solved by the wiles of reasoning. Every reading of the *Wake* may set out to solve the riddling words, but it can succeed only by involving more strands within the knot. Contemplating a knot, as a Zen student meditates nondiscursively on a koan, one is released from one's own concentrated efforts to organize and discipline the text. Joyce cultivates this verbal ground by preserving the precarious balance of credulity and skepticism, cosmic illumination and chaotic darkness. Joyce's reading of the Cartesian syllogism uncovers this combination of faith and doubt: "Cog it out, here goes a sum. So read we in must book. It tells. He prophets most who bilks the best" (304.31–305. 02). The mathematical "sum" underlies the metaphysical *sum* of *cogito, ergo sum,* revealing that Descartes' apparently prophetic remark was simply a boyish sum, a "bilk" that passed to his profit. Descartes' real prophecy, Joyce suggests, is concealed in his name, which states that subjectivity, the self, is a product of chance and reincarnation: *rené des cartes:* "As I was saying, while retorting thanks, you make me a reborn of the cards" (304.27). Descartes was a card in a world of chance who tried to stack a deck. As Joyce admitted, "Some of the means I use are trivial—and some are quadrivial." [42]

Begun in the years of cultural crisis described by Valéry following the slaughter of the Great War, written in the years of *l'entre deux guerres* which saw the flowering of psychoanalysis, quantum mechanics, and "modernist" art and literature, and published in 1939 at the beginning of the end of the imperial era, *Finnegans Wake* was appropriately conceived as a "dream of world history . . . the dream of old Finn, lying in death beside the river Liffey and watching the history of Ireland and the world—past and future—flow through his mind like the flotsam of the river of life."[43] Joyce's dream-book extends the premises of the tradition of dream literature, which includes *The Divine Comedy* and the Alice books, by "putting language to sleep," word by word, and allowing it to dream a dream in which, as Joyce said, "the visions pass from the trivial to the apocalyptic, where the brain uses the roots of vocables to make others from them which will be capable of naming its phantoms, its allegories, its allusions."[44] To these comprehensive and technical qualities of dream, Joyce could add both its ancient, prophetic, and its modern, neurotic attributes. He thus elaborated on Freud's conception of dream as a rebus, a sign language of puns, metonymies (which laterally displace unacceptable material), and metaphors (which vertically condense it), while also elaborating on Jung's claim that dreams revealed the collective unconscious—a chaos of displaced wishes and a cosmos of integrated forms. Both of these aspects of dream cross each word of the *Wake* to form "my Jungfraud's Messongebook" (460.20), equally lie and dream, deceit and prophecy. *Finnegans Wake* may be seen, then, as the reconciliation of Shem and Shaun, the two warring brothers of psychoanalysis, one that affirms Freud's scientific skepticism but also validates Jung's faith in the numinous power of symbols.

Joyce was convinced that life was finally and inevitably mysterious, and this conviction led him to assimilate psychoanalytic and physical theories of the mysteries of the unconscious and of matter itself. It also led him to combine physical laws derived from Newtonian mechanics and concepts and procedures derived from quantum mechanics with mythic laws derived from a variety of cultures. Throughout the *Wake*, for instance, there is really only one date: 1132, a number which combines the rate at which bodies fall in a vacuum (thirty-two feet per second per second) to the number eleven, which implies renewal; thus every year in the *Wake* is poised at the still point between the domains of life and death, falling and rising: "The oaks of ald now they lie in peat yet elms leap where askes lay. Phall if you but will, rise you must: and none soon either shall the pharce for the nunce come to a setdown secular phoenish" (4.14–17). The fallen tree becomes the soil for its successors, and so the "fall" of one man is the rising "phall" or phallus of his son: each "f" (as in "fall" or "finish") sounds the "ph" of the "phallus" or "phoenix." Just as the *kappa* of "kosmos" is crossed by the *chi* of "chaos," the "f/ph" coupling assists in the mythologizing of the fundamentally historical and empirical qualities of modern English. Attending to the homonymic relations between words and letters, Joyce is unwilling to say where one word "ends" and when another "ands." He thus sides neither with Newton's reversible nor strictly with Prigogine's irreversible "physics." Instead Joyce demonstrates a cyclical physics of falling and rising bodies wherein each movement forward is also a movement backward.

These well-known qualities of the *Wake* should be seen as a part of a mythic critique of modernity, not a "modernist" use of myth. The latter view was popularized by Eliot's "*Ulysses:* Order and Myth," an essay which more or less repeated the standard modernist attitude toward myth established by Francis Bacon's *The Wisdom of the Ancients.*[45] Bacon and Eliot both imply that myths are illustrations of certain philosophic problems or narratives of certain archetypal events. Eliot justified the apparent chaos of *Ulysses* by claiming that Joyce had introduced a technique (the mythic parallel) which could "organize" contemporary experience. He authorized this "technique" in acceptable terms by comparing it to a scientific discovery. While Eliot was mainly interested in smoothing the reception of the book, his comments suggest that myth is little more than a story once told unironically in the comfortable environment of what Lukács called an "integrated society." They also initiated the new critical and archetypal tendency to see the work of Joyce, Pound, and Eliot as a kind of rationalized and modernized literary "experimentation," slighting its profound critiques of modernity's intellectual foundations. Joyce, Eliot, Pound, and others may have started with myth as "props" or "trellises," but their works, like *The Waste Land, Ulysses* and the *Cantos* establish their own intrinsic, textual means of support. In any case, the mythic parallel is not a new technique: Dryden and Pope both used it to "organize" and ironize "Absalom and Achitophel" and "The Rape of the Lock." Joycean myth is more properly a critique of the modernist ideology of technology, instrumentalism, and control which Eliot's essay inadvertently repeats. Neither Joyce nor Eliot possessed the critical language to describe the ways in which *Ulysses,* the *Wake,* the *Cantos,* and *The Waste Land* are indeed mythic.

After the work of Benjamin Whorf and Claude Lévi-Strauss, it is easier to see that myth, in the general sense, is less a plot than a language that binds observed facts to intuited integrities. It is not an "explanation" of nature (a view which certainly reveals the modernist presumption that nature must be accounted for); it is a version of the world upon which the human mind (its desires, languages, dreams) is superimposed. Myth is an example of what Bateson and Prigogine would regard as a participative universe— a universe which is unified and completed only through observation and representation. Where modernist literature sought to define the subject and define the object, post-Enlightenment literature—whether one means Blake, Hölderlin, or Joyce—insists upon the ways in which water, air, earth, rats, eagles, and fish, all the phenomenal world and the tropes of language and consciousness, form an unbreakable network of significant relations. As languages become "modern," these mythic elements become segregated within the domains of "art"—and it is at this point that they become irrelevant to the dominant ideology of "realism." Lévi-Strauss reminds us, however, that "every civilization tends to overestimate the objective orientation of its thought and this tendency is never absent."[46] "Objectivity," in other words, measures the degree to which a culture is alienated from the sensible, rather than the intelligible, aspect of its language—the numbers, the words, the figures. And, as Whorf writes, "Languages differ not only in how they build their sentences but also in how they break down nature to secure the elements to put in those sentences."[47] Mythologies, which are so engrained in languages such as Chinese, Apache, Sanskrit, and Egyptian as to be unparaphrasable, thus reflect on the sensuous figures of consciousness which languages cast upon the "real." Lévi-Strauss writes that myths and rites "preserve until the present time the remains of methods of observation and reflection which were (and no doubt still are) precisely adapted to discoveries of a certain type, those which nature authorized from the starting point of a speculative organization and exploitation of the sensible world in sensible terms. . . . Mythical thought is therefore a kind of intellectual 'bricolage' [meaning a heterogeneous repertoire of skills and media] (116-17).

The English language, associated since the seventeenth century with empirical, no-nonsense realism, is made to absorb dozens of languages and myths so that its exclusivity and pretense to empirical and imperial singularity and authority disappears beneath the sheer excess of Joyce's associations. By turning English into a host language, Joycean bricolage overpowers what Whorf calls "the bipartitional ideology of nature" reflected in modern Western languages. The *Wake,* if it were to fulfill Joyce's demands, had thus to be thoroughly porous, receptive to other languages, myths, *kosmoi,* even to accidents of composition, if it were not to remain within the Lockean and Cartesian categories of substantives and verbs, atoms and the void. Joyce constructed a language which, like Apache and Hopi, would not make artificial distinctions and practical categories and which, like the unconscious, seemed to link the most discrepant meanings through the apparently accidental laws of resemblance and association. Joyce thus sought to establish a chaosmic universe by releasing the occulted powers of signs into a new discourse. Whorf recognizes the link between syntactic and cosmic structure and indicates the ways in which native American languages "do not paint the separate-object picture of the universe to the same degree as English and its sister languages [and] point toward possible new types and possible new cosmical pictures" (241).

It is along these lines that *Finnegans Wake* was designed, according to Eugene Jolas, as a "pansymbolic, panlinguistic synthesis of a 4D universe."[48] And according to Umberto Eco, "In *Finnegans Wake* Joyce establishes the possibility of defining our universe in the 'transcendental' form of language. He provides a laboratory in which to formulate a model of reality and, in so doing, withdraws from *things* to *language.*"[49] Such a synthesis, by virtue of its "panlinguistic" nature, can only be enacted in a polymorphic and polyphonic language. But in writing such a contrapuntal text, Joyce has practiced mythic thinking. According to William Irwin Thompson "we need to understand that a myth is not a linear code, but a polyphonic fugue. . . . A mythic narrative works through a system of correspondences, so a god is at once a principle of order, a number, a geometrical figure, a dancing measure, a mantram, a special planet, and a heavenly body."[50] In order to achieve such a network of correspondences, Joyce had to stratify his words the way mythic languages do: through punning and play. The Egyptologist R. T. Rundle Clark makes this relationship explicit in the course of a discussion of hieroglyphic punning. In Egyptian writing and myth, melody, geometrical figures, numerology, and archetypal imagery are all combined: "This strange proceeding is no longer part of our conscious thinking, but the psychologists have shown that similar verbal exercises underly the free association of ideas. It is, of course, the technique of James Joyce in *Finnegans Wake*."[51]

Joyce's conception of myth was mainly derived from Vico's speculations about the origins of metaphysics in the poetic wisdom of early men and women and demonstrates what happens if the body and the brain of a person becomes the language and code of the universe itself. Joyce's break with Cartesianism follows Vico's break with Cartesianism by placing the body of language into the universe of thought. Joyce, like Vico, dismantles scholastic and rationalist metaphysics through a rigorous materialism which refused to see the soul or spirit as a shadow of the real: instead Joyce sought to rediscover the fundamental spirituality of the body and the fundamental corporeality of the spirit. As a writer, this meant that Joyce located the physical and the metaphysical realms within the body of the sleeping Finn. Vico claims that "poetic wisdom, the first wisdom of the gentile world, must have begun with a metaphysics not rational and abstract like that of learned men now, but felt and imagined, as that of the first men must have been, who, without power of ratiocination, were all robust sense and vigorous imagination."[52] Joyce adopted these claims by reorienting the entire cosmos of modern reality within the dreaming mind of an ordinary man which could recover the robust figures of the giants at the dawn of history. "Vico's premise," John Bishop observes in the course of a discussion of Vico and Joyce, "completely breaks with such forms of Enlightenment belief as Cartesian rationalism and Lockean empiricism, both of which regarded 'Reason' as an eternal manifestation of laws of nature determined if not by a benevolent deity than by a transcendent order."[53] The Joycean chaosmos is similarly aligned with the natures of the body, language, and myth as it persistently pushes ideas back into words, and words back into tropes, and tropes back into bodies.

The chaosmos could be described as a lexical and syntactic interiorization of the flux of material existence. The Joycean "collideorscope" (143.28) is both an atomic collider and a kaleidoscope which displays the root compositions of etyms and transforms the ordinary world of objects moving in space into a constant flux and field of ever-new reorientations and relationships. Its "logic" could be likened in general to Bateson's conception of difference-as-relationship and specifically to Derrida's description of the play of *différance* within language: "Within a conceptual system and in terms of classical requirements, *différance* could be said to designate the productive and primordial constituting causality, the process of scission and division whose sunderings and differences could be constituted products or effects."[54] Each word in the *Wake* is more or less a difference, not only from any potential referent, but from "itself" or its proper, undistorted form. The indeterminacy of meaning in the *Wake* derives from the absence of a frame which could restrict and direct its language toward a center or a conclusion. *Différance* describes the way in which death and rebirth are involved in each atom of *Finnegans Wake*. *Différance*, Derrida writes, "is what makes this movement of signification possible only if each element that is said to be 'present,' appearing on the stage of presence, is related to something other than itself but retains the mark of a past element and already lets itself be hollowed out by the mark of its relationship to a future element" (142). Despite its technical description, Derrida's "nonconcept" of *différance* strains the limits of logical or purely abstract thought. By seeking to explain how meaning happens, Derrida produces what, in other contexts, could be likened to a mystical scheme of the continuous and inevitable reincarnation of meaning, what in *Finnegans Wake* is aligned with the "riverrun" of eternity. It could also be linked with the creative power of "noise" and "interdisciplinarity" which William Paulson sees in cybernetic systems, the way in which deviation (or metaphor) leads to new possibilities.[55] The chaosmos reveals in mythic forms the production of meaning as an eternal process of drafting significance from other sources and eroding the apparently permanent mountain of the past with the living (dissolving) water of the present. The cosmic scheme in the *Wake* dramatizes the microphysics of language which Derrida calls *différance:* birth, death, and resurrection occur within the alphabet of its elements.

Amid the many motifs compacted on the first page of the *Wake* one finds "Nor avoice from afire bellowsed mishe mishe to tauftauf thuartpeatrick" (3.9). I want to trace the phrases "mishe mishe" and "tauftauf" because they demonstrate how Joyce dismantles and reconstrues metaphysical values such as the self *(Mishe,* Gaelic, "I am") and naming *(taufen,* German, to baptize). "Avoice from afire," a voice from a fire, from afar, is the voice of Yahweh addressing Moses—but it also suggests Jesus' naming of Peter and St. Patrick's annunciation. These moments of calling, spanning the centuries of Judeo-Christian tradition, are condensed in one sentence which suggests that "god" (whose divinity inheres in namelessness: "I am that I am") calls (and masters) the bearers of his Word, and in so doing changes them. This archetypal linkage of Israel/Moses, Ireland/Patrick, the Church/ Peter also foretells that the water of baptism will be the water of grace: the dissolution of identity, name, and sin into the river of eternity: whether Lethe or Liffey, river water can memorialize or forget. Notice, then, that the divine origin of identity—and the *source* of all other kinds of identity—is already a stutter *(mishe mishe, tauftauf)* that garbles the communcation of the divine with the human. The emergence of the name and of language are involved with duplicity, stuttering—or sin. In this sense, sin is the inimitable difference "between" words, a *difference* which is described as a *fall.* All subsequent versions of this motif both aggravate and compensate for the divine act of identity which has fallen into repetition.

The phrase "Swishawish satins and their taffetaffe tights" (12.22) transforms the *mishe* of identity into a whirl of satin and the *tauf* of baptism into a taffeta sheath. Naming is compared to dressing and supplements the previous sense of naming as an equation of insides and outsides or bodies and sheaths, where one can "put on" a name like a dress. Thus the "satin" of divine naming gives way to taffeta, a cheaper (human) substitute. "A tofftoff for thee, missymissy for me" (65.31) renders a jazz age version of the father-daughter incest which the *Wake* associates with the unnamable sin—in contrast with the ineffable name of Yahweh. At this stage an explicit note of sin appears and infects the idea of identity, so that *mishe* becomes *missy*, the young girl who lures the father to sin so that he becomes "the father of fornicationists" (4.14), the patriarch of wrongful coupling, the father of his daughter, the fornicationist. The sexual turn is furthered in a repetition of the sin's telling: "in the old gammeldags, the four of them, in Milton's Park under lovely Father Whisperer and making her love with his stuffstuff in the languish of flowers and feeling to find was she mushymushy" (96.9–12). Here language is made to languish, as the baptismal *tauftauf* becomes the "stuffstuff" of the invaginated penis and the *mishe mishe* becomes *mushy mushy*, the sign of an aroused and receptive vagina—as well as the Japanese telephone greeting, which suggests analogies for the receiver: baptismal font, vagina, telephone. The gradual erosion of the initial meaning and the accumulation of sexual and corporeal signs interprets the "ideas" of the subject and the name. Further transformations elaborate the sound-shape of the signs, as the tempting daughter Izzy becomes identified with the *mishe* motif because of her narcissism. These elaborations include "toughturf . . . mishymissy (145.7–8); "Mishy Mushy . . . Toft Taft" (277.11); "messy messy . . . douche douche" (605.2–3). With this last transformation, one hears that the accumulated sense of sin as identity and sexual arousal *(mishe, mushymushy)* has produced the "messy messy" that only the douche of baptism can absolve, wash, and shower away. Thus, after the primary role of water in the baptismal naming, the "douche" of unnaming is necessary to dissolve the sexual accumulation of sin. Sin and fall, the moral terms for this *différance,* are inscribed from the beginning in the divine tautology ("I am that I am") which demonstrates the limits of language when it addresses the infinite. According to Derrida's famous essay, *différance* means, then, that "every concept is necessarily and essentially inscribed in a chain or system, within which it refers to another and other concepts" (140). As its medium and argument, *différance* comes close to expressing the

night-logic of *Finnegans Wake:* the perpetual differing and defer-
ring of the processes of life and language, the perpetual presumption of an origin or foundation always thwarted by the apparent
effects of such an origin.

It should not be surprising, then, that *Finnegans Wake*
should have come to play its own part in the unfolding of twentieth-century physics and its quest for a fundamental physical particle. When the physicist Murray Gell-Mann sought to explain
the behavior and structure of hadrons (quanta which the bom-
bardment of protons had produced) he postulated the existence of
what he called "quarks." In explaining his theory he pointedly
drew attention to a passage from *Finnegans Wake* where seabirds
flying above the ship carrying Tristan and Isolde "quark" (caw,
croak, squawk) in response to the cuckolding of old King Mark:

> —*Three quarks for Muster Mark!*
> *Sure he hasn't got much of a bark*
> *And sure any he has it's all beside the mark.*
> (383.1–3)

Although Overstreet complains that Gell-Mann chose a "random onomatopoetic word instead of a deeply meaningful oxymoron" (67), I think that, whether through chance or design, the
physicist picked the word from an interesting and suggestive passage. Gell-Mann indicated a passage concerning the cuckolding
of old King Mark by the young Tristan possibly to demonstrate
that the "old mark" (the hadron, the proton, the nucleus, the
atom) has to yield to a new "mark." King Mark is given "three
quarks" by the "shrillgleescreaming . . . seaswans" (383.15) when
his faithful emissary Tristan betrays his trust with "Usolde."
Beside the cuckoo's cuckolding song, the three quarks suggest the
curd or curds *(der Quark)* fed to an impotent, toothless old man.
Could Gell-Man have seen the scientists, like Mark, reduced to
an unsatisfying, unsubstantial meal of "curds" or "quarks"? Or was
he invoking the elusive cries of birds?

The fact that Gell-Mann entitled the octet of hadrons "the
eightfold way" suggests that there is indeed more to "quark" than

a silly word, although it is indeed that.[56] The "noble eight-fold path" lays out the eight rules of behavior established by the Buddha. More significantly in this context, however, is the fact that the eightfold way is the fourth of the Buddha's Four Noble Truths. Gell-Mann thus implies the infolding of eight within one and one within four, the folding of paths within truths, and truths within the Dharma, which is both the Law and the Truth of Buddhism. Gell-Mann showed that hadrons could be explained as the various compositions of three "quarks" ("up," "down," and "strange"—as well as their respective antiquarks) which produce eighteen different kinds of hadrons. At present, the various flavors of quarks have yet to be isolated and are confined to the hadron curd or "molecule." Emblematic of this transformation of the individuated particles into a pattern of relationship is Gell-Mann's explicit solicitation of Buddhist thought. And here certainly is a curious "Indianization" (as Husserl puts it and of which we will see more in this study) of Europe's quest for an indivisible and determinate ground for its truth.

One of the most stunning challenges to this desire came about, ironically enough, by attempts to reassert the fundamental premises of the physical sciences. In the 1930s Einstein, unhappy with Bohr's conclusion that objective reality was always at the same time an observer-restrained reality, proposed (with colleagues Podolsky and Rosen) the so-called EPR thought-experiment. Einstein and his colleagues pointed out that quantum mechanics leads physicists to make a choice between maintaining "local causality" (the premise that there are no physically unmediated causal relations between distant objects) and the easier conclusion that quantum mechanics was an incomplete theory, a conclusion that opened the door to so-called "hidden variables" which would provide the basis for a truly determinist and objective physics. This challenge was unresolved until 1965 when John Bell showed that quantum mechanics could not have passed over any hidden variables: either the world was not objective or it was not governed alone by "local causality." If the world is not objective the entire premise of the physical sciences is endangered, and if nonlocal causation is breeched then "action at a distance," a determinism unmediated by any known material reality and/or a faster-than-light signaling between particles, is inevitable. Remarking on the significance of his famous theorem, called by Henry Pierce Stapp the "most profound discovery of science," Bell says "I think it's a deep dilemma, and the resolution of it will not be trivial; it will require a substantial change in the way we look at things."[57] Whichever way physical science eventually develops, Bell's theorem seems to stand in the way of a simple working out of the fundamentalist model that has guided science since the atomists.

The late physicist David Bohm's thinking was far in advance of experimentation and his views are considered very speculative, but his metaphoric model of reality strikingly complements the Joycean chaosmos and suggests ways in which the conflicts between local causation and action-at-a-distance, the objective and the subjective, the part and the whole, are potentially resolvable. Bohm, a former collaborator with Einstein, begins by questioning the nonscientific, ideological premises of physical science and offers a general critique of Western languages and the scientific method. The fundamental problem, as he presents it, is the "almost universal habit of taking the content of our thought 'for a description of the world as it is, a habit which inevitably construes the world as pervaded with differences and distinctions which ought to be attributed to our language."[58] Division of labor and specialization, however useful for research, are not conducive to a coherent or rational vision: as our knowledge increases, our understanding becomes increasingly fragmentary. Bohm insists that "what should be said is that wholeness is what is real, and that fragmentation is the response of this whole to man's action, guided by illusory perception which is shaped by fragmentary thought" (7). To make this shift, we might consider how modernity has impoverished reality by equating the real with communally achieved measurements.

The Cartesian tradition, in its search for the indubitable, implicitly defined the true as what could reify the authority of the scientist: by a process of excluding the immeasurable or ungovernable, truth emerges as a kind of residue. Precise measure-

ment was invaluable to this enterprise because it was able to subsi-
tute data or facts for knowledge or truth and produce the modern
discourse of "information," the product of technical enquiry.
Etymologically related to *measure* and *modern* (from the Indo-
European root *med*) is the Sanskrit *maya*, the veil of illusion, of
plausible reality, a desire-constituted reality. Thus Bohm writes,
"Whereas to Western society, as it derives from the Greeks, measure, with all that this word implies, is the very essence of reality,
or at least the key to this essence, in the East measure has now
come to be regarded as being in some way false and deceitful" (23).
The modernist world-picture could be called the maya of measurement, the supreme fiction of scientific culture. Any significant
movement beyond modernism would thus require a means of
eluding the insistent fictions of measurement, the belief in the
actuality of discrete "things," and the alienation to which they
lead.

Bohm's argument follows Whorf and others who see conventional Western language shot through with the divisive traits
that culminate in science. Discounting the practicality of inventing "a whole new language implying a radically different structure
of thought," Bohm proposes the *rheomode,* a kind of deconstructed language which would cause the categories of subject-verb-
object to flow (*rheo,* Greek, to flow) into a continuum: "We are
often able to overcome this tendency toward fragmentation by
using language in a freer, more informal, and 'poetic' way, that
properly communicates the truly fluid nature of the difference
between relevance and irrelevance" (34). Bohm proposes new
uses of the verb, new formations meant to demonstrate the relatedness (or irreality) of categories and concepts. By altering these
elements of the verbal universe, language can be made more
receptive to the fluidity of nature, less a measure of reality and
more a part of it. "The meaning of a communication through language depends, in an essential way, on the order that language is.
This order is more like that of a symphony in which each aspect
and movement has to be understood in the light of its relationship
to the whole, rather than like the simple sequential order of a
clock or ruler" (41). The *rheomode* would facilitate an intrinsic

relationship between a universe in flux; it would borrow the "riverrun" of mythic and poetic representation to perform the tasks of genuine science. Bohm sees no final barrier between these intellectual realms: "Intelligence and material process have thus a single origin, which is ultimately the unknown totality of the universal flux. In a certain sense, this implies that what have been commonly called mind and matter are abstractions from the universal flux, and that both are to be regarded as different and relatively autonomous orders within the one whole movement" (53). Thus the apparent contradictions between local and nonlocal causation, objective and observer-constituted reality, are dilemmas if one maintains the rigid distinctions of philosophical and scientific dualism; otherwise they could be seen as evidence of the inevitable complementarity of opposites such as difference and relationship.

John Bell recognizes that the consequence of his "deep dilemma" is not necessarily a choice between alternatives but a profounder questioning of the thinking that produces paradoxes. Commenting on Alain Aspect's experimental proofs of his theorem, Bell says that "it is very difficult to say that any one experiment tells you about any isolated concept. I think that it's a whole world view which is tested by an experiment, and if the experiment does not verify that world view, it's not so easy to identify just which part is suspect and has to be revised."[59] Thus for Bell the distinction between an object and an observer is uncertain: spectacles, microscopes, and other instruments are objective certainly but they are also used as extensions of subjectivity. And in a larger sense, the question of determinism or the lack of it in the world has to include the physicist's own mind, choices, and inclinations. "One of the ways of understanding this business," Bell says, "is to say that the world is superdeterministic. That not only is inanimate nature deterministic, but we, the experimenters who imagine we can choose to do one experiment rather than another, are also determined" (47).

Such sensible and yet profound observations offered by Bell and Bohm, coming from quite different intellectual orientations, have usually been considered too "metaphysical" or vague to be useful to scientific work. Cartesian premises were employed for centuries because they proceeded from an ordinary sense of self-identity and because they were useful, and so led to communal findings. Descartes' arguments could never have been enough in themselves and even so their metaphysical aspects gradually eroded so that not only did God disappear but so did the idea of the "cogito" itself—what was left was that vastly complex *res extensa*, the Newtonian world-machine which lay, without any subjective mediation, beneath one's eyes. And in such a world using words like "machine" or "mechanism" or "device" to designate organisms or organs was not metaphorical, even if no one really believed that such artefacts had artificers: these are simply the self-evident tropes of a mechanical world.

Bohm has to provide other "models," however limiting, in order to convey some determinate aspects of the "flux" linking mind and universe. Since the two major models of twentieth-century physics (relativity and quantum) have not been and probably cannot be reconciled, Bohm has offered the *implicate order:* "one may say that everything is enfolded into everything. This contrasts with the *explicate order* now dominant in physics in which things are unfolded in the sense that each thing lies only in its own region of space (and time) and outside the regions belonging to others" (177). Bohm compares this *implicate order* to the record made by holography in which "each part contains information about the *whole object.*" Although Bohm provides the holographic figure simply as a model, "the actual order itself which has thus been recorded is in the complex movement of electromagnetic fields, in the form of light waves" (177). For Bohm "particles," the rudiments of explicate physics, are thus "abstractions" to which he would oppose the implicate order whose "holomovement" is an "unending flux of infoldment and unfoldment, with laws which are only vaguely known" (185).

Finnegans Wake could be said to present a rheomode proceeding from the mythic mind of the dead Finn (and the sleeping H.C.E.) which serves as a holograph for both center and periphery of time and space: "Face at the eased! O I fay! Face at the waist! Ho, you fie! Upwap and dump em, ᴛɹace to ꟻace! When a part so ptee does duty for the holos we soon grow to use an all-forabit" (18.35–19.02). For Joyce, of course, "holograph" could only have meant a document written wholly in the handwriting of the person whose signature it bears, since the idea of the holograph as a three-dimensional photographic record was not conceived by Dennis Gabor until 1947—six years after his death. Yet he saw in the original term an image of his hero and his work: "The great fact emerges that after that historic date all holographs so far exhumed initialled by Haromphrey bear the sigla H.C.E. and while he was only and long and always good Dook Umphrey for the hungerlean spalpeens of Lucalizod and Chimbers to his cronies it was equally certainly a pleasant turn of the populace which gave him as sense of those normative letters the nickname Here Comes Everybody" (32.12–19). Joycean holography is spelled out in the elements of the alphabet, in the languages which form an infinity of names: "samething is rivisible by nightim, maybe involted into the zeroic couplet, palls pell inhis heventh glike noughty times ∞, find, if you are not literally cooefficient, how minney combinaisies and permutandies can be played on the international surd!" (284.10–15). For Joyce the "zeroic couplet" of the *Wake* was the double-nought, the ∞, which signifies the infinity of variations on the "surd"—both a sum containing an irrational number and a voiceless sound— which Joyce saw and heard in the "map of the souls' groupography" (476.33).

A certain analogy between holographic photography and Joycean composition indicates how splitting and fusing etyms can be understood as a chaosmic event. A laser (a beam of light whose wavelengths are coherent) is focused on an object and then is reflected upon a photographic plate. A second laser of identical wave frequency, the "reference beam," is reflected from a mirror and arrives at the same photographic plate, forming an interference pattern which is recorded on the plate. When the reference beam alone is trained on the plate the original object appears to float in three dimensions.[60] Most of the words in the *Wake* are in a sense interference patterns produced by training at least two word-shapes on a single "plate," and like the holographic image the effect is to produce a three-dimensional "word." The "words" in Joyce's prose thus resemble the smeared plates where a pattern of interference is described. They may either produce the illusion of substantiality (they may appear to float above the page and one may be tempted to look "around" them) or of movement (they may cause the reader to have a tactile impression of transience, fluidity, or nebulousness), but in either case, Joyce wrenches them from the explicit dimension of simple reference and gives them a certain autonomy and expansiveness.

For Joyce, the universe is revealed in each of its minutest particles and syllables. Consequently it is so saturated with human perception and forms that its own progression from genesis to equilibrium is described within the pattern of an individual life: birth, marriage, burial, and fecund decay. Like Bateson, Bohm, Prigogine, and others, Joyce insists that human form-making is a part of reality, and that subjectivity, along with language and art, need not be placed under the rubric of fiction. Heisenberg remarked, "The same forces that have shaped nature in all her forms are also responsible for the structure of our minds."[61] The brain, mind, and consciousness must be considered within the larger cybernetic mind of nature. Within the mythopoetic and planetary scope of its language one can thus read in *Finnegans Wake* a prophecy of the continuity of life and death: "Signifying, if tungs may tolkan, that, primeval conditions having gradually receded but nevertheless the emplacement of solid and fluid having to a great extent persisted through intermittences of sullemn fulminance, sollemn nuptialism, sallemn sepulture and providential divining, making possible and even inevitable, after his a time has a tense haves and havenots hesitency, at the place and period under consideration a socially organic entity of a millenary military maritory monetary morphological circumformation in a more or less settled state of equonomic ecolube equalobe equilab equilibbrium" (599.09–18).

John Bishop writes that Joyce's book "absorbs Vico's vision of history to make its readers conscious on every page of the universe of people who have generated the possibility of his individual existence" (211). The action of the *Wake* is driven by a comic, cosmic economy in which causes and effects chase one another in an endless cycle, where the seeds and signs of the dead engender the living in "the semitary of Somnionia" (594.08). For Joyce, in other words, a cemetery of decomposing bodies is also a fertile scattering of signs: the cemetery/semitary of sleep and the unconscious features the unending return of the repressed, the resurrection of the dead, and the recomposition of their words in the dreams of the living. The dead are thus very much alive in the *Wake* because they have become us: we exist as figures carrying forward the momentum of other lives, their wills, desires, and especially their words. The "semitary" animates our own words and bodies with the legacy of the past, which can no longer be seen as "past." "Bloody certainly have we got to see it ere smellful demise surprends us on this concrete that down the gullies of the eras we may catch ourselves looking forward to what will in no time be staring you larrikins on the postface in the multimirror megaron of returningties, whirled without end to end" (582.16–21). Joyce's "whirled" begins and ends with "deaths" involved with births, for once one recognizes that the self is a linguistic knot, a point of contraction and oblivion, and that language is itself a system of infinite referral, death and birth fold into one another. As one reads in the *Lankavatara Sutra,* "All that can be said, is this, that relatively speaking, there is a constant stream of becoming, a momentary and uninterrupted change from one state of appearance to another."[62] Reincarnation is a mythic explanation for the process by which individual subjects form the living fabric of the whole continuum of life: "The untireties of livesliving being the one substrance of a streamsbecoming . . . whereinn once we lave 'tis alve and vale, minnyhahing here from hiarwather, a poddlebridges in a passabed, the river of lives, the regenerations of the incarnations of the emanations of the apparentations of Funn and Nin" (597.07; 600.07–10).

We might begin, then, to consider other Joycean fusions, such as H.C.E. with Howth in Dublin and A.L.P. with the river Liffey as more than allegory and personification. Especially if we see the ways in which some scientists, James Lovelock in particular, have suggested that the earth can be seen as a dissipative structure, a self-organizing unity: "The Earth's living matter, air, oceans, and land surface form a complex system which can be seen as a single organism and which has the capacity to keep our planet a fit place for life."[63] The living earth has a "settled state of equonomic ecolube equalobe equilab equilibbrium" because it appears, as Lovelock argues, to manage the conditions of its existence. Humans share in this vast theme linking the big bang and our daily bursts of energy: "The most primitive and old-fashioned Geiger counter will indicate that we stand on fall-out from a vast nuclear explosion. Within our bodies, no less than three million atoms rendered unstable in that event still erupt every minute, releasing a tiny fraction of the energy stored from that fierce fire of long ago" (16). In *Finnegans Wake*, itself a dissipative structure modeled upon the recursive movement of a river, these events are not really separated from aeon to aeon—they can be felt in one's own life: "eggburst, eggblend, eggburial and hatch-as-hatch can" (614.32–33). The ancient myth of a cosmic egg and the scientific hypothesis of a big bang tell the story of an originary catastrophe whose effects we are: "heavengendered, chaosfoedted, earthborn" (137.14).

Joyce's vision of a holographic and self-organizing world, a living chaosmos, concludes by turning eastward to the sunrise, the rebirth of the world after another historical cycle, and toward the concluding and originary complementarity of West and East, long cultural emblems of the conflict in the human mind between body and spirit, self and selflessness, science and wisdom. Joyce collapses this opposition. In the geographical condensation typical of the book we read of an Irish "yogpriest" celebrating "the primal sacrament of baptism or the regeneration of all man by affusion of water" (606.10–12). Drawing on an old tradition that the druids were descendants of the Brahmans, Joyce presents both a likely scenario for an age after modernity (the fusion of Western and Eastern religions) and an ancient echo of a forgotten age. Sanskrit and English, Christianity and Buddhism, East and West enjoy a union and reunion, a renaissance, in the waters of Joycean prose. And it is there that "we may plesently heal Geoglyphy's twentynine ways to say goodbett and wassing seoosoon liv" (595.06–08). Paradoxically, the great healing of earth and writing which Joyce attempts can only begin with the splitting of the etym and the ear by the thunder which, in Vico's *New Science,* announces a new age: "Take thanks, thankstum, thamas. In that earopean end meets Ind" (598.15–16).

ᒍ—The Chaosmic Self

In spite of all appearances to the contrary, we discern in the present unrest the gradual dawning of a great light, a converging life-endeavour, a growing realization that there is a secret spirit in which we are all one, and of which humanity is the highest vehicle on earth. . . . Science has produced the necessary means for easy transport of men and communication of thought. Intellectually the world is bound together in a web of common ideas and reciprocal knowledge.

—S. Radhakrishnan, "The World's Unborn Soul" (1940)

Resonances

The first nuclear fission explosion in the New Mexico desert during the summer of 1945 was suitably apocalyptic. The test occurred only after a thunderstorm threatened delay. Near five o'clock on the morning of July 17 "a silent blast" illumined the desert night like a minor sun, followed finally by a "thunderous roar" that signaled the success of the test. J. Robert Oppenheimer recalled that a "few people laughed, a few people cried, most people were silent."[1] For each of the three responses one could suppose a certain state of mind, a certain audition and understanding of this artificial apocalypse—rather like the gods, men, and devils listening to what the thunder said in the oldest of *Upanishads*. Oppenheimer's own reflections are seared into the psychic history of the twentieth century: "There floated through my mind a line from the *Bhagavad-Gita* in which Krishna is trying persuade the prince [Arjuna] that he should do his duty: 'I am become death, the shatterer of worlds'" (162).

Such explicit and implicit coincidence of Western science and Hindu scriptures would appear to stage a kind of archetypal

99

meeting of East and West, of the most advanced instance of science's passion for divisive probing of the innermost structure of
matter and Eastern thought's quest for the dissolution of human
divisiveness and passion. In another sense, the scene signals and
sounds a union or a reunion of the founding thunder of the Upan-
ishadic wisdom and the annihilating thunder of technological
death within the audition of the elemental Sanskrit syllable DA
that to Indian ears is the sound of thunder. The horrible irony and
promise of Radhakrishnan's vision, cited in the epigraph to this
chapter, is that the "great light" illumining and linking the Western
and Eastern hemispheres is both that of nuclear terror and philosophic and scientific convergence. Just as Bohr saw in the subatomic realm an epiphany of various eastern conceptions of unbroken
wholeness and the merging of opposites, so others nearly from the
beginning saw in nuclear physics potentially the greatest force for
an assertion of Western power over the rest of the world.

One finds at the conclusion of the *Brihadaranyaka Upanishad* an uncanny forshadowing of the scene at Los Alamos, a
fable which serves to summarize the *Upanishad's* treatise on the
delusory nature of individual identity:

> The classes of Prajapati's sons lived a life of continence with
> their father, Prajapati (Viraj)—the gods, men, and asuras.
> The Gods, on the completion of their term said, "Please
> instruct us." He told them the syllable "DA" (and asked),
> "Have you understood?" (They) said, "We have. You tell us:
> Control yourselves." (He) said, "Yes, you have understood."
> Then the same men said to him, "Please instruct us." He
> told them the same syllable "DA" (and asked), "Have you
> understood?" (They) said, "We have. You tell us: Give."
> (He) said, "Yes, you have understood?" Then the Asuras said
> to him, "Please instruct us." He told them the same syllable
> "DA" (and asked), "Have you understood?" (They) said,
> "We have. You tell us: Have compassion." (He) said, "Yes,
> you have understood." That very thing is repeated by the
> voice, the cloud, as "DA," "DA," "DA": "Control your-
> selves," "Give," "Have compassion Therefore one should
> learn these three—self-control, charity, and compassion."[2]

Like those who cried, laughed, and remained silent in Oppenheimer's account, these ancient students of thunder are driven to
hear something within themselves and then to reveal that something. What Oppenheimer heard in the voice of the thunder was
his own fatal apotheosis into a personification of a new kind of
death. In another sense, he had heard a violent and ultimately
divisive expression of Western science fusing with an ancient
mythological scripture—both audible in the brute utterance of a
"syllable" that lies at the philological origin of Western and Eastern languages.

When Jacques Lacan spoke in Rome eight years later he
recalled this "moment" after teaching the assembled psychoanalysts the necessity of returning to Freud's actual writings in order
to grasp his shattering truth. The disciples of Freud "understood"
their master in a way that had led to theories of depth and ego
psychology, founded on the assumption of a root self or ego, unal-
tered by the traffic of signs along the systems of the conscious,
preconscious, and unconscious mind. The celebrated *Discourse of
Rome* begins with a passage from Browning that evokes the
nuclear event: "'Flesh composed of suns?' How can such be, exclaim the simple ones" and concludes with the passage from the
Upanishad cited above. "That," Lacan says, "is what the divine
voice caused to be heard in the thunder: Submission, gift, grace.
Da da da."[3]

Freud heard *Da* in the teaching, not of his grandfather, but
of his grandson—as if his truth meant listening to the voice of the
unconscious, and not to the demands of patriarchal consciousness. Freud heard in the syllable *Da* the desire to control presence,
as in the game he witnessed his grandson playing in order to feel
he could control the disappearance and the return of his mother,
Freud's daughter. In *Beyond the Pleasure Principle* Freud offers his
own primordial fable:

> "One day I made an observation which confirmed my view.
> The child had a wooden reel with a piece of string tied round
> it. It never occurred to him to pull it along the floor behind

him, for instance, and play at its being a carriage. What he did was to hold the reel by the string and very skillfully throw it over the edge of the cot, so that it reappeared with a joyful 'da.' This, then, was the complete game—dissappearance and return."[4]

When the reel is retrieved, then, the child's pleasure is expressed by the cry of *Da*. If *Da* could be "there," could be "present," then absence could be supplemented and controlled by this game of representation.

In the second edition of *Beyond the Pleasure Principle*, yet another resonance from India is registered by Freud. Explaining how the death drive first articulated in that speculative work responds to "a need to restore an earlier state of things," he had in the first edition alluded only to Aristophanes' tale, recorded in Plato's *Symposium*, that in the beginning human beings were composed of both sexes. With their separation, Aristophanes explains, desire was born. In a footnote added to the next edition, Freud claims that there is an Indian precedent to this ancient Western myth in the *Brihadaranyaka Upanishad*, which speaks of the original Atman who is both man and woman in one body. Speculating about an original state to which the individual psyche desires to be restored, Freud is drawn into an apparently irrelevant controversy about the source of Plato's and Aristophanes' myth. "In contradiction to the prevailing opinion, I should hesitate to give an unqualified denial to the possibility of Plato's myth being derived, even if it were only indirectly, from the Indian source, since a similarity cannot be excluded in the case of the doctrine of transmigration" (52). But of course this question of sources points to a vast cultural demonstration of the argument of his book, one which resounds with other syllables from the same *Upanishad.* For what Freud heard in the Platonic myth, with the help of Heinrich Gomperz who alerted him to the parallel, was a precedent to the death drive in the Hindu traditions espousing union with *Brahman* or the Buddhist quest to attain *Nirvana.* Such a common precedent would represent a certain victory over the father of Western thought, making them heirs to the same "grandfather."

The year the second edition of *Beyond the Pleasure Principle* was published in Zurich (1921), T.S. Eliot journeyed to Switzerland to recover from a nervous collapse: a bad marriage, sexual inhibitions and failures, vocational doubts, and the desire to finish a long poem begun in London led Eliot to the mountains to take his recovery. There he was able to finish *The Waste Land* (1922), the conclusion of which turns upon three imagistic tableaux that interpret this same fundamental syllable, *Da*.[5] For these reasons, Hugh Kenner considers the poem to be a "romantic quest for the primitive, for early man giving tongue to impassioned communion with thunder and falling water . . . united with Romantic Orientalism (Xanadu) to draw the philological imagination back through Sanskrit to Indo-European roots."[6]

Such a quest could characterize Joyce's penetration to the oldest of these languages, to Sanskrit, which rises with the sun at the end of *Finnegans Wake:* "Vah! Survarn Sur! Scatter brand to the reneweller of the sky, thou who agnitest! Dah! Arcthuris coming! Be! Verb unprincipant through the trancitive spaces!" (594.01-.03). As the dream ends, the night is filtered with streaks of Sanskrit (*Vah:* flow, *Agni:* a fire god, *Dah:* burn, give) which announce the sun's renewing and clarifying gift—as well as the loss of *karma* which bathing in the Ganges promises. The Joycean "Dah!" joins the Vicchian thunder to Eliot's thunder—both signaling kinds of *recorsi*—and adds to them the purifying power of fire and its promise of rebirth: "The Phoenician wakes" (608.32). The end of the Joycean night demonstrates the rebirth of the self, of the planet, of the word through the explosive, thunderous, scorching "Dah!"

Martin Heidegger's philosophical enquiry into the possibilities of authentic being would be impossible without the "philological imagination" which led him to question the etymological, the poetic aspects of the philosophical vocabulary of the Greeks. Like his predecessor Nietzsche, Heidegger found in comparative philology a way back to the hidden splendor of ancient words. The hero of *Being and Time* is *Dasein,* the human being whose historical fate is to be thrown into existence, placed in the Da of cultural existence, rather than *Being.* Heidegger hears in this ordinary

expression *(Dasein)* the existential plight of historical man, situated in the surrounding world of contingency: "This entity which
each of us is in himself and which includes inquiring as one of the
possibilities of its Being, we shall denote by the term *Dasein*. If we
are to formulate our question explicitly and transparently, we must
give a proper explanation of an entity *(Dasein)*, with regard to its
Being."[7] Like the children of Prajapati, Heidegger's *Dasein* must
inquire into the sounds of his existence and discover, beneath the
layers of "idle talk," an original word of Being: the *Da* of his *Sein*.

Jacques Derrida makes of *Dasein* and the *Fort/Da* instances
of a deconstruction of the *proper* and the *proper name*, terms which
disguise the means by which an intruding other takes the place of
presence. Accordingly, a *da* trails after each reiteration of Derrida's name, linking him to Freud and to Heidegger, whose works
resound and are re-sounded in Derrida's work. For Derrida the
Da of *Dasein* and the *Da* of *Fort/Da* mark the complementarity of
philosophy and psychoanalysis, distance and proximity, difference and relationship. In *The Post Card* (1980), a book concerned
with the dispersion of meaning, the posting of letters, and the
"beyond" which awaits Socrates and Freud alike, Derrida writes,
"Beyond the metaphysical categories of the subject, of consciousness, of the person . . . this movement of propriation would come
back to the *Da* of the *Sein* and the *Da* of *Dasein*. And the existential analytics of Da-sein is inseparable from an analysis of dis-
tancing and proximity."[8]

These resonances can serve as introduction to an intertextal
articulation and commentary on three auditions and inscriptions of
a fundamental Sanskrit syllable. Eliot, Lacan, and E. M. Forster
compose, respectively, a poem, a psychoanalytic discourse, and a
novel upon the way that hearing and repetition contribute to the
constitution and the dissolution of the self, the formation and discovery of a "chaosmic self" extended across space and time. The
path which *Da* describes from India to Vienna, Zurich, Rome, and
elsewhere, from the ancient world of India to the modern wasteland can describe the vast panorama wherein one can track the
intersection of European and Indian subjectivity—according to
this apparently arbitrary anthology of quotations.

This network of associations thus suggests powerful links between Western modernity, Eurocentrism, and subject-centered philosophy which are also evident in poststructuralist analyses of subjectivity that confine themselves to a half-dozen French and German figures. Any significant movement beyond the metaphysics and ideologies of Cartesianism and logocentricity will require a marked extension of reference and a real confrontation with the great sources of non-Western thought, whether it is China, Japan, ancient Egypt, Islam, or India. There is no substitute for a philosophical and critical inquiry into non European theories of the subject, reality, time, language, and subjectivity and a careful reappraisal and qualification of Western critiques of modernity. The chaosmic self presented here is both a theoretical neologism meant to condense the dynamic contradictions of subjectivity and a crossing of epistemologies, literatures, and languages from two different hemispheres. Without this admittedly difficult détente and rapprochement the West and the world will continue to suffer from the effects of this "philosophical amnesia," a forgetting which, for the culture as for the individual, has proved so indispensable to Western identity—and identity in the West.[9]

Eliot's Upanishad

For the writers of the American Renaissance, the East in general and India in particular often appeared as an alternative to the Mediterranean classical cultures which sustained European literature. Attempting to establish their own literary identities and "American" identity in general, Emerson, Thoreau, Whitman, and Melville were often attracted by alien conceptions of subjectivity and alien scripts, such as the recently deciphered Egyptian hieroglyphics: references to both, however different in provenance and significance, appear frequently in their works as if to reorient American subjectivity to a wider world of identification. "Thus it appears that the sweltering inhabitants of Charleston and New Orleans, of Madras and Bombay and Calcutta, drink at my well," Thoreau writes in *Walden*. "In the morning I bathe my intellect in the stupendous and cosmogonal philosophy of the Bhagavat Geeta, since whose composition years of the gods have elapsed, and in comparison with which our modern period and its literature seem puny and trivial."[10] Like Thoreau, Emerson and Whitman invented a literature of the transcendental subject that drew from India, just as Melville turned again and again to ancient Egypt as if looking for some vast antiquity that could dwarf even Athens and Rome.

Since its publication in 1922 *The Waste Land* has been seen as the paradigmatic *modernist* work, the exemplary response to the expressive poetics of romanticism. Ezra Pound believed that it was "the justification of the 'movement,' of our modern experiment, since 1900." For I.A. Richards in 1926 the poem was a "music of ideas." By the thirties, F.R. Leavis had attempted to justify its puzzling form and obscurities by elaborating on the poem's "orchestration" and "musical organization." Cleanth Brooks established the New Critical approach by claiming, against all appearances, that the poem was "unified," like the great poems of Donne and Wordsworth, by its "central symbols." In the fifties and sixties, source studies such as Grover Smith's and archetypal readings such as Northrop Frye's supplemented formalist approaches. And by the eighties, deconstructive critics approached the poem well-equipped with theories of decentered form and intertextuality.[11]

When current concerns about such critical schools have faded, The *Waste Land* may be seen as a direct heir to Emerson, Thoreau, and Whitman, a central American poem which not only books, but makes, Whitman's "passage to India." And if Harold Bloom is right in suggesting that sacred genres begin as powerful literary achievements and only later, according to the entropic process of weak reading, become "religous," perhaps *The Waste Land,* still so radical after more than seventy years, will have its own place in a future global canon about thich we can only guess.[12] *The Waste Land* has certainly functioned as a kind of secular scripture for decades, at least for literary intellectuals, but some of its significance and power has not been recognized.

I see the poem as a kind of textual passage from the West to the East, a passage that moves in both directions, and as a necessarily fragmented quest, modulated by both the grail romances and one of the scholarly romances of the nineteenth century—the search for an original language.

For the fundamental source of the poem, including both its linguistic origins and the spring Eliot discovers in the arid wastes of modern culture, is simply language itself—if, that is, one thinks of language as the elemental framework of human experience, and not as a substitute for a supposedly unmediated experience. Eliot's poem is in fact an inventory of the seven major languages (Sanskrit, Greek, Latin, Italian, French, German, and English) that form the legacy of the so-called proto-Indo-European language, the hypothetical original language whose scattering reflects the fable—in philological terms—of the Tower of Babel. This supposition of one original language spoken somewhere on the plains of Asia was one of the nineteenth century's many acts of devotion to the idea of a determinate origin, scientifically achieved, able to replace the stories of divine, scriptural origin. Eliot was quite aware of this philological quest, having studied Sanskrit at Harvard and Oxford, when he wrote *The Waste Land.* Eliot's poem can be seen as a fantasia on these themes, on the Indo-European resonances that could lead the imagination of Europe and America back to Asian origins and a knowledge summarized in a single elemental syllable.

Eliot's studies were not of course free of the imperialist context of his time. David Trotter has pointed out one resemblance between the plot of *The Waste Land* and the late nineteenth-century, early twentieth-century literature of empire in which Europeans find spiritual renewal by confronting the savage and timeless vistas of the Eurasian plains. "Eliot's poem resembles these fictions of Empire in one respect only; it begins in London, the dead heart of the system, and it ends on the frontier. It shows an 'Unreal City,' a journey, a muted and perhaps empty promise of regeneration."[13] Eliot fused this plot with the quest plots of medieval romances in order to search out a source and a spring for the replenishment of European culture which necessarily must be outside of it or in its past: India was strangely both of these things, both alien and a long-lost element in its linguistic and philosophic ancestry. The revelatory or apocalyptic nature of *The Waste Land* springs from this attempt to form the axis of a new planetary mythology, a mythology at the same moment premodern, modern, and post-modern, in which Augustine and the Buddha, the Thames and the Ganges, English and Sanskrit are aligned to the same archetypal and contrapuntal logic. This was not an easy synthesis of the elements of world religions and languages, however. Eliot's later reactionary attempts to outline the principles of a Christian society and a classical tradition indicate his own resistance to the transcultural qualities of his major poem.[14]

The Waste Land, unlike Eliot's earlier poems or the later ones, is persistently polyphonic, polylingual, and dialogic because of such interests and themes, not simply because Eliot was striving to advance the modernist experiment, as Pound and many critics saw it. This exemplary "modernist" text may well be less the triumphant discovery and deployment of a new poetic technique celebrated by Richards, Leavis, and Brooks than the radical demonstration of the chaos to be found within the normative and supervisory languages of Western culture.[15] *The Waste Land* is not only speech and inscription, it is a preternatural kind of hearing and listening *into* the languages of the Indo-European legacy, registering montage, polyglossia, and dissonance. The poem thus provides a cubist soundscape which records and amplifies the decadence of modern culture through a keen attention to its many languages, genres, dialects, and idiolects, both in the stream of consciousness proceeding from the "mind of Europe" and a single, tormented typist. The thunder that finally speaks in Eliot's text, then, gives both ethical and philological closure in its *Da:* the sound of the thunder, a child's first approach to the father, but also the syllable closest to the theoretical root *Do,* the source of words for "giving": *datta* (Sanskrit), *didonai* (Greek), *dare* (Latin), *dacha* (Russian), *donner* (French), *donate* (English). This is the hearing of what the thunder said to the human grandsons of Prajapati, the first speakers of Sanskrit.

Eliot's studies in Sanskrit were derived from one of the major philological researches of the nineteenth century that culminated

in *The Sacred Books of the East* and *The Harvard Oriental Series*.[16] At
the origin of this collective project one finds the English jurist Sir
William Jones, renowned as the greatest linguist of his time as well
as a poet and philosopher. Jones announced the results of his study
of Sanskrit to the British Asiatick Society in 1786:

> The Sanskrit language, whatever be its antiquity, is of a
> wonderful structure; more perfect than the Greek, more
> copious than the Latin, and more exquisitely refined than
> either, yet bearing to both of them a stronger affinity, both in
> the roots of verbs and in the forms of grammar, than could
> possibly have been produced by accident; so strong indeed
> that no philosopher could examine all three without believ-
> ing them to have sprung from some common source, which
> perhaps no longer exists.[17]

The linguist Murray B. Emeneau has argued that Jones's insight
into this relationship between Sanskrit and Greek and Latin was
derived from a reading of the ancient Sanskrit grammarian
Panini. This grammar "allowed him to see relations between
Panini's explicitly stated morphemes and the similar, implicitly
intuited basic morphemes which he already knew in the classical
languages." Not only was Sanskrit a philological mine for western linguists, it was also their tutor. Emeneau argues that "the
slow growth of a competent Western descriptive linguistics in
the nineteenth century and the first half of the twentieth century
owed much, if not all, to the Hindu grammarians."[18]

Sanskrit was both, according to Jones, superior and anterior
to the founding languages of Western culture. The "common
source" or spring that could refresh a wasteland may no longer
exist, except within the memories and amid the resonances of
modern languages. Sanskrit appears to have the benefit of this
source, both in its linguistic refinement and antiquity, and in its
philosophic discourses. It is the Da of the thunder that promises
rain in token of a lost and forgotten vitality, and it is to that desert
land that Sanskrit brings the teachings of the Vedic mysteries, the
Brihadaranyaka Upanishad, which literally means "the teachings

of the forest." Paul Deussen, whose German edition of the *Upanishads* Eliot cites in his notes, claims that this *Upanishad* is the richest and oldest, the source of all the others, bringing to perfection what would later be the teachings of Christ, anticipating the thought of Plato, Kant, and Schopenhauer.[19] It is in this context that we should consider the importance of Indian thought in one of the literary landmarks of the twentieth century.

Eliot's poem ends with the teachings of the forest because it is focused on the delusions and pain that comes from unreflected egocentric existence. The torments dramatized in the poem all spring from a concentration on the desires or fears of ego-centered existence, the insistent seeking for unity and satisfaction or the fleeing of contact and relationship. The drama of fragmented voices has one consistent theme: the dilemmas of subjectivity, of isolated existence—whether one thinks of the Sybil of Eliot's epigraph from Petronius who only wants to die or of the "young man carbuncular" who is interested only in fornicating.

In this regard Eliot also draws on the Buddhist texts, no less fundamental to the psychology and the poetics of the poem, translated by Henry Clarke Warren.[20] Warren's *Buddhism: In Translations,* cited by Eliot in the notes to the poem, includes two headings that Eliot may well have been drawn to: "There is no Ego" and "All signs of the Ego are absent." These scriptures argue that the ego is nothing more than a name for abstracted sensory data that have no continuous, no real existence. The "ego" is simply the Latin "I," which linguists call a "shifter," that becomes an entity, as such, only when its linguistic status is forgotten. In this way the English translations of Freud's second psychic topography essentialized the "Ich" into the "ego." Under the heading "There is no Ego" in Warren's edition one reads, "in the absolute sense there is no living entity there to form a basis for such figments as 'I am,' or 'I'; in other words, in the absolute sense there is only name and form. The insight of one who perceives this is called knowledge of the truth."[21] The follower of the Buddha's teaching realizes: "I am nowhere a somewhatness for any one, and nowhere for me is there a somewhatness of any one. . . . Thus, inasmuch as he sees that there is no Ego anywhere, and that he has none to bring forward to be a somewhatness to himself, he has grasped the fourfold emptiness" (145– 46). In another passage: "When there is form, O priests, then through attachment to form, through engrossment in form, the persuasion arises, 'This is mine; this is I; this is my Ego'" (157).

Thus Eliot's poem is not attached to "form," its characters are, dwelling in desire, dread, lack, and delusion, confined by the imaginary dimensions of the self:

> I have heard the key
> Turn in the door once and turn once only
> We think of the key, each in his prison
> Thinking of the key, each confirms a prison.
> (lines 412–415)

The "key" of desire creates and confines the ego in the same act, and the "key" that would free the inmate can only aggravate his attachment and confinement—until the very terms of subjectivity and self-identification are cast aside. It is in this context perhaps that we should interpret Eliot's famous definition of poetry: "Poetry is not a turning loose of emotions; it is not the expression of personality but an escape from personality."[22]

The Buddhists saw the absolute emptiness of the ego through an analysis of sensory data. It is the function of both the Buddha's and Eliot's "fire sermons" to show that the senses are on fire with desires (and demands for gratification) and it is the climactic recognition of this fact that leads to enlightenment, the extinction of the fiction of the self, and *Nirvana*. The episode in the hyacinth garden dramatizes the failure of sexuality as a failure of desire, but it also affords a glimpse of non-ego-centric being:

> I could not
> Speak, and my eyes failed, I was neither
> Living nor dead, and I knew nothing,
> Looking into the heart of light, the silence.
> (lines 38–41)

Although these lines may seem to exemplify the failure of action and feeling in Eliot's wasteland, they also indicate a real moment of insight. As language, sight, and identification with life and knowledge disappear, the young man has a powerful epiphany into silence. Twenty years later, in *Burnt Norton*, a similar scene recurs, but here the value of the insight into emptiness is clear:

> Dry the pool, dry concrete, brown edged,
> And the pool was filled with water out of sunlight,
> And the lotos rose, quietly, quietly,
> The surface glittered out of heart of light . . .
> (lines 35–38)

Here certainly it is out of the empty and dry pool, out of a direct confrontation with emptiness, that the ecstatic moment arises. Eliot's meditations on the delusions of subjectivity in the earlier poems are fearful and unusually pessimistic, but by the forties and *Four Quartets* they have become visionary and at times rapturous.

If Buddhism contributes to the psychological poetics of *The Waste Land*, Hinduism and the *Brihadaranyaka Upanishad* provide a mythic language necessary to bring the poem to a conclusion. Like the great *Upanishad*, Eliot's poem is fragmented, anecdotal, philosophic, and ritualistic by turns. In order to understand the fable of the thunder toward which Eliot's poem moves, one must understand the fundamental teaching of Vedic wisdom contained here. The eighth-century philosopher, scholar, and saint Shankaracharya, in his introductory commentary on the *Upanishad*, remarks, "for the removal of the ignorance of a man disgusted with the universe, this *Upanishad* is being commenced in order to inculcate the knowledge of *Brahman* which is the very opposite of ignorance."[23] Beginning with the epigraph from Petronius expressing the Sybil's disgust for life and desire for death, *The Waste Land* ends with the core of this *Upanishad's* teachings.

Addressed, as it were to the characters of *The Waste Land*, the *Upanishad* teaches this knowledge and recounts the difficulties encountered by those who would acquire it. The originating moment of ignorance and its consequent fear and suffering is the splitting (and creating) of self and other. The original man was afraid: "Therefore, people 'still' are afraid to be alone. He thought 'If there is nothing else but me, what am I afraid of?' From that alone his fear was gone, for what was there to fear? It is from the second entity that fear comes" (I.IV.2). Unreflected solitude is fearful until it can create an Other for company; but, when it has done so, it substantiates and eternalizes its fear, which then becomes involved with its desire. The second entity, the Other, constitutes the self strictly as a "difference within the real" and sentences it to desire and suffering, the emotions that accompany the attempt to recover its lost unity. The primal Indian subject, like Descartes and Adam, seeks certainty and freedom from fear by constituting and desiring a finally subdued and satifying world, but in doing this it also and necessarily leads to its own frustration. All knowledge, and the language that represents it, is thus a kind of division, and so the instigation of desire and suffering demands that there be a division between what one senses and the sense. This demand divides the subject from its object precisely because to be objective and trustworthy, the object must be separate from the untrustworthy subject. "When there is duality, as it were, then one smells something, one sees something, one hears something, one knows something. (But) when to the knower of *Brahman* everything has become the Self [the world-subject], then what should one smell, and through what, what should one see and through what. . . . Through what should one know that owing to which all this is known—through what, O Maitreyi, should one know the Knower?" (II.IV.14). Ignorance of *Brahman*, the principle of undividedness, not only means suffering, it also means the repetition of suffering for those who see only difference and not difference-as-relationship: "Through the mind alone (It) is to be realized. There is no difference whatsoever in It. He goes from death to death, who sees difference, as it were, in it" (IV.IV.19).

The Vedic authors realized that this difference and division in *Brahman* was not only the result of the mind but also a function of language. Eliot emphasizes the divisive nature of language by allowing the literatures of the world to speak in their own voices and by refusing to organize a consecutive, linear narrative or exposition according to the presumed centrality of a single subjectivity. So too, the English language breaks into Elizabethan, baroque, Augustan, romantic, aristocratic, working class, and academic languages, just as individual characters are presented only as inferences from verbal fragments. The narratives and natural languages remove *The Waste Land* from the illusion of self-centeredness and from modern conventions of literary order: instead a kind of chaosmic montage emerges.

The *Brihadaranyaka* claims that "this (universe) was then undifferentiated. It differentiated only into name and form. So to this day it is differentiated only into names and forms" (I.IV.19). The appearance of "chaos" in any vision of the world is the product of a conflict between language and experience, between the conventions of predictable order and multivarious, abundant detail. Any vision (and fear) of anarchy or chaos thus registers the homogeneity of the perceiving subject and its resistance to noise, chance, and spontanaeity. The chaosmic nature of *Finnegans Wake* and *The Waste Land* is a necessary feature of Joyce's and Eliot's refusal to constitute their own authority with respect to a temporal-spatial given. Neither Joyce nor Eliot have, to recall Husserl's words, "Indianized" themselves: they have "othered" themselves by allowing other cultures and languages to brush the English language and its conventions against their grains.

The last section of *The Waste Land*, "What the Thunder Said," is entrusted with the audition and representation of an originary and natural "speech." The poem may thus be seen as a hermeneutical unfolding of this informing syllable from the massive detail, the related but alien lexicons of the Indo-European languages. This last section, then, passes from an impressionistic snapshot of Christ's journey to Emmaus to the grail quest suggested by Eliot's notes. Both Western narratives are left unfinished, as the poem's designed fragmentation blocks their movements toward the satisfaction of desire:

There is the empty chapel, only the wind's home.
It has no windows, and the door swings,
Dry bones can harm no one.
Only a cock stood on the rooftree
Co co rico co co rico
In a flash of lightning. Then a damp gust
Bringing rain.

(lines 389–395)

But no rain comes, except in the form of Eliot's adaptation of the fable of the thunder—and such is the only rain that will come to this wasteland. For it is at this point that a "flash of lightning" illumines the "empty chapel" of Christianity and that, after a suitable delay, the thunder of India speaks. In the gap between the two strophes, Eastern and Western myths meet in silence and the quest for the grail reveals, not an empty chapel and a chalice, but the Vedic scriptures in an abbreviated yet apocalyptic flash.

The *Brihadaranyaka* arrives at the fable in as abrupt a fashion as Eliot's poem. The Da interpreted accordingly by the three classes of beings provides the ethical source for human conduct. James N. Powell writes, "For Eliot, speaking to the lost postwar generation, the Word, the voice of God, the thunderclap that contains all wisdom necessary to correct the spiritual dislocation of the generation, is contained in a single syllable, DA."[24] In Eliot's polylingual, chaosmic text, the *Da* functions as a chiasmus of philological and ethical truth—all compacted in something that is less than a word and more than a sound, a primal voice of the earth heard by all mythological peoples as demanding interpretation, obedience, and reverence. Powell comments that the "seer of the Great Forest Teaching simply used DA, the sound of thunder, to represent the voice of the Father of All Creatures striking down the knot of egoity" (55). The superior syllable at the beginning of the linguistic imagination, at the source of natural speech—along with the sound of waves, streams, other creatures—is thus already one and many, heard as one and repeated differently. Gods, humans, devils hear the same syllable but what they understand, and what is measured, are themselves. Thus the languages of Europe are deliberately displayed by Eliot in their relational difference—fragmented and tormenting discourses that alienate selves as well as civilizations.

Deussen explains that one of the meanings of the word "Upanishad" is "secret word, secret text" (16). *The Waste Land* resembles such a word, especially at its conclusion, which describes the effects of the fall of an original language before it cites the speech of its highest source:

> Datta. Dayadhvam. Damyata.
> Shantih   shantih   shantih
> (lines 433–34)

Eliot's final note, explaining that Shantih "repeated as here is a formal ending to an Upanishad," suggests that his poem could be considered an *Upanishad,* a secret text. The poem's whorl of languages, centered in the last strophe, is suddenly and paradoxically pacified and quieted by the Brahmanic syllable *Da* that, according to Raimundo Pannikar, "is the primal sound which, sounded at the beginning, resounds in every portion of the Vedas, which are nothing but echoes of this."[25]

Lacan's Mystical Ejaculations

Jacques Lacan's "The Mirror Stage as Formative of the Function of the I as Revealed in Psychoanalytic Experience" (1949) concludes with a remark that has not been sufficiently noted: "In the recourse of subject to subject that we preserve, psychoanalysts may accompany the patient to that ecstatic limit of the 'Thou art that,' in which is revealed the cypher of his mortal destiny, but it is not in our mere power as practitioners to bring him to that point where the real journey begins."[26] Here certainly is a citation, and an important one judging by the deference Lacan has for its authority. But Lacan's editors, translators, and annotators have nothing to say about it, as if they they had not, or could not, hear or see what was being said.[27] Lacan does not oblige his readers with even so much as as a gesture toward India and the *Upan-*

ishads, but it is there that one must turn for an understanding of this oddly humble yet masterful caveat poised at the entrance way into his labyrinthine *Ecrits.*

"The 'thou art that'"—Lacan cites these words as if his audience and readers would recognize them immediately, as they would, for instance, "In the beginning was the word" or "I think, therefore, I am." One need not be a Vedantist to recognize this phrase, translated from the Sanskrit *Tat tvam asi,* as a central expression of what Aldous Huxley, after Leibniz, called the "perennial philosophy," the collective insights of the mystic traditions from around the world.[28] The phrase is the central motif of the *Chandogya Upanishad,* which presents a critique, in dialogue form, of the self, a critique that Lacan more than anyone else returned to intellectual currency and respectability in the humanities and social sciences. And yet the vast majority of discussions of the "fading of the subject" (or the "death of the author") proceeds as if this were a recent intellectual development, perhaps going as far back as Nietzsche. And yet at this crucial moment Lacan himself points out the antiquity of the question. Indeed Lacan's indication of the Vedic and Buddhist parallels to and precedents for his work is not limited to this address from 1949—such parallels are indicated throughout his work.

The central thesis of the *Chandogya Upanishad* is that, whenever one describes the self, one is in actuality describing something else. The point is presented through a series of echoing phrases: "Thou art that. . . . And thou art that."[29] In this way, the ego is offered a panorama of the phenomenal world and, at the same time, of its own transcendental dissolution into that world. *Brahman* is glimpsed when one begins to lose touch with the supposed reality of one's own self, its limits, its center, its essence. So *Brahman* is neither an empirical nor a metaphysical principle; it is rather an indication of the finally meaningless nature of such linguistic artifacts as self/other, soul/body, and so forth. Lacan links the question of the subject (with its Cartesian and Freudian associations) with the motif of *Brahman* in order to dismantle the very idea of "identity" as a unitary or originative principle. As the word's other forms indicate, "identity" requires an equation between an empty figure of dividuation (the "I," the "self," the "soul") which everybody is and has and the referred objects, attitudes, views, and qualities that fill it or mask it. *Identity* is the residue of an arbitrary act of *identification* that becomes a metaphysical principle only through repression and effacement of the solicitation and acquisition of representations. *Brahman* refers to both the fullness and the emptiness of this subject, and as such it extends beyond the "ecstatic limit" which the fictional identity has agreed not to cross in exchange for the privileges of selfhood. In this limitation is inscribed what Lacan calls the "cypher of his mortal destiny." This strange envoi indicates the limits of psychoanalytic practice, which are also the limitations of speech in the constitution of the subject. Psychoanalysis can only lead to and then indicate this ultimate emptying out of the subject (which emptying is also enlightenment) that follows any radical expulsion of the signs which constitute our subjectivity. Only at that point can the "real journey" begin. Poststructuralist commentators are understandably put off stride by such language, seeing in such "metaphysical" phrasing remnants of a Heideiggerian faith in authentic being or of the Hegelian road of the spirit in *The Phenomenology of the Spirit*.[30] But the *Chandogya Upanishad* provides a more pertinent instance of the journey in the description of Indra's education. In the *Upanishad* the journey illustrates the ego's futile quest for the satisfaction which can come only by renouncing the ego's demands. The signifier is destined to a fruitless search for an ever-retreating signified, and the ego is destined never to achieve its desires for satisfactions by the laws of *karma* which require that repressed actions in previous lives must return until they are thoroughly worked through. "The ego," Lacan writes in his *Discourse of Rome*, is "frustration in its essence" (42). This suggests that the loss of the ego (in the achievement of a knowledge of *Brahman*) would also mean the end of suffering, anxiety, and, simply enough, *need*. The "real journey" would then begin with the ecstasies of the realization of the *thou art that* and lead either to a reinvestment in the mirroring languages of the world or to the final collapse of the ego-bubble, an event toward which psychoanalysis can only point in silence.

Lacan's pointed statement of the limitations of psychoanalysis in this address is easily overlooked or uneasily ignored, but in his next major address it is unavoidable.

The major declaration of the Lacanian project, "The Function and Field of Speech and Language in Psychoanalysis," delivered in Rome in 1953 (the *Discours de Rome*), turns from the *Chandogya* to the *Brihadaranyaka* and beyond. Like Eliot, Lacan recognizes *The Upanishads* as a dissertation on the power of speech and its role in the constitution of the subject. "Through the word—already a presence made of absence—absence itself gives a name in that moment of origin whose perpetual recreation Freud's genius detected in the play of a child. And from this pair of sounds modulated on presence and absence . . . there is born the world of meaning of a particular language in which the world of things will come to be arranged" (65). The pair of sounds *Fort/Da* joins Freud to Eliot and the *Brihadaranyaka* in an apparently fortuitous play on the syllable that announces presence and the representation of presence (and absence) in language. The Eliotic resonances thus link Lacan to the critique made in the *Upanishads*—millenia before Descartes introduced his axiom (I think, therefore, I am) at the "dawn of the historical era of the ego." In the same way, the utterances of the grandfather Prajapati resound when Freud's grandson plays his game. The echo chamber of *The Waste Land* communicates these effects to Lacan's address, while "The Hollow Men" presents, through Lacan's citation, the most graphic exposition of how the ego is made: "We are the hollow men/We are the stuffed men/Leaning together/ Headpiece filled with straw. Alas!" This poem, an exemplary expression of modernist disenchantment, broadly satirizes the construction of modern subjectivity, both hollow and full, scarecrows that scare no one but themselves. Eliot shows that any naming of the self is also a misnaming and a corporealization of the straw of language—whether one is talking about tabloids or quarterlies: "language is not immaterial. It is a subtle body, but body it is. Words are trapped in all corporeal images that captivate the subject" (87). Because of language's "subtle body" (a term taken from theosophy), its divisions and classifications are that much more persuasive and enticing. The child is driven to a mastery of speech in order to master, or at least represent and command, the objects of his desire. But this mastery is double-edged: *"Fort! Da!* It is precisely in his solitude that the desire of the little child has already become the desire of another, of an *alter ego* who dominates him and whose object of desire is henceforth his own affliction" (104). The child's experience is also the human experience of language according to the Vedantic perspective, where existence itself is synonymous with desire. "Thus the symbol manifests itself first of all as the murder of the thing, and this death constitutes in the subject the eternalization of his desire" (104). Such is the *karma* of attachment to the body of language, which displaces the elusive body and so torments those who accept language as real. As one reads in the Buddhist *Lankavatara Sutra:* "the ignorant cling to names, signs, and ideas; as their minds move along these channels they feed on multiplicities of objects and fall into the notion of an ego-soul and what belongs to it. . . . As they thus cling there is a reversion to ignorance, and karma born of greed, anger, and folly, is accumulated. As the accumulation of karma goes on they become imprisoned in a cocoon of discrimination and are thenceforth unable to free themselves from the round of birth and death."[31] Although the Hindu and Buddhist conceptions of subjectivity are radically different (the Hindus holding that *Atman* or the individual expression of *Brahman* is quite real, the Buddhists holding that there is, from an absolute standpoint, no soul or ego at all) both show how language, as in Lacan, creates a simulacrum which inhibits union with *Brahman* or the achievement of *Nirvana.*

Eliot's poetics, as we have seen, suggest an escape from the emotions and desires that constitute egocentric existence. Lacan follows in the direction that Eliot indicates by introducing poetic condensation and allusiveness into the scientific discourse of psychoanalysis. In this way Lacan attempts to awaken the psychoanalysts gathered in Rome to the power of speech, the enigma of the sign, and the knotty nature of the symptom. Thus "that supreme pinnacle of the aesthetics of language, poetics" must be added to the disciplines that Freud required of analysts: "the history of civilization, mythology, and literary criticism" (76). Thus *The Waste Land* resounds in the *Discours de Rome,* just as *The Upanishads* resound in Eliot's poem. The climax of these echoes is reached in the third section of Lacan's Discourse, entitled "The resonances of interpretation and the time of the subject in psychoanalytic technique," with epigraphs which echo "The Hollow Men" and Eliot's epigraph to *The Waste Land* from Petronius' *Satyricon.* Lacan's citation of Eliot's citation of Petronius' citation of the Sybil's express desire to die *(apothanein thelo)* is a preface to Lacan's urging the assembled analysts to learn "to play on the power of the symbol by evoking it in a carefully calculated fashion in the semantic resonances of their remarks" (82). These epigraphs, moreover, introduce the fable of the thunder and imply that the teachings of Freud and Prajapati resound with the same syllable. The intertwining of American poetry and Vedic scripture, Latin decadence and Parisian glamour is no accident: Lacan's text is no mere scientific or psychiatric discourse; it offers the auras of poetry and the sacred, of poetics and prophecy.

In Sanskrit poetics, resonance, both the ability to hear it and to initiate it, is called *dhvani,* "the property of speech by which it communicates what it does not actually say" (82). Lacan paraphrases a tale from the Indian tradition that demonstrates this property:

> A girl, it begins, was waiting for her lover on the bank of a stream when she sees a Brahmin coming towards her. She runs to him and exclaims in the warmest and most amiable tones: "What a lucky day this is for you! The dog that used to frighten you by its barking will not be along this river bank again, for it has just been devoured by a lion that is often seen around here. (82)

Despite the girl's "amiable tones" and apparent meaning, her words resound with an unspoken menace that the Brahmin cannot but hear. Her words also exemplify *dhvani* by showing how the barking of the dog, like her own words, is obvious and significant but a mere distraction: the silence and absence of the lion, like her own unsaid words, speak more loudly. "The absence of the lion, " Lacan comments, "may thus have as much importance as his spring would have were he present, for the lion only springs once, says the proverb appreciated by Freud" (82). *Dhvani* thus assumes as part of its meaning precisely what it refuses to say, what saying would in effect unsay. Such a resonance issues from thunder, from *Da*, and informs the poetic text that analysts must attend, Lacan advises, if they are to understand and use the "resources of language" (83).

In this regard, Lacan's own text is exemplary, as it inscribes its messages in the enigmatic and circular utterances that resound within themselves before they have even begun to resound in the ears and minds of his auditors: "I identify myself in language, but only by losing myself in it like an object. What is realized in my history is not the past definite of what was, since it is no more, or even the present perfect of what has been in what I am, but in the future anterior of what I shall have been for what I am in the process of becoming" (86). In this way the subject is not declined like a noun, but conjugated like a verb. Identity ceases to signify at all, except insofar as the dissemination of reference, *Brahman,* can define the self only in the act of absorbing it. Lacan's admission of the limitations of his practice is understandable if one ponders for a moment what the Lacanian "cure" could possibly be: given his entire analytic orientation, it is difficult to see him interested in returning neurotics to the illuson of subject-centered existence. Lacan says that he is not "the only one to have remarked that analysis ultimately becomes one with the technique known as Zen, which is applied as the means of the subject's revelation in the traditional ascesis of certain Far Eastern schools" (100). Where analysis remains committed to the powers and limitations of speech, Zen Buddhist practices seek to mock it and to discover in silence a superior expression of its realization. One can recognize in Lacan's highly condensed discourse and his lecture antics an attempt to bring as much of the Zen master's repertoire into psychoanalytic use as possible.

Yet the psychoanalyst cannot, in *propria persona,* move into that space where the "real journey begins." The analyst, Lacan advises, should "be well acquainted with the whorl into which his period draws him in the continued enterprise of Babel, and let him be aware of his function as interpreter in the discord of languages" (106). Where better to turn for such training than Eliot's great poem, where the Babel of voices is finally quelled by the Sanskrit syllable that Lacan hears in Freud?

In Joyce and Eliot, and Lacan and Oppenheimer one can see how the drive for literary and scientific mastery seems chastened. Instead of attempting to dominate the word, the self, and the material world, these very different figures have allowed them to ramify and resound without limit. In *Finnegans Wake* thunder sounds ten times in the hundred-letter words that, according to Vico, drove the first people into the caves where family and culture could begin. These Joycean "thundreds" roll across the text with a mixture of humor and bluster, signaling the human Fall and Vico's historical cycles. But in the thunder that Oppenheimer heard and turned from, the voice is humorless and terrifying, portending a new age of nuclear terror and death for the people of Hiroshima and Nagasaki. One can see that the modern devotion to technological transformation of the world and intervention into matter itself could not occur without a consequent emptying out of subjectivity, as evinced in Oppenheimer's reflections at Los Alamos. Thus in his 1964 seminar Lacan remarks that "there really must be a series of crises for an Oppenheimer to question us all as to what there is in the desire that lies at the basis of modern physics."[32]

One can see in the Joycean "abnihilisation of the etym," Eliot's apocalyptic representation of the West, the epochal Oppenheimer episode, and Lacan's ambitious attacks on Cartesianism a genuine crisis of the modern project. All that happened from Descartes to Oppenheimer, within this unfolding adventure of technologically interventionist modernity, is the development of Cartesian method and the consequent return of its originating doubt and fear. Following Descartes' advice to "divide the difficulties" with the blade of science, Oppenheimer discovered how the difficulties multiplied with such an act—how the moral dimension of science returned with a vengeance.

Lacan notes that Descartes does not search for truth or knowledge so much as he searches for certainty. Cartesian "doubt" is an epistemological prop designed to produce a theatrical vision of certainty. "Scepticism is something," Lacan writes, "that we no longer know. Scepticism is an ethic. Scepticism is a mode of sustaining man in life, which implies a position so difficult, so heroic, that we can no longer even imagine it—precisely perhaps because of this passage found by Descartes, which led the search for the path of certainty to this very point . . . of alienation, to which there is only one exit—the way of desire" (ff. 224).

Cartesian theatrics in *Meditations on First Philosophy* and the *Discourse on Method* led to a modern presumption that certainty— which means mathematics, mechanical predictability—was preferable to doubt or the self-sustaining skepticism that holds one away from credulity, either in the powers of analytic reason or of faith. The Cartesian subject confuses its own *desire* for certainty, its own demand or need for a vision unsullied by doubt, falsity, or superstition, with the alienated knowledge it stoically proclaims. But even so Descartes' legacy should not be confused with what he actually argued, for he argued not only for a metaphysical *res cogitans* but for God. Descartes, Lacan tells us, made of God the "subject supposed to know" and so "inaugurated the initial bases of a science in which God has nothing to do" (FF 226).

Throughout the 1964 seminar Lacan alludes to this signifer "God" in another sense entirely, as if it were a ground or "other," a vast and unconscious principle—in a number of irresolvable ways that suggest that he is attempting to understand this signifier/subject, this "God," outside of the dialectic of scientific certainty and metaphysical doubt—to understand "God" without regard to the modern tradition of Its disappearance. This "God" represents a kind of knowledge, both ground and subject, before or beyond the rules of Cartesian method, a postmodern God detached from the existentialist context of the absurd, the death of god, and bad faith. Lacan thus corrects the atheistic claim that "God is dead": "The true formula of atheism is *God is unconscious*" (FF 59). Such a revisionary atheism would relinquish the doubter's reliance on God's death or disappearance and fully align

It with the vast unconscious processes in the subatomic realm, the regular movement of bodies in space, and the autonomic functions of the body. If the atheist's real objection is that human beings made God in their image, this revision of atheism would indeed be its "true formula."

Lacan's questions about "God" are at the same time, of course, considerations of how one is to conceive of subjectivity after the death of the subject, and how to conceive of psychoanalysis with respect to the Cartesians moorings of modern science. He asks the rather strange question, "Can psychoanalysis be situated in our science, in so far as this science is considered as that in which God has nothing to do?" (FF 226–27). In other words, "God" has something to do with psychoanalysis and It has even something to do with the science of Newton, Einstein, and Planck, whose work, Lacan says, "trac[ed] in the real a new furrow in relation to the knowledge that might from all eternity be attributed to God" (127). Psychoanalysis, then, is neither privileged to instigate the "real journey" nor is it ready to accept a position in a Cartesian science with which God has nothing to do. Psychoanalysis would appear confined to the guardianship of the signifier's place in the economy of the subject. Lacan is even willing to align his own practice, at least implicitly, with Spinoza in a striking way: "Pantheism is simply the reduction of the field of God to the universality of the signifier, which produces a serene, exceptional detachment from human desire" (FF 275). Lacan shifts atheism and pantheism from the childlike realm of anthropological characters to the field of relations between consciousness, unconsciousness, and language. Lacan's remarks suggest that a release from the naïve or ignorant infatuation with the linguistically created world might lead to an ecstatic dislocation of the subject and a glimpse of a "God-face."

Thus in the 1972 seminar Lacan rather abruptly announces that the "mystical is by no means that which is not political. It is something serious, which few people teach us about, and most often women or highly gifted people like Saint John of the Cross. . . . Mystics sense that there must be a *jouissance* [sexual pleasure] that goes beyond. This is what we call a mystic."[33] This valuing of mysticism is at odds with Freud, of course, Charcot, and others who argued that mystical experiences should be understood in terms of sexual energy finding expression under difficult circumstances (isolation, illness, monasteries, convents, caves). Lacan implies, however, that *jouissance* is a better figure for this unrepresentable experience than "insight," "knowledge," and "vision": "The essential testimony of the mystics is that they are experiencing it but know nothing about it." One may say, indeed, that they know nothing, precisely because they have experienced the eclipse of language: *Brahman,* the Unconscious God, the field of signifiers—and Thou art That.

These remarks from 1972 are the fulfillment of Lacan's cryptic allusion to the *Chandogya Upanishad* in 1949. The "mystic" aspects of Lacan's works are persistent and central to his critique of rationality and its commitment to a decisive and analytic ego prior to and uncontaminated by the contingencies of language. But this is not to say that Lacan, any more than Joyce and Eliot, "Indianized" himself and renounced reason or analysis or science. The chaosmic aspects of *Ecrits* are evident enough: Lacan was simply not afraid (although clearly on the defensive) of combining "Cartesian" rigor with mysticism—any more than Descartes himself was. Indeed it would appear that, for Lacan, mysticism is an ally of reason and performs a specific function in the critique of representation. Since for Lacan language is a critique of experience, and psychoanalysis is a critique of language, an even greater skepticism is required for a transcendental ironization of psychoanalysis: this is the role of mysticism.

Lacan's writerly discourses, characterized by a constantly allusive and riddling play against an easy and untested comprehension, are meant to avoid the traps of metalanguage and metapsychology, which catch anyone who speaks as if his own words and reasoning were not involved in the field of complex relations he is attempting to describe. In fact by 1972 Lacan is no longer willing to maintain a difference between his own writings and this "other tradition": "These mystical ejaculations [by St. Theresa] are neither idle gossip nor mere verbiage, in fact they are the best thing you can read . . . note right at the bottom of the page. *Add the* Ecrits *of Jacques Lacan, which is of the same order."* For a difficult writer, this last comment is rather simple to grasp: *Ecrits* should be understood within the tradition of "mystical ejaculations."

In 1955 Lacan expressed the kernel of his discursive practice: "The trade route of truth no longer passes through thought: strange to say, it now seems to pass through things: riddle, it is through you that I communicate."[34] Pronounced like the riddles of an adept, these ejaculations cannot simply engender truth in the ears of their hearers. Like *The Waste Land* and *The Upanishads,* they illumine by dazzling, enlighten by stunning, speak by deafening. "You are all going to believe that I believe in God" Lacan taunts his audience in 1972. But neither the presence nor the absence of "God" can be derived from his writings: such belief in presence is an example of a degraded modern skepticism. Instead, Lacan simply asks a question that subverts other questions which require affirmation or denial, questions which, in any case, are asked so that their answers may be forgotten: "Might not this *jouissance* which one experiences and knows nothing of be that which puts us on the path of ex-istence? And why not interpret one face of the Other, the God face, as supported by feminine *jouissance?*"

Forster's Permanent Parabasis

The chaosmic self is heard in the dissonance of limited and unlimited, centered and decentered, Cartesian, Hindu, and Buddhist principles of subjectivity. In the works of Eliot and Lacan, in the anecdotes from Freud and Oppenheimer, as in Forster's *A Passage to India,* this dissonance is heard as what could be called a "revelation," if that word did not suggest a visual and spatial unveiling or manifestation. Just as the word "chaosmos" is in itself a dissonance that is heard rather than a referent that is grasped, so the "self" that emerges in these moments is heard as a kind of "annunciation," if that word did not suggest a divine naming. The "self" understood in all of these instances results from a diffusion and reorientation of the Cartesian "I" and its European milieu when it is brought into radical contact with what it imagines to be entirely Other: India. So what is involved is not simply a personal epiphany but a union or reunion of civilizations no less significant than the European rediscovery of its classical heritage during the Renaissance.

Considering the world outside its boundaries as an alien, perhaps a dangerous threat, the West has since the Greeks denied its relationship, perhaps its derivations, from Egypt, from Phoenicia, from Persia, from India. At the same time, Europeans have since the days of Pythagoras and Plato, considered India in particular, and the "East" in general, as the source of deep truths and (at least for them) "forgotten" wisdom. The coexistence of these attitudes suggests a persistent doubleness in European consciousness, a demand for exclusive identity and a longing for a release from it.

John Drew's history of European literary relations with India, ranging from Pythagoras to Coleridge, shows how deeply Western ideas of imaginative truth are bound with what Coleridge called "inmost Ind."[35] The idealism of Plato, Plotinus, the Gnostics, Christianity, Schopenhauer, and the American transcendentalists are all profoundly indebted to Indian sources, just as the organicist conceptions of nature as a self-organizing process are indebted to China. This combination of colonial disdain and exotic longing, so well described by Edward Said, could be the result of a conflict between the prestige to be gained by domination and the secret personal longings for self-dissolution. In the case of T.E. Lawrence (of Arabia), self-dissolution could be achieved by an exotic affiliation with Arab nationalism, while in the case of George Gordon (of Khartoum) a quite literal self-dissolution could be found by a fanatic martyrdom achieved by resisting it.

Said's powerful studies demonstrate how Western scholarship and literature presented an exotic and barbarous Orient that could be colonized with ethical certitude.[36] But by emphasizing the conniving and self-serving nature of these discourses, Said—undoubtedly with an intentionally polemical rhetoric—tends himself to essentialize Western responses to the East. Arrogance, greed, and conquest have, like other forms of behavior, psychological and historical origins: they are no more intrinsic to Europe than deception, fanaticism, and cruelty are intrinsic to the East. Orientalism as a psychological and political ideology could be seen as Europe's profoundly anxious confrontation with its own sense of belatedness with respect to the East. In confronting Asia in the last three centuries, European intellectuals have had to wonder if their cultural "superiority," their belief in the unprecedented nature of Greek culture and Jewish moral law, was an adolescent self-deception. For Jones and Deussen, India represented a tremendous opportunity for deepening their knowledge, not only of another classical culture, but of their own. In evaluating Europe's general reluctance to recognize the possibility of its debt to Asia, John Drew concludes that "Europe will not fully understand the more imaginative productions of its own culture until it has first discovered the imaginative depths of the Indian" (122–23).

Exoticism has its good uses, then, but only if it can serve as a preliminary feeling of dissociation from one's dedicated sense of cultural and personal identity and an enticement toward a wider field of associations and relationships. One of the central themes of imperial romances, the threatened chastity of a colonial woman, turns on this theme of exoticism. Supported by a whole range of ideological assumptions, the unironized romance presents male intellectuals and women as the weak links in the colonial order: the first are in danger of "going native" due to some misplaced sympathy or interest in the natives and the second are in danger, because of their weakness and fragility (associated with moral superiority), of falling "ill" due to the harsh climate or being sullied by native contacts, a fear which combines a feeling of native abjection and an unspoken fear of the sexual whims of women. Such themes suggest a good deal more than the "loss" of a white man or the "pollution" of a white woman: they suggest the penetration of the colonial ear by the alien and seductive voices of Asia and their menacing repercussions in Europe. In *A Passage to India* (1924) Forster treats the symptom of this imperial fear, the supposed rape of an English woman, Adela Quested, and the seduction of an English intellectual, Cyril Fielding by the same

Indian physician, Dr. Assiz, identifying it with a perennial Western attraction to and dread of the kind of exotic revelations that can change one's understanding of both worlds.

The medium of such putative revelations in the novel is echoing or resonance, and Forster's own subtly ironic adoption of *dhvani*. In his *Sanskrit Poetics* Krishna Chaitanya describes *dhvani* in this way: "If, after the appearance of the expressed sense, either the sound *(Sabda)* or the meaning *(Artha)*, completely subordinating itself, gives rise to another sense, it is said that, in those cases, word and meaning suggest another sense."[37] Lacan describes this "other sense" as the resonance that speech prompts in the subject through a momentary access to the unconscious. The subject, in that moment, may be said to resound and produce a meaning quite different from the one intended or articulated. Chaitanya continues, "This rise of the suggested sense can be likened to two phenomena: resonance *(Anunada)* and echo *(Pratidhvani)*. It is only such metals as bronze which, when struck, give rise to ripples of resonance and it is only a few special spots like caves where the voice produces an echo, similar yet so subtly different" (120). As the analysand resounds to the analyst, the reader to the poet, and gods, men, and devils to the voice of the thunder—so Forster's characters, Adela Quested and Mrs. Moore are drawn to listen to themselves in the "extraordinary" Marabar caves. It is only then that they begin to walk, in Lacan's phrase, "the path of ex-istence."

At the center of Forster's novel, then, are these barren caves whose sole interest is their ability to reduce and extrapolate whatever is spoken within them. "Nothing, nothing attaches to them," Forster's narrator writes, "and their reputation—for they have one—does not depend upon human speech. It is as if the surrounding plain or the passing birds have taken upon themselves to exclaim 'extraordinary' and the word has taken root in the ear, and been inhaled in mankind."[38] From the center back to its beginning and forward to its end, *A Passage to India* seduces and resounds with a visionary or auditory promise of revelation that is finally expressed in a "meaningless" choice of syllables: *boum, ou-boum* "—utterly dull," as Forster's narrator drily comments.

These matters are unwound in the course of what only superficially resembles an English novel of manners, "a work," Paul Armstrong writes, "of much greater epistemological complexity than its seemingly conventional narrative form suggests."[39] Perhaps Forster began the novel with the generic premises developed in his previous fiction, but by the time he had finished it, they served to restrain his novel from drifting, with its increasingly complex patterns of resonance, beyond novelistic bounds altogether. Committed as the genre is to the rudiments of empirical reality and character, it can only with difficulty absorb the kind of derealizing themes that Forster impressed upon it. *Finnegans Wake*, a novel only in the sense that it is a work of prose fiction, clearly presents itself as a book like no other: encyclopedic, mammoth, a vocation for its readers. *A Passage to India* seems to pursue a more sinister route, treading well-worn novelistic paths but doing everything to show the uncanny aspect of its novelistic chores and to dematerialize the geographical rootedness of its setting.

The three parts of the novel—Mosque, Caves, Temple— imply that cultures are kinds of enclosures which attempt to limit and shape significance. Within these enclosures, the illusion of meaning can be maintained, if one has been taught how to understand the ways in which confined (and repeating) syllables "make sense." These divisions inaugurate cultural epochs by diminishing and reducing the field of signifiers to suit a particular interpretation of life. The contained echoings of Mosque, Cave, and Temple constitute, in this forgetting, the cosmologies and religions that thrive on exclusive words and particular practices. But at the origin of both Islamic and Hindu beliefs are the elemental caves buried in the Marabar Hills. The hills are "like nothing else in the world, and a glimpse of them makes the breath catch. They rise abruptly, insanely, without the proportion that is kept by the wildest hills elsewhere, they bear no relation to anything dreamt or seen" (124). Unformed even by imagination, these hills conceal caves that a visitor leaves "uncertain whether he has had an interesting experience or a dull one or any experience at all" (124). Mosque and Temple inadvertently refer to the primeval audition of sounds which form a natural litany whose meaning is not even "uncanny," for that "suggests ghosts, and the caves are older than all spirit" (124). Forster's genealogy of constituted forms thus leads, past the trope of "spirit," to a pair of elemental syllables. To these timeless sites Forster conducts a pair of middle-class British women in quest of "the real India."

Mrs. Moore's path leads toward a general alienation from human confinements and concerns—her death is plotted from her first appearance as "ghost" in the mosque where Assiz muses after his humiliation at the British Club. After reciting a passage from a Persian poem, the doctor considers "the secret understanding of the heart" the poem reveals. "He repeated the phrase with tears in his eyes, and as he did so one of the pillars of the mosque seemed to quiver. It swayed in the gloom and detached itself. Belief in ghosts ran in his blood, but he sat firm" (20). When Mrs. Moore appears, instead of a moving pillar or ghost, we realize that she has been invoked by the poetic phrases sounded in the mosque, and in this sense she could be said to be the resonance of Assiz's "heart." Stopped by Assiz who assumes she is violating the mosque, Mrs. Moore impresses his religious sentiments when she says that "God is here." It becomes apparent that she shares with him a "secret understanding of the heart," and draws Assiz to her as if she were already the goddess she will later become for the crowds at his trial.

The old woman's reluctant observations about India and the British Raj show that she is prepared for the audition in the caves that will consummate her growing indifference to English, and finally, human affairs. Hearing that the crocodiles in the Ganges consume the cadavers floating down from Benares, she says, "What a terrible river! what a wonderful river!" (32). Terror and wonder, like fear of losing the ego and an eager anticipation of losing it, coincide in her response to the "India" organized by the British with their convenient racism and disdain. Responding to her son's imperialist banalities, she tells him that "God has put us on earth in order to be pleasant to each other. God . . . is . . . love" (51). The silly comment about being "pleasant" leads to another hesitant formula, far from the imperialist mythology of a just

God and Britain overseeing an immature or simply barbarous India: "She must needs pronounce his name frequently, as the greatest she knew, yet she had never found it less efficacious. Outside the arch there seemed always an arch, beyond the remotest echo a silence" (52). Though she tries to maintain her proper (novelistic) role (seeing to it that her son is engaged to Adela), Mrs. Moore is drawn toward the "silence" beyond "the remotest echo," a silence more "efficacious" than the name of God. Like Forster's novel, she forsakes the traditional task of marrying the young and affirming the real, and assumes that there is a vocation in that "silence." *A Passage to India* was, of course, Forster's last novel, published nearly half a century before his death.

Despite the apocalyptic premonitions, her experience in the caves is neither visionary nor revelatory in an expected sense. It is both a devastation and a transcendence of human language—as well as the ethical precepts that derive from language:

> Professor Godbole had never mentioned an echo; it never impressed him, perhaps. There are some exquisite echoes in India . . . . The echo in a Marabar cave is not like these, it is entirely devoid of distinction. Whatever is said, the same monotonous noise replies, and quivers up and down the walls until it is absorbed into the roof. "Boum" is the sound as far as the human alphabet can express it, or "bou-oum," or "ou-boum,"—utterly dull. (147)

Her interpretation of the experience in the cave is comparable to existential critiques of humanism: "Coming at the moment when she chanced to be fatigued, [the echo] had managed to murmur, 'Pathos, piety, courage—they exist, but are identical, and so is filth. Everything exists, nothing has value'" (149). Value, then, appears inseparable from the divisive, hierarchichal nature of "language." The confounding of language, the reduction of all syllables to one, prompts Mrs. Moore to quasi-Niezschean reflections that link "values" to "words." The most threatening aspect of the caves is that they cannot be displaced into sacred, revelatory, or erotic registers: "no one could romanticize the Marabar because it robbed infinity and eternity of their vastness, the only quality that accommodates them to mankind" (150). Mrs. Moore experiences the collapse of human speech which entails the collapse of Western values. Among these is the informing role of speech in the Judeo-Christian ideas of God as Logos: "divine words from 'Let there be light' to 'It is finished' only amounted to 'boum'" (150).

Mrs. Moore's experience in the caves allows her to discard languages and laws, as well as her mission to India—which was, in effect, to join two people within the bonds of language and law. Only when Adela mentions she has heard an echo since their visit to the caves does she awaken any interest in Mrs. Moore. When Adela asks that she explicate the echo, Mrs. Moore responds like one adept in the yogic disciplines: "If you don't know, you don't know; I can't tell you. . . . As if anything can be said!" (200). The idea of testifying at Assiz's trial becomes suddenly absurd to her: "I have nothing to do with your ludicrous law courts" (200). Equally absurd to her is the distinction society makes between marriage in a church and seduction in a cave: "And all this rubbish about love, love in a church, love in a cave, as if there is the least difference, and I held up my business over such trifles" (202). Refusing to *hear* the speech of culture, whether in a law court or a church, she accepts the audition in the cave as their original, undivided source. This detachment from cultural speech is confirmed, appropriately enough when the magistrate informs the attorneys, "I must repeat that as a witness Mrs. Moore does not exist," for it is at this moment that she dies aboard ship in the Indian Ocean (226). Adela explains that Mrs. Moore died "when they called her name this morning," so that she passes away, as she first appears in the novel, as an effect of speech (249). Her ghost "followed the ship up the Red Sea, but failed to enter the Mediterranean," forsaking the West's cultural origins, and resounding in the jubilant chants of the crowds celebrating Assiz's acquittal (256). Although she has done "nothing" to help him (or because she has), she becomes in the speech of the Indians of Chandrapore, "Esiss Esmoor, a Hindu Goddess" (225).

Whereas the "boum" leads Mrs. Moore to prepare for death, it awakens Adela to the living death that marriage to Mrs. Moore's son Ronny Heaslop, the local magistrate, would be. Death and love, "bo-oum" or "ou-boum," the echoes of Marabar direct both women to heed impulses muffled and contained by the laws and the words of their culture. Adela is described "looking through a nick in the cactus hedge at the distant Marabar Hills, which had crept near, as was their custom at sunset" (45). As hints of the "real India," the hills and their hidden caves are associated with her own undiscovered sexuality which is in danger of remaining so should she acquiesce to her colonial life with Ronny. Adela imagines that such longings would disappear, just as "the true India slid by unnoticed" (47). As India is colonized by British power, British power threatens to colonize Adela, who continues to gaze at the hills as if toward an assignation with her most repressed desires. This identification is borne out by her decision not to marry Ronny after seeing his condescending behavior to Dr. Assiz and Godbole, and after Assiz's trip to the caves has been proposed. India, and the caves, are associated with her own fears of being dominated, and thus her experience there can be seen as a desire to be seduced by India, her own double.

As Assiz leads her toward the cave entrance, the earth speaks for her: "The air felt like a warm bath into which hotter water is trickling constantly, the temperature rose and rose, the boulders said, 'I am alive,' the small stones answered, 'I am almost alive'" (150–51). The ascent and her thoughts of marriage make her realize that "she and Ronny—no, they did not love each other" (152). The stones speak and then Adela does, to ask Assiz if he is married, as his hand and hers are joined in her ascent toward the cave. She assumes that Assiz, like other "Mohammedans," would "insist" on four wives. Her vulgar projection of her own sexual desire onto Assiz angers the Indian, who is insulted by her remarks. Having alienated both her British and Indian contacts, Adela is brought closer than ever before to her own desires, and it is at this point that she imagines being assaulted and runs down the hills to "safety." It is also at this point that Forster shifts his point of view, abandoning Adela to her fantasy. Rather than

representing or interpreting the fantasy or the echo Adela complains of, Forster's narrative simply echoes the echoes: "What was
the 'echo' of which the girl complained?"; "No one understood
her trouble, or knew why she vibrated between hard common
sense and hysteria"; "Adela was always trying to 'think the inci-
dent out'. . . . For a time her own logic would convince her, then
she would hear the echo again, weep, declare she was unworthy of
Ronny, and hope her assailant would get the maximum penalty"
(191, 193, 194).

Lacan's explanation of a *jouissance* of the beyond might
describe both women's experiences about which "they know
nothing." Lacan says that one has only to look at Bernini's statue
of St. Theresa "to understand immediately that she's coming,
there is no doubt about it. And what is her *jouissance,* her *coming*
from?. . . I believe in the *jouissance* of the woman insofar as it is
something more. . . . Might not this *jouissance* which one experiences and knows nothing of, be that which puts one on the path
of ex-istence? And why not interpret one face of the Other, the
God face, as supported by feminine *jouissance?*"[40] Lacan is careful
to distinguish the mystic's experience from a simple case of displaced libido. In the instance of Forster's two female characters,
one sees that the *jouissance* of woman is displaced into a death
wish and a desire to be seduced, wishes which can at least be
interpreted and acted upon. A second displacement by Adela can
be observed in her charging Assiz, India, and her own repressed
self with the crime against her social existence as a British
woman.

The effects of these events on Fielding, the endangered
intellectual who expresses an impotent and aesthetic disavowal of
imperialism and religion and can only threaten to "go native," is
divided between a determined repression ("The original sound
may be harmless, but the echo is always evil") and an uncharac-
teristic suspicion about his own skepticism: "he lost his usual sane
view of human intercourse, and felt that we exist not in ourselves,
but in terms of each other's minds" (276, 250). Like the "insane"
Marabar caves, which insist upon a radical reverberation and
reinterpretation of all the words of value, Fielding seems to

resound with the dubious, the supposedly hysterical and senile fantasies of Adela and Mrs. Moore.

This fearful idea that the self exists only by virtue of a violent, lingusitic splitting (maintained only at great psychic cost) might also characterize the way in which Forster's novel resonates from its own empty center. The caves respond to whatever is spoken within them with "bo-oum," or, more simply, *OM*. Vasant A. Shahane writes, "While *Om* or *Oum* is believed to signify the nondualist *Vedanta*, *Ou-boum* has been interpreted as the voice of the dualistic point of view. Both of these sounds either help or hinder the process of the characters' attempts at merging with the Absolute."[41] Thus Forster would appear to dismantle the "words" of the Judeo-Christian tradition while inscribing the syllables of the Hindu tradition, for the Brahmic word *(Om* or *Aum)* opens *The Upanishads* by absorbing the reader's voice and subjectivity within a single sound. Swami Nikhilinanda explains that "devoid of names and forms, the universe is *Brahman;* it is these that distinguish it from *Brahman.*"[42] Whatever is spoken, the caves reduce and expand to "bo-oum," a sound that Western ears hear as a sign of the absurdity of all human endeavors. But, as Swami Prabhavananda explains, "The syllable O*M*—symbol of *Brahman*, or God—is, to Hindus, divine; and in their rituals, it is uttered with a solemn resonance, indefinitely prolonged."[43]

Lionel Trilling wrote, with reference to the episode in the caves, "However we may interpret Forster's intention in this web of reverberation, it gives his book a cohesion and intricacy usually found in music."[44] Most readers would probably see in such "intricacy" a typically modernist irony, through which Forster is able to remain superior to the dramatic tension between true revelation and hysteric projection. But this attitude reflects a rather recent and simplified sense of irony, one touching on superior indifference. Edward Said, ignoring the profounder sources of Forster's skepticism, considers that he is of the imperialist's party without knowing it, because the end of *A Passage to India* seems to insist on the unalterable difference between Fielding and Assiz, between "us" and "them." The real obstacle to such union, Said claims, is Forster's "style" of "compact definition."[45] The Indian critic Rustom Bharucha is less certain. Bharucha claims that Said's reading has less to do with the subtleties of character in Forster's fiction than with the programmatic argument of Said's book, *Orientalism:* "Yes, there is separation in the final moments of *A Passage to India,* but it is so subtly juxtaposed with intimacy that one might say that Assiz and Fielding have acquired a mutual understanding of each other for the first time—perhaps because of the separation."[46] This ironic movement toward intimacy through alienation is less an allegory of Indian/English relations than an example of all human relations which dramatize the dialectic of difference and relationship.

Forster's ironic narrative derives from a subtler approach to the issues than the indifference or racism which Said suggests, one for which Friedrich Schlegel could be the spokesman: "True irony—for there is also a false one—is the irony of love. It arises out of the feeling of finiteness and one's own limitation, and out of the apparent contradiction between the feeling and the idea of infinity which is involved in all true love."[47] The echoes from the caves are, in this sense, truly ironic. In another context, Schlegel describes irony as an "permanent parabasis," which appears in fiction, as Paul de Man has indicated, in the self-conscious narrator. By disturbing the reader's ready acceptance of narratives and judgments, the novelist allows his work to be penetrated by an irony that allows both himself and his reader freedom from naïve identifications with the illusions of realism. De Man claims that such a device "serves to prevent the all too readily mystified reader from confusing fact and fiction and from forgetting the essential negativity of the fiction."[48] Since Hinduism and Buddhism are essentially critiques of naïve identification with an internalized ego, Forster's narrative cannot simply be said to be "ironic" except in this Schlegelian or Indian sense. "The essential negativity of the fiction" in Forster's novel does not, then, cast doubt on the value or significance of the experience in the caves: the caves have already done this by denying any link between human signs and ultimate reality. Hindu qualified identification with all aspects of the phenomenal world (*"Tat tvam asi,"* "Thou art that"), and the Buddhist negation of linguistic and subjective identifications (*"Neti, neti,"* "not that! not that!") are joined at this point. By writing an ironic narrative, Forster rejects any simple adherence to Indian "revelations," which would indeed constitute a naïve orientalism. John Drew makes a similar distinction: "The irony in the novel is not just the comic irony of the sceptic; it is the cosmic irony of the idealist who has discovered that the formulations of language do not permit idealism to be differentiated from materialism—or mysticism from scepticism."[49]

The Chaosmic Self

The disappearance of the subject, the death of the author, the dehumanization of "man," the passing of the Eurocentric world —these eclipses of a certain kind of subjectivity and a certain kind of reality have been seen ambivalently by some theorists and with unalloyed horror by others. The ambivalent postmodern response tends toward a modulated, ironized melancholia, a rear-guard sizing up and description of retreating forces: the punctual subject, the competent sign, the representable world. Focused on the last three centuries of European history and thought, any other life-world tends to be seen as an abyss of signs, an unrelieved field of discursive fictions. The defensive humanist reaction has been to shore up the fragments of our ruins, to bolster the Eurocentric heritage, to insist upon the necessary and practical, if not the metaphysical, reality of the subject, the sign, and representation in general.

The chaosmic self, as a term, designates a principle of subjectivity no longer strictly punctual, expressive, or interior. The chaosmic self, as an aspect of a self-organizing, organic process, is expressed at different levels of reference and within different temporalities by corresponding contexts. One could say that this "self" is the expression of a series of interinvolved, temporally and spatially imbricated environments. The male and female aspects in *Finnegans Wake,* to cite the exemplary chaosmic text, emerge as a series of structural patterns and atomic instances, ranging from the organic world to the unconscious, from a mountain and a river to periodic and peritactic syntaxes. To insist upon the exclusive reality or significance of a "single" environment is to confine and amputate it. The current critical emphases on gender, class, and racial determination have transformed the exclusivist and airy platitudes of individualist humanism, which sought to deny that such things could significantly restrain artistic genius, into the exclusivist and materialist platitudes which celebrate the liberation of categories. Both descriptions, following the Cartesian bifurcation into souls and bodies, express the limitations and values of their categories: the first pretends that social determination is dissolved by genius, and the second ignores the fact that texts become "literary" or studied because they *are* exceptional rather than generic, able to characterize and perhaps elude—once gaining the material opportunity—ideological determinants. My goal in this book is to get as many of these environments involved as possible, to grasp the actual dimensions of self and world: organic, material, subjective, intellectual, cultural, and literary.

Without the insights guarded by poets and mystics alike, words do not merely represent the self and the world, they transform the fluent world of *relations*—of which they are interanimating aspects—into opposed *things*. By translating the English words and values of a metaphysical heritage, stretching from *Genesis* to English law, into the thunderous echoes of "ou-boum" or "bo-oum," the Marabar caves and *A Passage to India* open the orderly self-centered cosmos of ideological constructions to a chaotic chorus of voices, both individually different and yet indistinguishable from one another, both a cartoonish onomatopoeia (Boom!) and the most sacred of Sanskrit sound-words: *Om, Aum*. The legible appearance of Sanskrit within all these texts is both an invasion of the other and a return of the scattered elements of a single family of languages—both a literal incorporation and a reincorporation of the other into the self.

One begins to see the other within the familiar everywhere, the world within the self, the self within other selves, one language within another, one name within another, one world within another. Thus the Da, which Derrida hears in Heidegger's *Dasein* and Freud's *Fort/Da* and in his own name and language, resounds in the

voice of the thunder in the *Brihadaranyaka,* echoes across the mil-
lennia in *The Waste Land* and the *Discourse of Rome.* These resonances resemble the roar that frightens Mrs. Moore and Adela
Quested and leads Oppenheimer to consider an ancient scripture at
the very moment when modern technology had achieved its most
momentous intervention within the physical world.

The sites of these resonances and auditions are more or less
arbitrary, but the events they articulate are not. These moments in
Western culture, the moments when modernity saw for a moment
beyond and back to itself, cannot be described exclusively as the
apocalypse of technology, either scientific or aesthetic. Nor are
they simply the points when modernity's triumphs imploded or
exploded with the splitting of the subject and the word: they can
also be heard in the conjunction of India, America, and Europe, a
meeting whose thunderous syllables may announce the union and
vocation of a planetary, a chaosmic, subject.

ᴖ—Chaosmoi

Wouldn't the apocalyptic be a transcendental condition of all discourse, of all experience itself, of every mark or every trace? And the genre of writings called "apocalyptic" in the strict sense, then, would be only an example, an exemplary revelation of this transcendental structure.

—Jacques Derrida

The Apocalyptic Tone

In 1966 Michel Foucault concluded a monumental critique of modernist knowledge (what he calls Classical thought), with these remarks: "As the archaeology of our thought easily shows, man is an invention of recent date. And one perhaps nearing its end."[1] This end or death of the invention called "Man" is coterminous with the collapse of a matrix of intellectual assumptions, an *épistemè*, and of the ahistorical, egocentric demand for independant or individual existence. This end would necessarily represent the end of a conception and thus would present an opportunity which Foucault describes with relationship to the death of another conception: "Thus, the last man is at the same time older and yet younger than the death of God; since he has killed God, it is he himself who must answer for his own finitude; but since it is in the death of God that he speaks, thinks, and exists, his murder itself is doomed to die; new gods, the same gods, are already swelling the future Ocean; man will disappear" (385). Jacques Derrida considered in those years "the ends of man" and a "future" which "can be anticipated in the form of an

143

absolute danger . . . a sort of monstrosity" whose birth is "in the offing, only under the species of the non-species."[2] So too, at the end of his life, Adorno considered how the death of philosophy portended an "afterlife" haunted by its unsatisfied desire: "Philosophy which once seemed obsolete, lives on because the moment to realize it was missed."[3] Philosophy will "live on" in the interminable and futile repetitions of a ghost haunting the unredeemable grounds of its frustration. I cite these oracular remarks, not in order to analyze them (a risky task), but in order to sound their portentousness and consider the remains of the sixties' zeitgeist. For there can be little doubt that Foucault, Derrida, and Adorno presumed in the midst of a period of cultural crisis to imagine a world—after modernity.

The apocalyptic tone of these remarks, like those of Lacan and Heidegger, suggests a metaphysical longing, a longing for and a fear of a new age, ungoverned by the fictions and metaphors of modernist thought. The death of the subject and the "return" of language seemed to threaten and enrapture at the same time, to portend a liberation from the confinements of reason, the prison of the empirically "real," and a humanism defined by the project of technological modernization. Foucault foresaw "the explosion of man's face in laughter, and the return of masks; it is the scattering of the profound stream of time by which he felt himself carried along and whose pressure he suspected in the very being of things; it is the identity of the Return of the Same with the absolute dispersion of man" (385). Foucault, like Derrida, recognized that the "absolute dispersion of man" is both an opportunity and a threat, that could lead to a "monstrous" birth, like the beast of Yeats' "Second Coming," making us long for the old humanist compromises.

I think that these remarks, and others by Derrida and Lacan, indicate a tone of poststructuralist thought that has not been adequately remarked because it seems to insinuate and foreshadow more than analyze and predict. The apocalyptic or oracular tone, always a temptation in philosophic discourse, may be intentionally enigmatic in order later to gather to itself a certain prescience or necessarily enigmatic because one simply doesn't know what one thinks and the tone registers this as well as the complex emotional intensity of the desire and the need to speak. So the apocalyptic tone has a risible aspect, inevitably because it is dispatched from the moment and the self, without any possibility of certainty, into the future and to others. Despite the unprecedented severity of Foucault's and Derrida's work, their grindingly thorough and yet enigmatic undercutting and cross-questioning of the humanist values (the self, the sign), there is also a momentary exhilaration, neither in accord nor in dissent, with apocalyptic prospects: the passing of "man" and "modernity" and the advent of something truly other, neither utopian nor distopian, but rather carnivalesque, if not grotesque.

The poststructuralist and deconstructive enterprises, one might conclude, assumed or were assigned a general purpose, the dismantling of metaphysical thought, which did not fulfill their initial apocalyptic demands and their own potential for a motivated reconceptualization of the old humanist project. Instead they fell into familiar modern forms, the demystification of idealisms: where Bacon and Galileo "deconstructed" the scholastic universe of fixed forms and essences, the poststructuralist and deconstructive projects were satisfied by the ever-renewed aim of deconstructing the aesthetic and philosophical machinery of modernism: the author, the closed work, the dominant ideology. When the notably abstract complexion of early theory began to pall, the metaphysics of presence and logocentrism discerned in texts were literalized as political and cultural repression. The initial political opacity of the works of Derrida and Foucault was clarified throughout the late seventies and eighties and was oriented by many as kinds of liberation theory. This "modernizing" of the uses of theory was accompanied by a marked professionalization of literary criticism, complete with the necessary technicalities, protocols, and jargon. Of all the terms that Derrida used to describe his own work, drawing on anatomical, botanical, astronomical, literary, pharmacological, psychoanalytical, archaeological, and zoological vocabularies, it was the word "deconstruction" which was seized on, if only to undercut the very notion of structure. The material and technical connotations of "construction" and "deconstruction" suited both critics and students of deconstruction. Out of this terminological consensus, Derrida's work was aligned, wrongly I think, with the standard modernist project of demythologizing our knowledge of the world [4]

The reasons for this modernist reading of Derrida's work can be located in the confusion of two different understandings of "metaphysics," both of which are pejorative: a) the scholastic nomenclature of philosophies which have no interest in the empirical findings of the natural sciences; b) the artificial categories, internalized by an ideology, academic or cultural, which organize perceptions, representations, and interpretations of the world. Thus a physicist may condemn Heidegger's *Being and Time* as pure "metaphysics" because Heidegger cannot demonstrate that concepts like *"Dasein,"* "Being," "Falling," and "Thrown-ness" are anything more than words. On the other hand, a philosopher may consider the knowledge of physicists to be simply a metaphysics inscribed in the languages of mathematics. The world, he could claim, is not composed of quantity or number; any "knowledge" predicated upon the discipline of describing and predicting the relations of such mathematical entities is no less "metaphysical" than discussions of "Being."

The discussion becomes meaningless because it is based on a false distinction between the physical and the metaphysical, between the realm of natural process and the realm of human consciousness. Obviously, metaphysics, understood as a discourse beyond or after or superior to "physics," can mean little definite unless physics as a discipline was complete. Considering Bell's theorem should lead anyone to relinquish any self-confidence about being able to tell the difference between physical and non- or metaphysical phenomena.

Seventeenth-century physics, it should be remembered, was in effect a "deconstruction" of theological, scholastic knowledge associated with Aristotelian and Ptolemaic physics and astronomy. Indeed, Newton's revolution could be viewed as the first essentially modern intervention within the onto-theology of natural science, because it disregarded the place of the Book within a physics now oriented to mathematical revelations. Physicists, in any case, began to doubt seriously the purely physical model of quantum reality by the 1920s and thus joined a general critique of the Cartesian legacy. One must ask, then, what pure or exclusive meaning metaphysics could have after the destructuring of the atomic model and the deterministic laws of classical, modern physics describing a fundamental, atomic *physis*. Without admitting as much, those who have set themselves the task of undermining metaphysics make a pact with a physics that is no longer synonymous with nature. Rather than attempting to escape or deconstruct metaphysics, we should recognize that the "conceived" or "significant" or even the "measured" existence of the world is necessarily *metaphysical* in the sense that it is finally thought, and thus an aspect of Bell's "superdeterminism."

Henry Pierce Stapp describes the Copenhagen (Bohr's) interpretation of the non-Newtonian findings of quantum physics this way: "[It] was essentially a rejection of the presumption that nature could be understood in terms of elementary space-time realities. According to the new view, the complete description of nature at the atomic level was given by probability functions that referred, not to underlying microscopic space-time realities, but rather to the macroscopic objects of sense experience. The theoretical structure did not extend down and anchor itself on fundamental microscopic space-time realities."[5] Bohr and Heisenberg, moreover, claimed that the physical—in the sense of an irreducible ground—could no longer be posited as a given in nature. In postulating a "probability wave" to account for the possible outcome of physical relations between particles, Bohr was offering, as Heisenberg puts it, "a quantitative version of the old concept of 'potentia' in Aristotelian philosophy." These scientists thus "introduced something standing in the middle between the idea of an event and the actual event, a strange kind of physical reality just in the middle between possibility and reality."[6] Resistance to this interpretation by Einstein and others could not refute the findings that experimentation had produced. Opposition to the Copenhagen interpretation thus exposed all the more patently the significance of presumption, even within the "hardest" of sciences. Material reality and the idea of objectivity became, in the context of quantum research, increasingly "theoretical" and bound to certain methods of measurement whose premises could not be validated by experimentation. The simply "physical" could make sense, at the quantum level, only through disregarding the means of conducting the experiment and the means of expressing its results.

One could say that quantum physics, by pursuing the functional model astutely and patiently, had uncovered the fictive nature of "ground," "basis," and "origin" insofar as these terms had been linked to what Whitehead calls "brute matter." Physics had become, to the extent that it went beyond the physical model, metaphysical in positing the existence of a realm of mathematical forms, "potentia," and revoking the logical law of excluded middles. The metaphysics of Plato, like the physics of Bohr and Heisenberg, relied on a mathematical formalism which could not be actually observed or translated into natural languages. As Heisenberg points out, "the elementary particles in Plato's *Timaeus* are finally not substance but mathematical. . . . In modern quantum theory there can be no doubt that the elementary particles will finally also be mathematical forms."[7] If physics, then, can no longer maintain its own foundation, as postulated by the aspirations of a detailed and final science of the real, what of other inquiries that can only allude metaphorically to the foundation or ground of their inquiries? Invoking large-scale regularities and predictability can only add to the stress on the fundamentalist premise of hard science by emphasizing the levels of physical organization and description. And with the recent emergence of chaos theory, yet another level of stochastic dynamics emerges. Physics, like twentieth-century literature, would seem to have allowed its own double to emerge, a metaphysics that, like metaliterature, would begin to critique its own aesthetic pretentions to validity. In the context of twentieth-century science the "deconstruction of metaphysics" appears as an oddly retrograde, a *modern*, task.

If one thinks of metaphysics as a synonym for the tendentious discipline of unprovable assertions and arbitrary definitions that characterize medieval scholasticism, then it is certainly overdue for deconstruction. But Jacques Derrida was never interested in simply banishing metaphysics, despite suggestions to that effect—any more than he was interested in substituting absence for presence, writing for speech, play for structure. Indeed his work has always been far too complex to be reduced in such ways and continually demonstrated how such summary projects would necessarily mirror what they sought to undo. Indeed, only after the "deconstruction" of metaphysics have the questions of "origin," "end," "totality," and "presence" been so persistently raised and so passionately discussed by scholars. I would prefer to link Derrida's deconstruction of metaphysics not only with Heidegger and Nietzsche, but also with Kant and Hegel, who preserve one kind of metaphysics by dismantling another. And preserving metaphysics means keeping certain questions alive in an age quite ready to equate unreflected scientific data with a knowledge of the world.

Kant, for example, recognized that Newtonian science threatened traditional metaphysics and in his three *Critiques* attempted to preserve the "possibility" of a future metaphysics by putting ultimate reality out of play—specifically out of the grasp of the positive sciences. But Kant's preservation of the metaphysical site in the noumenal realm actually led to its entombment for two centuries, and with such a site both privileged and denied, the compromised notion of aesthetic experience gained circulation. From Kant to Husserl the critique of empirical or positivist sciences is constant and severe, but largely impotent because it relies on an epistemological revisionism—itself reminiscent of Descartes—that could not move to its promised project: a new comprehensive science or metaphysics. Out of this context comes the romantic genre of the prelude, the self-conscious concern with the artist's formation that has become in twentieth-century literature the metaliterary or self-destroying text. Wordsworth, Baudelaire, Flaubert, and Mann mirror in their works the effects of a metaphysical and cognitive stalemate that is evident in the works of contemporary writers terminally and exclusively concerned with the effects of discourse. The traditions of formalist art, from Kant to de Man, reflect this dilemma that the scientific tradition instituted precisely to avoid the stalemate and facilitate the appearance of progress. As the Cartesian bifurcation led to scientific mastery and social authority, art since Baudelaire has often made its own aesthetic concerns and resentments universal: the *poet maudit* leads to the cold war rebel without a cause.

Hegel saw the consequences of Kant's *preservation* of metaphysics long before it had assumed the consequences I have sketched—even as it inaugurated the tradition of a prelude to an unwritten or unwriteable treatise. He countered the Cartesian and Kantian dichotomies with the essentially mystical concept of the *Aufhebung* which appeared to reconcile opposition and denied the alien nature of the Thing-in-Itself (the Noumenon). In place of the object and subject, preserved and destroyed at the same time, Hegel sought to revitalize the *Geist:* "The Spirit shows itself so impoverished that, like a wanderer in the desert craving for a mere mouthful of water, it seems to crave for its refreshment only the bare feeling of the divine in general. By the little which now satisfies Spirit, we can measure the extent of its loss."[8] "The bare feeling of the divine" characterizes the compromise of a merely aesthetic experience and suggests the extent of the loss that Spirit has experienced in the modern era.

Death, in both subjective and epochal terms, is thus critically important in Hegel's dialectics of Spirit because it is the one indisputable confrontation with the metaphysical horizon of individual existence and history. Heidegger's philosophy similarly demands a resolute advancement-to-death in order for *Dasein* to realize its own destiny as a complete and authentic Being. The forgetting of death, like the naïve predilection for the "positive" that Hegel condemns, characterizes the ideological discourse that Heidegger calls "idle talk" *(Gerede).* "The expression 'one dies' spreads abroad the opinion that what gets reached, as it were, by death is the 'they.' In Dasein's public way of interpreting, it is said that 'one dies,' because everyone else and oneself can talk himself into saying that 'in no case is it I myself,' for this 'one' is *the 'nobody.'"*[9] This kind of ideological expression "provides a *constant tranquillization about death*" and cultivates a "superior indifference" which "*alienates* Dasein from its ownmost non-relational potentiality-for-Being" (298). The ideological appropriation of existentialism by the intelligentsia has similarly *forgotten death* by publicly interpreting it as the determinate feature of the absurd. Death is appropriated and made to signify an end, which is precisely what "idle talk" requires.

Heidegger and Derrida approach death in a different way, by appreciating its intimate relations with representation, and more specifically with the act of inscription. Heidegger asserts that "we must characterize Being-towards-death as a *Being towards a possibility*—indeed towards a distinctive possibility of Dasein itself" (305). In other words, Heidegger refuses to limit the meaning of death to the terms of life—for death cannot be understood simply as the termination of the subject. It is, inevitably, an event of representation, translation, and inscription. Death is represented to us in fictions and experience, and when we are dead we will become represented as dead for those who remain. The dilemma of death is that it offers an apparent totalization of the life-experience that occurs only to be lost in the passing away of the subject who knows. Heidegger writes, "When Dasein reaches its wholeness in death, it simultaneously loses the Being of its 'there'" (281). Death could be said to exemplify or allegorize the act of perception in which the living moment dies into representation: in the same way that the world-in-itself is always beyond our grasp, so too is death, and without a knowledge of death we can never know the context or frame of life, and without a recognition that we don't know what death is we cannot know that we do not know what life is. Conceiving a world would seem to require a remembering of death.

The dead necessarily present themselves to the living as an epistemological problem whose solution can only lie in inferring the idea, at least, of an *other* world—not necessarily a "beyond" or an "afterlife" (too easily imaginable as a phantomized version of our own world), but an inflection of this world. Death presents the possibility, then, of seeing "this" world as necessarily an "other" world. The modernist faith in the absolute dissolution of the subject remains simply that—a too simple resolution of the epistemological problem par excellence.

"Death," Heidegger continues, "does indeed reveal itself as a loss, but a loss such as is experienced by those who remain" (282). Whether death is a loss for the one who is, according to the living word, "lost" cannot be determined. "Ending does not necessarily mean fulfilling oneself. It thus becomes more urgent to ask *in what sense, if any, death must be conceived as the ending of Dasein*" (289). Heidegger's reflections form a central part of his conception of an authentic "freedom towards death," but such freedom and authenticity depend upon the possibility of a death with the dialectic of termination and transcendence. The analysis of *Dasein*'s totality "has shown only in a *negative way* that the 'not-yet' which Dasein in everycase *is*, resists Interpretation as something still outstanding" (290). Heidegger, however, warns that a "metaphysic of death lies outside the domain of an existential analysis of death," but maintains the "possibility"of death within his analysis of *Dasein* (292). Like Lacan's announcement of the limitations of psychoanalysis, Heidegger's announced limitations of "existential analysis" do not encourage the naïve hope for the persistence of the ego's "existence"—they imply a radical reinterpretation of subjectivity without regard to its mere being or non-being.

For Derrida death is akin to the act of writing, because both engender spectral and significant kinds of existence—neither physical nor metaphysical. Life and death are coexistent and, in a sense, inhabit each other. Meaning for Derrida is bound up with unending returns—of the ghosts of intention, of conception, of the presence of a subject no longer present. The subject is always an anticipation of its own death. Each time that one expresses oneself, a surrogate (a ghost, a delegate, a revenant) is granted an uncanny existence, neither alive nor dead, neither at home with its origin nor alien to it, and each is dispatched, as it were, into the other: both other minds and futures. "This concept of the ghost is just as difficult to grasp, in person, as the ghost of the concept. Neither life nor death, but the haunting of one by the other."[10] Death is a critique of the concept, as Heidegger implies, because it maintains the possibility of a totalizing and disappearing perspective. Just as logocentrism, which puts speech and conscious intention before the differential structures of writing, is deconstructed by grammatology, which deciphers the inscriptions within speech, so death is haunted by the effects of life and life is haunted by the effects of death.

In *Schibboleth*, Derrida writes: "What one calls poetry or literature, or even art . . . in other words a certain experience of language, or color as such, can only be an intense familiarity with the ineluctable originarity of the spectre."[11] Since phantoms, spectres, and revenants are representations, as opposed to souls and spirits which are supposedly originary, Derrida's remarks here certainly deconstruct while reconstructing a kind of metaphysics of representation. Similarly, and much earlier in his career, Derrida's analysis of Husserl situates death in the act of self-representation and writing: "The statement 'I am alive' is accompanied by my being dead, and its possibility requires the possibility that I be dead; and conversely. This is not an extraordinary tale by Poe but the ordinary story of language."[12] Interpreters doubtlessly read "death" here as a figure for the alien position of the linguistic shifter, the way in which the one-who-speaks dies when "it" is represented by the "I." But perhaps Derrida *means* death in this argument: "*The history of metaphysics therefore can be expressed as an unfolding of the structure or schema of an absolute will-to-hear-one-self-speak. This history is closed when this absolute appears to itself as its own death. A voice without différance, a voice without writing, is at once absolutely alive and absolutely dead.*"[13]

If the "absolute" desire of metaphysics has been insufficiently modulated by the play of presence and absence, of the "I" and the passing of the "I," then the "death" of metaphysics in Derrida's work must also be its reinscription within the subtler discourse of its critique. "As for what 'begins' then—'beyond' absolute knowledge—unheard of thoughts are required, sought for across the memory of old signs. . . . In order to conceive of this age, in order to 'speak' about it, we will have to have other names than those of representation" (102–3).

Otherwise metaphysics simply describes the effort to claim general validity for the representational discourse of a single discipline. When one reads Plato or Hegel, the *Brihadaranyaka*

Upanishad or the *Lankavatara Sutra,* one finds exactly this critique of such "metaphysics," yet these are the texts which many would consider the axes of Western and Eastern metaphysics. In both East and West, the history of metaphysics has always been a history of the critique of metaphysics. The chaosmos explored and described in this study follows what Paulson acutely sees as the insistently antitheoretical and antiexclusivist effects of literary texts, and embodies a critique of singular metaphysics of this sort while answering their totalizing impulses through a general intertextuality crossing disciplines as well as cultures.[14]

We have seen in previous chapters the chiasmic interanimation and complicity of chaos and cosmos in the Joycean chaosmos and in the chaosmic self in Eliot, Lacan, and Forster. In the deconstructive analyses of Heidegger and Derrida one can see the analytical deconstitution of the idealisms of representation allied with a call for a new kind of "representation." Heidegger's early explanation of the need for another lexicon and grammar for his philosophical enterprise led to the unique discourse of *Being and Time* and then, later in his career, to another philosophical discourse clearly poetic and inclusive rather than analytic and exclusive. Derrida's inventive formal and antiformal philosophical languages have distinguished his work from the start, most prominently in *Glas* where he writes a double-columned work examining and demonstrating the double voice of philosophy and literature, showing the relationship between organic and linguistic kinds of reproduction and representation.[15] The "literary" aspect of Derrida's work has not been as widely discussed as the supposedly extricable philosophical stances. But it is as a writer that I think that one can see the fulfillment of his earlier soundings of the "apocalyptic tone," for a new way of writing and thinking, something other than "representation." These deconstructive and apocalyptic aspects of Derrida's work appear to come together and fall apart with a kind of chaosmic economy, for it would be difficult to know what purpose a "new" or "other" manner of philosophical writing could have if it could not be said to be—not answerable or corresponsive or representative—imbricated in the mutual interanimation of the chaotic and cosmic functions in nature, the subject, writing, and reading. And I think it is this perpetually off-balance, off-center movement between the apparently disruptive and the apparently unifying, the deconstructive and the totalizing, which any work which opens itself to the chaosmos—which is neither—will display.

The *other* worlds written into being by Mailer, Merrill, and Lessing and examined below have no explicit relationships with these specific philosophical contexts, or with each other, except for their own marked originality or eccentricity. Compelling attempts at combining the critique of representation and the meaning of modern death with the recovery, revelation, and imagination of other worlds, other ages, and other selves, they could be called chaosmological works.

Mailer's Ancient Egypt

Where modern cultures have understood art in relationship to the sciences which surpassed it, ancient Egypt considered science and art to be aspects of what one might call a single "technology." Heidegger reminds us that "there was a time when it was not technology alone that bore the name *technē*. Once that revealing that brings forth truth into the splendor of radiant appearing also was called *technē*. Once there was a time when the bringing-forth of the true into the beautiful was also called *technē*. And the poiesis of the fine arts also was called *technē*."[16] Art has become, since the triumph of science and the demise of religious authority, aligned with craft, cunning, and a pleasing, but false knowledge. This sense which Prigogine and Stengers have recognized in the familiar terms "mechanical" and "engineer" has become exclusively linked with the *aesthetic,* a term that arose in the eighteenth century to describe the merely "apparent" or "perceptual" quality of the arts. Before the advent of science and the Cartesian segregation of subjectivty, Heidegger writes, "The arts were not derived from the artistic. Art works were not enjoyed aesthetically. Art was not a sector of cultural activity" (34). The whole of human activities was motivated by concerns with form, unity, and integration.

E. H. Gombrich has described such a *technē* in Egyptian "art" as a technology whose purpose was to reveal truth and to effect and influence nature. "If the likeness of the king was also preserved, it was doubly sure that he would continue to exist for ever. So they ordered sculptors to chisel the king's head out of hard, imperishable granite, and put it in the tomb where no one saw it, there to work its spell and to help his soul to keep alive in and through the image."[17] The tombs, the mummies, the stylized representations of the body were specifically designed to convey the souls of the dead to a beyond, implicitly where the referents, or "souls," of the dead persisted in eternity.

Thus Egyptian art, once seen by European art historians as primitive and incapable of realistic depiction, should be seen as a code designed to insure the communication of the metaphysical double, the *Ka*. Where humanistic art "immortalizes" the artist or the subject insofar as the *objet d'art* or poem is preserved, Egyptian technology buries its art in stone tombs so that its referents will continue to exist as a kind of eternalized signified. "On the other hand," Wallis Budge writes, "to destroy or 'blot out' a name was to wipe out of existence the being who bore it, and it was for this reason that in the earliest days of civilization in Egypt services in which the name, or names, of the dead were commemorated and were mentioned with laudatory epithets, were established."[18] The Egyptians thus did not maintain the familiar modern notion of a gap between sign and reference, between art and science. Their culture represents the type of a pre-Cartesian, pre-Newtonian thought that does not require a persistent distinction between that which is significant and that which is real, that which is dead and that which is living.

In *Ancient Evenings* (1983) Norman Mailer imagines this culture as free from the rationalist and technical ambition which cut the lived world into mental and physical aspects and invested the machine with the archetypal power and significance once invested in the body. It would appear that this novel is the realization of a desire which Mailer expressed decades before. "I wish to attempt an entrance," Mailer wrote in 1959, "into the mysteries of murder, suicide, incest, orgy, orgasm, and Time."[19] Through such an initiation into these mysteries, Mailer hopes to grasp a world unaffected by modern divisions between the physical and the metaphysical, the imaginative and the real, and so return to an era untrammeled by the ethical neuroses created by Greek rationalism and Christian contempt for the body. *Ancient Evenings* demonstrates the interdependence of the physical and the metaphysical, sexuality and death, critique and creation, within a narrative of one soul's imagination of its life, a life which includes a genealogy of Egypt beginning with the fertile slime and stench of the Nile and moving toward the perfumed rites of the dead.

Harold Bloom's review of the novel in 1983 argues that Mailer has attempted to detach himself and his audience from what he calls "post-Enlightenment reality," the especially inhibitory culture that Bloom's criticism has charted in the lives and ambitions of English and American poets.[20] Richard Poirier, one of the other few favorable reviewers of the novel, believes that "Mailer has imagined a culture that gives formal, and not overly anthropological sanction, to what in his other works often seems eccentric and plaintively metaphysical."[21] By giving himself completely to a metaphysical or cosmological theme, Mailer has written a massive prose epic which imaginatively recovers and displays the mythological semantics of Egyptian culture. But even while Mailer assumes this mythological task of fashioning a world and a cosmos he also undertakes an anthropological and theoretical analysis of this culture which linked immortality to *technē*—to architecture, painting, and, most of all, to writing. There is something oddly primordial and yet postmodern about this Egyptian sensitivity to the fragile relationship between representation and immortality, and Mailer is keenly aware of it.

Beginning with a tour de force, a monologue of "one man dead" and a retelling of the Osiris cycle, one of the most remarkable achievements of American prose fiction, *Ancient Evenings* follows in a tradition of American literature which John T. Irwin has decribed in *American Hieroglyphics: The Symbol of the Egyptian Hieroglyphics in the American Renaissance*.[22] Irwin's book studies the ways in which American writers of the nineteenth century were drawn to hieroglyphic writing and other emblems of a dead culture which, paradoxically, offered the means of their own imaginative birth—or rebirth. In the shadow of Wordsworth, Coleridge, Scott, and Keats, not to mention the ancestral figures of Shakespeare and Milton, American writers like Poe and Melville turned constantly if not obsessively towards these ruins of Egyptian representation as an alien source, a "possibility," in Heidegger's terms, for an authentic *Dasein*. The fact that this origin "is" death leads these writers to consider the necromantic aspects of representation and so inspires tales and romances which reflect on the nature of writing in general. "Egypt" is both the private source of imaginative nourishment and a country standing in the place of an England that is still vital and intimidating, the master of its own language and the master of those who use it. All the more strange, but understandable, that a "new" culture would be obsessed with the dead, the ancient, and the remote.

The journey that Poe's tales recount can be seen in this light as flights from domination from another literature. "For the writers of the American Renaissance, the hieroglyphics and the question of man's origins are implicit in one another: if you start with one, sooner or later you will be led to the other. Furthermore, because in pictographic writing the shape of a sign is in a sense a double of the physical shape of the object it represents, like a shadow or a mirror image, the essays and stories from this period dealing with the hieroglyphics and human origins are always, in one way or another, 'double stories'" (61). Irwin's analyses of Emerson, Poe, Thoreau, and Melville concentrate on the figure of the hieroglyph as a reflection *on* language *in* language. They also concern the attempt by American writers to discover their own origin and authority in this once secret script of an ancient land. Irwin's reading of *The Narrative of Arthur Gordon Pym* develops this thesis, concluding that "writing in search of its origin *is* the self-dissolving voyage to the abyss" (91). This writing as journey away from domination toward death, this fascination with pictographic scripts, also characterizes Pound's *Cantos* and Olson's *Maximus Poems*, poems that link conventional narrative chronology with the alphabet and thus with Platonist and Judeo-Christian metaphysics. Within the tradition, literary innovation and metaphysical reorientation are joined.

Mailer shares these ambitions, but his novel is less concerned with the hieroglyph as a sign than as a metonym, a ghost from a dead culture brought to life by Champollion. Mailer's Egypt is not a melancholy site but a culture which flourished in the shadows of its pyramids, its own monumental past, but still understood art as both technique and science. Egypt thus is the type of a culture firmly involved with its own body, its own excrement and its own corruption. Irwin writes, "As the empty tomb and the vanished body evoke the Judeo-Christian concept of an immortal self that is independent enough of the body to have dispensed with even a bodily image, so the monumental pyramid and the mummified corpse express the Egyptian sense that the immortality of the personal self is constitutively linked to the preservation of such an image" (145). Unlike Pound or Olson, who imagined the hieroglyph or ideogram as a superior cypher of presence, Mailer's hieroglyphic novel celebrates writing itself as an uncanny and perishable presence. Mailer's imagination of an unenlightened era leads him to the origins of language because they are origins unformed by the hierarchies of form and content, body and soul, instinct and reason, pictographic writing and phonetic speech. By accepting writing as a power similar to a mummified body, Mailer overturns modernist, existentialist dialectics. "The contrast between the Egyptian hieroglyphics and the Christian imageless Word," Irwin claims, "is simply the difference between the visible presence and the visible absence of the referent in the . . . opposition between god as graven image and god as disembodied voice" (146).

For these reasons, hieroglyphics, long considered the emblem of a priest-ridden culture, seemed to many a secret script when its pictographics actually copy the visible world. The hieroglyph's exotic and obscure associations indicate the degree to which a literal blindness constitutes enlightened sight. Thus Pound claimed that ideograms could be understood simply by

looking at them. Alphabetic writing, as Pound and Derrida recognize, is better suited to mystification, since it has *necessarily* an
internalized and phonetic meaning which its writing reveals only
to the initiated. Derrida explains: "What was invented 'for secrecy,' and for political secrecy, would thus be, according to this
hypothesis, phonetic writing, that which professed to be the
invisible (imageless) vehicle of a spoken word—and not the
hieroglyph in the strict sense, even if the functions could subse-
quently, in the course of revolution, be interchanged."[23]

Egyptian writing, thus bound to objects and natural forms,
is incapable of inscribing an ethics alienated from the world of
process. Mailer's novel, in approaching the power of hieroglyphic
writing, seizes on the body as its most fundamental trope for the
relationship between human meaning and natural meaning.
Mailer subverts the fundamental, modernist dualism of *Being and
Nothingness* by addressing the Sartrean conception of *nausea:*

> The perpetual apprehension in the part of my for-itself of an
> *insipid* taste which I cannot place, which accompanies me
> even in my efforts to get away from it, and is my taste —this
> is what we have described elsewhere under the name of *Nau-
> sea.* A dull and inescapable nausea perpetually reveals my
> body to my consciousness. Sometimes we look for the pleas-
> ant or for physical pain to free ourselves from this *nausea;* but
> as soon as the pain and pleasure are existed by consciousness,
> they in turn manifest its facticity and its contingency; and it
> is on the ground of this *nausea* that they are revealed. We
> must not take the term nausea as a metaphor derived from
> our physiological disgust. On the contrary, we must realize
> that it is on the foundation of this nausea that all concrete
> and empirical nausea (nausea caused by spoiled meat, fresh
> blood, excrement, etc.) are produced and make us vomit.[24]

Sartrean nausea is an internalized sense of the alien quality of the
body and yet of the mind's inextricable involvement with it. Existentialism could be said to represent the rotting or spoiling of the
Cartesian model of a divided mind and body, as Sartre both registers his commitment to the science of division and shows how

certitude has become disgust, and knowledge of God a knowledge of the absurd. Nausea thus functions as an especially privileged sign that aligns the body, consciousness, and physiological disgust upon a "foundation" that is neither concrete nor empirical. This fundamental legibility of a response joins Sartrean insights into existential dread with a metaphysical origin which can neither be questioned nor truly sensed. The body is the sign of this sign of nausea that signifies authoritatively, even if what it signifies is the "facticity" and "contingency" of consciousness. For Sartre, vomiting in response to a rotting corpse can only allude to the fundamental nausea of consciousness in response to its own existence.

Julia Kristeva's work contrasts, in this respect, with this existentialist sign of the absurd. Nausea, in the context of poststructuralism, could be regarded as a provocation for language and the formation of a metaphysics—insofar as it opens up a need or a lack that must be filled. Where Sartre sees the sign of all signs, Kristeva sees the lack into which signs fall and out of which they arise. Nausea, prompted by decay and, by inference, the very idea of change, leads to the division of the world into two categories: the present (the objective, changing, real) and the absent (the permanent, unchanging, ideal). Kristeva's analysis of this division in signification is based on "abjection," the way in which people become attached to what they find necessary to throw away:

> A massive and sudden emergence of uncanniness, which, familiar as it might have been in an opaque and forgotten life, now harries me as radically separate, loathsome. Not me. Not that. But not nothing, either. A "something" that I do not recognize as a thing. A weight of meaninglessness, about which there is nothing insignificant, and which crushes me. On the edge of non-existence and hallucination, of a reality that, if I acknowledge it, annihilates me. There, abject and abjection are my safeguards. The primers of my culture.[25]

Kristeva's *abject* silently reads Sartrean *nausea* according to the subtler, uncanny terms of an absurdity that always threatens but is always averted by conscious denial. This denial can act to organize language, subjectivity, and culture. The appearance of decay, excrement, blood, all that changes, egregiously, the notion of the proper (*le propre*, in Kristeva's French text) links the clean, the sane, and the proper name into a common and improper sin, demands the memorial engravings of the tomb, the white and proper toilet, the pure white cotton gauze and bandage. Yet such challenges to the living death of the proper (shit, blood, corpses) must be recognized in order to cultivate culture. Culture must continually recall the threat from which it remains temporarily safe—precisely by enshrining the abject in the white blankness of their difference. The objective, which is always sliding away from "itself" into the "abjective," can only perpetually delay our vomiting by showing us how the body of the world can be seen as a sign of the beyond. And this beyond is simply a place where nothing rots.

Mailer's novel, then, begins and ends in the Egyptian necropolis where funereal art not only memorializes the dead but works a kind of semantic transmission. Mailer's monumental novel, long promised and many times abandoned, is modeled on these tombs that once concealed in their centers a petrified and bound corpse explicitly in order to convert the locus of rot into a passageway to the timeless. In a similar way, the existentialist insistence upon viewing death as a token of the absurdity of existence is answered by a novel that explores every kind of imaginative and supernatural possibility. The voices of the novel echo within each other, beginning in ignorance and moving to another ignorance, but significantly evoked by the sensations of decay. Thus the narrative voice of the novel, Menenhetet II, recalls a past gradually through the sense of smell, the least mediated of all sensations:

> My memory, which had given every promise (in the first glow of moonlight) that it would return, was still a sludge. Now the air was heavy with the odor of mud. That was the aroma of these lands, mud and barley, sweat and husbandry. By noon tomorrow, the riverbank would be an oven of

moldering reeds. Domestic animals would leave their gifts
on the mud of the bank—sheep and pigs, goats, asses, oxen,
dogs and cats, even the foul odor of the goose, a filthy bird.
I thought of tombs, and of friends in tombs. Like the pluck-
ing of a heavy string came a first intimation of sorrow. (8)

The lyre and the tomb, like memory, transform the ongoing
decay of the present into symbolic and spiritual permanence,
a permanence achieved by art, death, and the art of death. Mailer's narrating soul, like the Hebrew Adam, is made of this red clay
from the riverbank, the clay which Yahweh fashioned into a body
and that the riverine cultures of Mesopotamia fashioned into the
first writing tablets.

In *Ancient Evenings* Mailer has imagined a culture formed at
the confluence of signs and being, humanity and mud, the sacred
and the profane, the pleasing and the disgusting. Human beings
are formalized mud, the meaning of mud, the tablets upon which
histories and annals are inscribed. Their pre-enlightenment subjectivities are so unformed and porous, so undisciplined by cate-
gorical imperatives, that they are not confined to spoken or
corporeal expression but move telepathically. Indeed, the hero can
intentionally father himself by copulating with a woman who will
become his own mother: he can copulate, expire, and conceive
himself in the same moment. The novel and Egypt thus derive
their power from an approach to and acceptance of decay, the profane, and the abject origins of human culture. The figure of this
crossing of the sacred and the profane is the narrator's corpse at the
beginning of the novel, for the corpse is, as Kristeva writes, "the
utmost of abjection. It is death infecting life. Abject. It is something rejected from which one does not protect oneself as from an
object. Imaginary uncanniness and real threat, it beckons to us and
ends up engulfing us" (4).

Writing is the fundamental means by which a culture con-
fronts the abject, and it is from this abjection that writing derives
its power, its uncanniness, and its sublimity. For writing, as Derrida has remarked, is a praxis of death (a thanatopraxis) that
embalms presence before its rot can spread to another presence,

and thus to the idea of presence itself.[26] The work of mourning and the work of art, like the works of dreaming and memory, are motivated by endless contamination by the abject, which is another term for everything that has yet to be written. In a similar vein, Mailer's novel demonstrates the ways in which the rites of embalming and encrypting replicate the rites and logic of inscription. Such an analogy is clear in the hieroglyph which, as Irwin reminds us, is "an image of organic unity derived from the limits of [man's body] that he projects on the world in order to render it intelligible" (62). The Greeks recognized this, implicitly at least, when they referred to Egyptian writing as *hierogluphoi*, sacred writings, or more precisely, sacred notching, hollowing, or carving. The sacred is necessarily constituted in the shadow or inscription of the abject object, and in this way the sacred retains its radical original meaning, which included the abject or profane.

Thus the *Ka*, the nominal spiritual self of Egyptian religion, means simply a "double," a kind of hieroglyph or shadowy pictograph of the corpse. Indeed, the metaphysical dimension of Egyptian thought is indistinguishable from the effects of writing and representation in general. Budge writes:

> From numerous passages in texts of all periods it is clear that the Egyptians believed heaven was in many respects a duplicate of earth, and, as it was supposed to contain a celestial Nile, and sacred cities which were the counterparts of those on the earth and which were called by similar names, it is only reasonable to assign to it a company of gods who were the counterparts of those on earth. (Vol. I, 91)

Menenhetet II, nicknamed Ka, remembers his life, in the opening pages of the novel, as someone else's: "I think some of us began to regret the nickname Ka, that we gave him. It seemed clever at the time, since it not only means twice (for Menenhetet Two) but is also our good Egyptian name for your Double when you are dead ... " (11). The metaphysical principle is a referent, a double or shadow, granted an extracorporeal, semantic existence.

Securing that principle requires a *technē* such as mummification to transform the fast-rotting human corpse into a stony edifice, a tablet for projecting the soul.

As the befuddled Ka of Menenhetet II gradually recovers his memory by encountering his great-grandfather Menenhetet I, he recalls his embalming, mummification, and entombment. The evolution of these funerary procedures and rites, like the evolution of hieroglyphic writing, is driven by the need to preserve, record, and make real what would otherwise be transient, lost, and unreal. This decay must be converted into the prominent display of the absence of life so that the prepared corpse would seem to be a willing accomplice to the act of death. In this sense, art, writing, and mummification are reactions to the abject. In *Powers of Horror* Kristeva writes:

> The various means of *purifying* the abject—the various catharses—make up a history of religions, and end up with that catharsis par excellence called art, both on the far and near side of religion. Seen from that standpoint, the artistic experience, which is rooted in the abject it utters and by the same token purifies, appears as the essential component of religiosity. That is perhaps why it is destined to survive the collapse of the historical forms of religion. (17)

The preparation of Menenhetet's cadaver thus condenses the aesthetic-religious transformation of the organics of decay into a transcendental semantics of survival.

This point is forcefully made when the narrator remembers the removal of his own brain after death: "A hook went into my nose, battered through the gate at the roof of the nostril, and plunged into my brain. Pieces, gobbets, and whole parts of the dead flesh of my mind were now brought out through one aperture of my nose, then the other" (26). This hollowing of the cranial cavity is the most dramatic figuration imaginable of the emptying out of subjectivity strictly as a principle of interiority. In these initial stages of mummification one sees the reinscription of voice into writing, subjectivity into intersubjectivity, as the body is translated from flesh into stone. Each detached part of the corpse thus opens the *Ka* more widely to a world of consciousness:

> Yet for all it hurt, I could have been made of small rocks and roots. I ached no more than the earth when a weed is pulled. . . . Once they even turned me on my stomach to slosh the fluids, and let the caustic eat out my eyes. Two flowers could have been plucked when those eyes were gone. . . . Bathed in natron, I became as hard as the wood of a hull, then hard as the rock of the earth, and felt the last of me depart to join my Ka, my Ba, and my fearsome Khaibit. . . . I was entering that universe of the dumb where it was part of our gift to hear the story told by every wind to every stone. (26-27)

This hollowing, petrifaction, binding, and entombment are aspects of a writer's practice, the ostentatious preparation and institutionalization of the human remainder. The purpose of these operations is simple: once the referent of the sign, the body now becomes the sign of the referent—the *Ka, Ba, Khaibit.*

This transliteration of one script into another can be read thematically in the context of Mailer's own passage from the existentialist and absurdist themes of his previous fiction to the transcendental, metaphysical scope of *Ancient Evenings,* a journey signaled by the novel's epigraph from Yeats' *Ideas of Good and Evil:*

> I believe in the practice and philosophy of what we have agreed to call magic, in what I must call the evocation of spirits, though I do not know what they are, in the power of creating magical illusions, in the visions of truth in the depths of the mind when the eyes are closed; and I believe . . . that the borders of our mind are ever shifting, and that many minds can flow into another, as it were, and create or reveal a single mind, a single energy . . . and that our memories are part of the great memory, the memory of Nature itself.

Yeatsian confidence of this kind derives from a pre-Cartesian sense of the inevitable falseness of any division in nature, just as

Sartre, especially in *Being and Nothingness,* represents the absurdist conclusions implicit in the modernist bifurcation of mind and nature. In this sense, *Ancient Evenings* mummifies the themes of existentialist literature in order to transliterate them into the Yeatsian realm of magic, metaphor, and the "memory of Nature."

Thus if one turns the sense of the epigraph upon itself, one begins to wonder who is speaking: is it Yeats speaking through Mailer or Mailer through Yeats? "The evocation of spirits" and the writer's encounters with them in order to preserve them within the uncanny boundaries of literary texts provide the foundations of art, a foundation which is also the spectre of a concept. So memories and imagination, according to Yeats and Mailer, are not simply the representations of remembered or unreal events exclusively: they are the means by which the "memory of Nature" becomes accessible to "herself"—which is to say, accessible to Yeats, Mailer, Menenhetet I and II, and to the readers of literature. The "single energy" of signs, bodies, and nature is indistinguishable in Mailer's imagination from the metamorphoses of nature into myth, myth into nature, signs into bodies, and bodies into signs. The organization of these aspects of energy under the authority of modernity constructed the objectively real by demanding the palpably false and imaginary: art. Mailer dismantles this organization and allows this energy fluent expression, specifically through the history of Menenhetet—which is also the history of Egypt, its gods and goddesses, and the great memory.

Nature is thus revealed in the novel as a chaosmic totality that includes human acts of self-representation, so that representations in general lose their secondary or parasitic position and join in the metamorphoses and ecology of life. "The Book of One Man Dead" opens the book and its evening with Menenhetet's first words: "Crude thoughts and fierce forces are my state. I do not know who I am. Nor what I was. I cannot hear a sound. Pain is near that will be like no pain felt before" (3). Thought, sensation, and being are unified as the *Ka* of Menenhetet II awakens to the knowledge of his death and history. Significantly, he experiences himself as a kind of unrefined but powerful fusion of thought and energy, a rhythm and drive within natural process. In this selfless state he discovers that thought and action blend into one another:

> I travelled with my thoughts through the long narrow shaft, my body sufficently supple to obey—a most peculiar sensation. I felt altogether alive. The whisper of the air before me had phosphorescence. Particles of light glowed in my nose and throat. I was more alive than I could ever remember and felt no yoke of muscle and bone. (7)

He recalls "priests who could concentrate their wrath enough to start a fire by the light of their light" and discovers that these powers are "natural." These experiences of incarnate consciousness and representation lead to a recovery of his own seven metaphysical principles: the Ren, the Sekhem, the Khu, the Ba, the Ka, and the Khaibit, which translate as the Name, the Power, the Angel, the Heart, the Double, and the Shadow. It is only with difficulty that he remembers the seventh: "That was Sekhu, the one poor spirit who would reside in my wrapped body after all the others were gone—the Remains!—no more than a reflection of strength, like pools on the beach as a tide recedes. Why, the Remains had no more memory, and no less, than the last light of evening recollects the sun" (25). The ill-prepared, rotting toe of the Sekhu, however, reveals that "I was nothing but the poor Ka of Menenhetet Two" (31). It is decay, then, that returns him to a sense of his isolated, human existence. The gradual interanimation of the great-grandfather and the great-grandson provides the overarching structure of *Ancient Evenings,* dramatizing in subjective terms the chaosmic totality that is evident in Egyptian *technē* and religion. Archetypal physical force and archetypal aesthetic mind merge in their union, just as Menenhetet I (according to Mailer's own imaginative vision, not any known feature of the ancient Egyptian religion) can join copulation and death in order to reincarnate himself. Indeed it appears that his aborted attempt to be reborn through his granddaughter Hathfertiti engenders Menenhetet II. His discovery of this identity, like that of death and life, represents the final stage of his education: "For if Menenhetet could die, yet become himself once more, so did I wonder if I was supposed to have been the fifth appearance" (162). Mailer does not insist on this point, and the paternity of Menenhetet II, like the source of the novel's voices, remains wrapped in metaphor. The unity of their mind and consciousness is not in doubt, however: "My mind felt like a bowl of water, and the least movement in Menenhetet's thought rippled through it" (137). Thus as they approach the final test and transit into the Land of the Dead, the young Menenhetet thinks: "If the souls of the dead would try to reach the heavens of highest endeavor then they must look to mate with one another" (707). Then "I felt the Ka of Menenhetet expire. With one convulsion, the power of his heart came into me, and I knew that my youth (my demonically thwarted youth!) would be strengthened by his will, strong as the will of four men, and he was strong indeed" (708). Despite the younger man's disgust and envy for the powerful and filthy old man, connoisseur of bat dung and magic, the two are ultimately revealed as a complementary unity.

The narrative of the younger Menenhetet's life is entwined but also overwhelmed by the narrative of the elder Menenhetet's life. In order to recall fully who he was, Menenhetet II must allow the life of Menenhetet I to be told, and it is the telling of this four-fold life that dominates Mailer's novel. Similarly, Menenhetet's first life, during which he ascends the hierarchy of the Pharaoh's court, dominates the telling of his subsequent lives. Realizing that one's immortality can be threatened by the destruction of one's mummy and funerary inscriptions, Menenhetet seeks another escape from mortality and finally discovers the magical techniques of self-engendering in order to prolong and develop his enormous energies and satisfy his unflagging appetites. But each subsequent life represents his own declining powers: he starts as a soldier, is reborn as a priest, then as a papyrus-dealer, and finally as a violator of tombs.

The declining power of his lives traces and extends the decline and ultimate ruin of Egyptian *thanatopraxes* and technology, which began with the massive and unprecedented erection of the uninscribed pyramids, then developed subterranean tombs covered with hieroglyphs, and finally yielded to papyrus and cursive writing, which meant that by the end of the civilization the earliest hieroglyphics had become incomprehensible to the Egyptians themselves. The apocalyptic conclusion of the novel reveals how the Egyptian world, following this decline, simply passes away. As they approach the other world, Menenhetet tells his great-grandson "[It] is no more than a ghost. But then you must understand that you have been dead for a thousand years. The Pharaohs are gone. Egypt belongs to others" (705). His great-grandfather continues: "Our Gods, if we speak of Ra and Isis, Horus and Set, are now in their possession. . . . For our land of the Dead now belongs to them, and the Greeks think no more of it than a picture that is seen on the wall of a cave" (705). But the "ghost" of the Egyptian cosmos and its engravings and hieroglyphs remain, even after the culture that imagined them has expired.

Like Whitman, Mailer begins with the solitary self, but he ends by turning that self inside out to show it as the fundamental atom and sign of the cosmos. In death, Menenhetet loses his identity and gains access to the "memory of Nature herself": "Is one human? Or merely alive? Like a blade of grass equal to all existence in the moment it is torn? Yes. If pain is fundament, then a blade of grass can know all there is" (3). "All there is" can be known through the pain or grief at the loss of the self, the experience of a cut "blade of grass." Like Whitman or Joyce, Mailer recounts the artist's education and concludes by showing that the ineffectual, artistic Menenhetet cannot be separated from the primal force of his great-grandfather Menenhetet. The whole of Menenhetet, like the starry coincidence of Stephen and Bloom at the conclusion of *Ulysses,* or the flowing of Anna Liffey into the ocean at the end of *Finnegans Wake,* is achieved in their journey into the Land of the Dead at the end of *Ancient Evenings*—a literary work, a galaxy of signs.

Merrill's Other World

In *The Changing Light at Sandover* James Merrill has written an original kind of metaphysical poem which, instead of trying to elude the limitations of writing, seems to be based on them. These revelations do not form a static cosmology—they are to be found within the interplay of rule and chance, the cosmos and chaos within the alphabet and the periodic table of elements. Among all the spirits attending this poem it is the angel Gabriel who reveals this medium to Merrill by "a grave, deliberate/ Glissando of the cup to rainbow's end":

ABCDEFGHIJKLMNOPQRSTUVWXYZ

DJ. What's all this?
JM. Looks like the alphabet.
GABR. THE NEW MATERIALS, YOUNG POET, FOR A NEW FAITH:
ITS ARCHITECTURE, THE FLAT WHITE PRINTED PAGE
TO WHICH WILL COME WISER WORSHIPPERS IN TIME[27]

These revelations are founded then on metaphor and the alphabet, the turning and knotting of elements that temporarily constitute an object, a self, a world, and then unturn them—in the way that words and figures are written and read. Merrill's prophetic or epic poem thus thrives on the capacity of language to project its own form, values, and system upon the world. Where traditionally metaphysical utterances, whether occult, scholastic, or visionary, have sought either to deny or transcend these linguistic qualities of language, Merrill's text discovers in them the perfect medium for an oscillating, yet synthesizing, revelation. Merrill's studied airiness and playfulness is quite serious, because his poem is devoted to a metaphysical vision that is based on the absence of all grounds, selves, and even words—for the alphabet, the arabic numerals, and their numberless combinations are the basis of Merrill's prophecy. So one could agree with Peter Sacks that "Merrill's astonishing achievement is to have transformed the experience of loss and fear to one of celebration and to have moved, in a series of arduous revelations, beyond the stances of resignation or fractured yearning to one of magnificent confidence."[28]

Merrill's poem begins, in effect, with a game of affirmation: a yes, a *oui*, a *ja* coming from a Ouija board, a parlor game that assumes that the dead can become accessible, if still absent, through the fortunate appearance of the proper medium. The ouija board of course displays the roman alphabet and the arabic numerals, as well as the words yes and no. Nineteenth-century spiritualists had merely to put their hands on this constellation of signs in order to give language to the dead. In effect, those who "had passed on" could use the living the way the living use language. When James Merrill and his partner David Jackson sat down at a Ouija board in the fifties, they began playing a game that, in a sense, dramatized the act of literature: seated before the alphabet, the poet can either await the muse and inspiration or despair of such and begin to play with words. Harold Bloom, whose books on poetic influence and imagination were published in the same years as the books that formed *The Changing Light at Sandover,* saw poetry in an oddly similar way: the spirits of dead poets, indistinguishable from the language they shaped and left behind to be internalized by living poets, rise up in the scene of writing. The living must battle with these ghosts, and even those strong enough to triumph over the dead will in a sense share their identities with them. "Strong poets," Bloom believes, "keep returning from the dead, and only through the quasi-willing mediumship of other strong poets."[29] Merrill's poem enacts this theoretical scenario in the most literal way, as poets from Homer to Auden spell themselves and their words at the living poet's desk. One of the dramatic struggles of the poem concerns Merrill's flagging resistance to their revelations, which gradually assume more space in the poem. Bloom's sense of these visitations is entirely different: "The apophrades, the dismal or unlucky days upon which the dead return to inhabit their former houses, come to the strongest poets, but with the very strongest, there is a grand and final visionary moment that purifies even this last influx" (141). Merrill's poem dramatizes poetic influence, verging on possession, and yet it does not follow Bloom's Oedipal logic of paternal-filial combat for possession of the mother-as-muse. Where Bloom's theory is governed by the essentially romantic figure of the poet as a personality, a hero, a kind of demigod, Merrill's poem is gradually rigged out as a masque in which such notions of

fixed identity are undone by the intertextual weaving and reincarnations of selves and words. We are not surprised to find, given
Eliot's and Bloom's poetics of tradition and the individual talent,
that Rimbaud was responsible for *The Waste Land.*

The Ouija transcripts upon which the poems are based are
real: they have been *trans*-scribed across a distance that this prefix can only suggest. In an interview Merrill has said that he tells
the curious, "I don't care whether you believe the revelations as
long as you believe that we had the experience."[30] The voices
sounding the alphabetic medium come either from some entirely
other place, such as the dead, or they come from the unconscious,
a site in which experience exists as a kind of perpetual presence of
the past:

> Jung says—or if he doesn't, all but does—
> That God and the Unconscious are one. Hm.
> The lapse that tides us over, hither, yon;
> Tide that laps us home away from home. (74)

The familiar Cartesian logic which asks that we assign these messages either an internal or external origin fails us here. Merrill, like
Lacan, transforms "God" from an exemplary principle of ultimate
self-identity into an endless web of punning relations. If the pun
has a place in eschatology, then language's capacity for doubleness
and ambiguity should be seen as its greatest strength, not its weakness. Merrill's plays on words and metaphors, though hardly as
intense as Joyce's in *Finnegans Wake,* oscillate between the simplest
figures of speech and the most capacious cosmologies.

The Changing Light at Sandover demonstrates how individual character is indeed a kind of mark, how the subject is indeed
a trope or knot of the energy of other lives, and how matter is
indeed a trope of energy read according to the substantiating perspective and language of Newtonian observation. At the quantum
level, toward which Merrill's poem will move, "things" are different. The physicist Henry Pierce Stapp tells how the physical
world is "not a structure built out of independently existing unan-
alyzable entities, but rather a web of relations between elements

whose meanings arise wholly from their relationships to the whole."[31] The knowledge imparted in the three sections of Merrill's poem is in an analogous way continually reinterpreted as the whole of the poem grows and expands: the revelations of the *Book of Ephraim* are modified by the different voices of *Mirabell's Books of Number*, and these modified revelations are themselves recast in *Scripts for the Pageant*. Tropes are turned and tuned differently each time, so that metaphysics, far from a scheme or framework, becomes more mutable and theatrical as the poem develops. The poet's and the readers' desire for a dogmatic and ultimate scheme is refined away as the details of the revelations accumulate. From the endless relationship within the subatomic realm to the reincarnational economy of Merrill's souls, these metaphysics are inseparable from the expansion and contraction of metaphor: between them lies the ordinary world of Newtonian objects and bodies in the spatial-temporal confines of human reality.

This theme appeared none too soon for Merrill, whose poetry was long known for its virtuosity but also for its effeteness. By turning toward death and the powerful traditions of poetic cosmology and prophecy, Merrill, almost despite himself, has found a place within the European epic tradition of Dante, Milton, and Blake and within the American tradition of Poe, James, and Stevens, who have most profoundly investigated the relationships between the self and style, subjectivity and spirits, and death and representation in general. The texts of these American writers are at times haunted by ghosts, the ghosts of style, as if to thematize the materializations of our own personal subjectivities and then their persistence after death. If imagination, memory, regret, and mourning can become the origins of the revenant in Poe, James, and Stevens, in Merrill style becomes matter, while the alphabet serves as its periodic table of elements.

Thus when Merrill begins the testament of his experience at the ouija board, the preliminary question concerns style:

> Admittedly I err by undertaking
> This in its present form. The baldest prose
> Reportage was called for, that would reach
> The widest public in the shortest time. (3)

Such a desire for clarity and accessibility is doomed from the start of course, not only by Merrill's own artistry and sophistication, but by the nature of the revelations. "Reportage" would subordinate form to content, and Merrill's cosmology is largely about reality as a kind of ongoing representational agon. The lapse into style at least gets around the reduction of the revelations to the empirical conventions of ordinary prose with its dedication to the laws of non-contradiction and temporal progression. With limpidity and simplicity, time and its laws are simply discarded:

> I alone was left
> To tell my story. For it seemed that Time—
> The grizzled washer of his hands appearing
> To say so in a spectrum-bezelled space
> Above hot water—Time would not. (4)

Merrill's "I" is set against time, the medium of a relentless progression, and so the *Book of Ephraim* combines the narrative of years at the ouija board with the narrative of the poem's composition. The metaliterary aspects of the poem are not a substitute for a theme, as is sometimes the case, but a necessary exploration of its argument.

The first lesson Merrill and Jackson learn is that no "I" is ever alone, since all "I's" are the reincarnations of previous letters, that the universe—like language—is the shuffling and reshuffling of the elements of a system. As words are composed or incarnate, so souls are composed of an alphabet of patterned energies that bridge the Cartesian gap between the sensible and the intelligible, the physical and the metaphysical. The appearance of Ephraim, their first contact with the dead, metaphorizes Merrill's own appearance on earth, for all selves are the effects of a signifying bond between one soul and another. As Ephraim's education of Merrill and Jackson proceeds, it becomes clearer that the self, as Lacan shows, is a representation that can become a subject for another representation:

> on Earth
> We're each the REPRESENTATIVE of a PATRON
> —Are there many patrons? YES O YES
> These secular guardian angels fume and fuss
> For what must seem eternity over us. (9)

(The uppercase letters throughout the poem indicate the speech of spirits.) As one advances through a system of nine stages of reincarnation, the mortal gradually enjoys—as in the Buddhist conception of Nirvana—"PEACE FROM REPRESENTATION" (10), a phrase that Merrill likens to a "motto for abstract/ Art." The isolated ego is thus shown to be an illusion of the uninstructed soul, and the very real weight of his own mortality. The histories of literary influence are representative of the porousness of subjectivity, for influence is understood to be an "intervention" by the powerful dead into the lives and works of the living. Merrill learns that a dead friend has spoken for him: "Hans/ has INTERVENED on my behalf/ As patrons may not. To have done so requires/ SOME POWERFUL MEMORY OR AFFINITY/ (Plato intervened for Wallace Stevens)" (24). So Stevens becomes an influence or inspiration in Merrill's poem, just as Plato did for Stevens.

As Merrill and Jackson attempt to understand the meaning of the words of their familiar spirit Ephraim, the familiar distinctions between credence and disbelief blur along with other rational dualities. Far from being credulous, Merrill dramatizes the twenty years of secrecy and doubt that preceded the publication of the *Book of Ephraim* in 1976:

> The question
> Of who or what we took Ephraim to be,
> And of what truths (if any) we considered
> Him spokesman, had arisen from the start.
> If he had blacked out reason (or vice versa)
> On first sight, we instinctively avoided
> Facing the eclipse with naked eye. (31)

If "reason" or the dismissal of reason were their only alternative, they could have made little of the revelations. It was Merrill's aesthetic inquiries that illuminated the question—not the rational or credulous temperaments:

> Like Tosca hadn't we
> Lived for art and love? We were not tough-
> Or literal-minded, or unduly patient
> With those who were. Hadn't—from books, from living—
> The profusion dawned on us, of "languages"
> Any one of which, to who could read it,
> Lit up the system it conceived?—bird-flight,
> Hallucinogen, chorale and horoscope:
> Each its own world, hypnotic, many-sided
> Facet of the universal gem.
>
>   (31)

Credulity and rationality are resolved by this insight into the many realities illuminated by various languages. Yet even this epistemological stance, so familiar in recent theory, cannot prepare them for the uncanny revelations to come: "NO SOULS CAME FROM HIROSHIMA U KNOW/ EARTH WORE A STRANGE NEW ZONE OF ENERGY/ Caused by? SMASHED ATOMS OF THE DEAD MY DEARS" (55). The "soul" is not simply a metaphysical trope—it exists the ways quarks and planets do, articulated within a haze of sub-atomic particles whose density establishes its talent or genius. Thus the world and its very real souls can indeed be destroyed. And it is largely to provide this warning that the spirits have come to Merrill.

In order to substantiate its claim for the power and persuasiveness of metaphor in this materialistic sense, the poem explores the relationship between atomic and literary kinds of "volumes," between atomic structure and poetic representation. In *Mirabell's Books of Number* Merrill records the forceful means by which a new group of spirit-voices compelled him to write a different kind of poem once *Ephraim* was completed:

UNHEEDFUL ONE   3 OF YOUR YEARES MORE WE WANT   WE
                                     MUST HAVE
POEMS OF SCIENCE   THE WEORK FINISHT IS BUT A PROLOGUE
ABSOLUTES ARE NOW NEEDED   YOU MUST MAKE GOD OF
                                     SCIENCE

TELL OF POWER   MANS IGNORANCE FEARES THE POWER WE
                                                    ARE
THAT FEAR STOPS PARADISE   WE SPEAK FROM WITHIN THE
                                                    ATOM
                                                    (113)

The elegiac style and tone of *Ephraim* are violently wrenched with the appearance of these new voices, muses who are fallen souls of another and earlier creation. The metaphoric truths of ancient poems are interpreted through crisp scientific explanations as visionary insight into the imagery of the premodern world:

INDEED JM WE HAVE ALWAYS SPOKEN THROUGH THE POETS
YET PARADISE WAS NO FIGURE OF SPEECH BUT A FRESH WORLD
IF ADAM WAS A FISH HE SWAM   IF EVE WAS LAND SHE BRED
THE DEVIL HAS BEEN DRIVEN FROM US INTO MAN   WE NOW
DRIVE IT OUT OF HIM   OUR TOOLS ARE MIND WORDS REASON
                                                    LIGHT
                                                    (114)

Through this kind of materialistic reading of metaphor, the authority of poetry is reestablished, most dramatically via its imaginative access to the relational nexus within matter itself:

WE MADE PARABLE & MYTH IN HARD
BIOLOGICAL TERMS   ADAM & EVE ARE IMAGES
FOR DEVELOPMENTS IN THE VERY NATURE OF MATTER
A WORLD NEGATIVE & POSITIVE DWELLS IN THE ATOM
                                                    (115)

Lancelot Law Whyte provides some historical background for these revelations:

Atomism originally stood for iconoclasm, impiety, and atheism, because the Greek atomists conceived a universe under the reign of chance. Indeed most atomic thinkers through many centuries neglected the order, harmony, and beauty, the adaptation of structure to function, the ordered dance of the atoms, which mark many aspects of the world and for

the religious are evidence of a divine design. If God is a principle of order, then chaos, the disorder and random collisions
of material particles, are the province of the Devil. . . . [32]

The fundamental struggle between the forces of mere order and
disorder, human fulfillment and human waste, begin in the atom
itself. Science, which once suggested that myth could be salvaged
as metaphor, is thus read back into myth and literature. But where
dualistic myths such as Milton's insist upon the absolute alterity
of these opposed principles, the atomic forces act to bind the
atomic structure, and so make the world possible. When they are
not interrelated, meaningless destruction and chaos occur.

The complex, exotic prophecies of Mirabell include word of
previous creations, a God known as Biology and his twin Nature
(or Chaos), a bureacracy of souls that provides for the cloning
of souls and various kinds of intervention into human affairs, a
nearly successful nuclear fission device in Akhnaton's Egypt, the
lost continent of Atlantis, and the like. Themes from the tabloids,
popular books on the occult, Dante, Milton, and *Genesis* all combine and mix. Merrill's earlier poetry, so high-toned and sophisti-
cated, could hardly be more alien from such apparent nonsense,
and Merrill is the first to recognize this. Even the skeptical and
Christian Auden, once he has joined the seance from the other
side, approves of the revelations and the poetry as a necessary
union of scientific and artistic imaginations.

Despite the eccentric and promiscuous inclusiveness, two
principles seem to operate in this cosmos: a) the synthesizing
nature of its spiritual and semantic processes; b) the absence of
mere accident or chance. The *Sandover* cosmology, however
immune to paraphrase (I have only attempted to give the basic
sense of it here), appears to observe what could be called aesthetic rules that Henry James, for example, might have endorsed.
James's famous advice to would-be novelists ("Try to be one of
those upon whom nothing is lost") is taken up by the universe in
Merrill's poem. When Mirabell informs Merrill that the nine
stages of Ephraim's reincarnational program are only a part of a
larger scheme, s/he echoes James' advice:

ALL WILL BE USED ALL A GLOW OF PARADISE
. . . .
NOTHING IS EVER EVER LOST THE WATERFALL WILL HOLD
YR 2 BRIGHT DROPS & YOU WILL SPLASH INTO THE GREAT
                                    CLEAR POOL
                                                    (116–17)

The economy of the cosmos is Jamesian in the sense that its relations are endless and nothing is lost or alien to its pattern: "A
BASIC PRECEPT U WILL NEED TO TAKE ON FAITH: THERE IS / NO
ACCIDENT" (179). Thus where modern cosmological and evolutionary theories are founded on the fecund possibilities of pure
chance, whether in the movement of atoms in space or of the
combination of two sets of genes, the aesthetic cosmology in
Merrill's poem is founded on the absolute absence of such an odd
principle as accident. The cosmic text is inscribed in all kinds of
characters, not limited to a single style or language, deriving from
a single and solitary individual. The coherent economy of this
baroque world resembles an infinite semiotic chain of material
elements, souls, and signs. As Milton integrated the alien codes
of Hebraic, Christian, and classical mythologies, Merrill articu-
lates metaliterature, pop culture, poststructuralist theory, religous
myth, and aspects of quantum physics into a single poetic argument. And, the spirits tell him, "THE ATOM IS THE KEY," indicat-
ing that the elemental nature of matter, always elusive, physicists
have found, remains a kind of trope, a turn in the endless knotting
and unknotting of subatomic traces, the chaosmos.

Like other major poetic prophecies in the Western tradition,
The Changing Light at Sandover does not simply relate an
unchanging state of affairs in which souls seek advancement or
suffer debasement. It describes the universe in conflict between
the forces of God Biology (the spirits' name for the principle or
seat of ever-increasing order and self-realization) and the eroding
of these forces by mere chaos and nothingness. In *Mirabell,* Merrill and Jackson are told how the poem revealed and being written
will play a part in this cosmic struggle:

WHAT IS IN YR HAND COMES TRULY   DO NOTHING FORCED 2
                                                    GODS
GOVERN   BIOLOGY & CHAOS WHICH EMPLOYS FEELING

WE ARE NOT EVIL BUT IMPATIENT   FEAR US NOT   WE TOO
ARE SLAVES BOUND TO THE IMPLACABLE UNIVERSALL WHEEL
RAISE A SONG TO OUR REAL ORDER   MYND AND NATURE
                                 WEDDED
                                                    (113)

The "REAL ORDER" is a deep union of "MYND AND NATURE" which
the poem must describe and embody. Our failure to recognize
this "necessary unity" (to cite Bateson) will inevitably and finally
lead to a nuclear disaster and the destruction of the "LAB," the
earthly realm where souls are encouraged by the bureacracy to
develop their genius and realize their greatest potential for
enlightened order:

THE WARRING PRINCIPLES PRODUCED WARRING HEIRS   SO EVIL
PREVAILD   IN YR AGE IT BEGAN IN AD 1934
WITH FERMI   URANIUM FISSION WRECKD THE GREENHOUSE
                                              ONCE
500 MILLION YEARS AS YOU KNOW YEARS AGO   GOD B
GAVE US A 2ND CHANCE   MAN FROM THE COOLING SEA
                                     EMERGED
& THIS TIME SAT CHASTEND & ATTENTIVE ON HIS THRONE   WE
INVENTED THE SCRIBE   WE TOLD HIM THAT ANCIENT HISTORY
And he wrote *Genesis?* Oh I mean to say . . . !

                                                    (116)

Much more than an exotic hybrid, Merrill's poem links the
themes of cosmological literature, creation, the fall, apocalypse,
and redemption, to the nuclear age. While Milton's poems rely on
the spiritualized mechanics of Platonized Christianity and
Blake's on a spiritualized "thermodynamics" in opposition to
Newtonian mechanics, Merrill has exploited twentieth-century
physics in an even more explicit way than Joyce does in the *Wake*.
But unlike Joyce, and like Blake and Milton, Merrill's poem has a
clearly didactic purpose. *The Changing Light at Sandover* attempts
both to widen our sense of the possible and to alert us to the conflict between the technological exploitation of nuclear energy and
the ecological demands of a living planet.

   The complementary yet oppositional relationship between
biological order and nuclear energy resembles what Prigogine and
Stengers explain as the increasing organization of living systems

and the increasing entropy or chaos in merely physical systems. The spirits warn the poet that physicists and biologists carry on this primordial struggle:

FOR NOW THE PHYSICIST IS DRAWN UNWITTINGLY TO
FIRE EXTINCTION THAT ANCIENT GLAMOR & COULD AGAIN
WRECK THE LAB   THE BIOLOGIST SEEKS THE FRUITFUL UNION
(115)

The moral of this conflict concerns the differing values of purely atomistic thought and motivation and the realization that life, in order to flourish, must agree to a molecular organization and interdepedence leading to greater and greater complexity. The complexity of the DNA molecule and the split atom: these are emblems of God Biology and chaos:

THE ATOM   IT IS ADAM & LIFE & THE UNIVERSE
LEAVE IT TO ITSELF & LET IT BREATHE   THE STRUCTURE
NEEDED
FOR MAN TO GAIN PARADISE ARE MOLECULAR & CAN
AT LAST BE USED TO BREAK THE CHAIN OF BLIND & WASTEFUL
LIVES
(118)

The atom is composed of those forces which hold the world together, and so necesarily it comprises the forces which can tear it apart: "THE ATOMS APPLE LEANS PERILOUSLY CLOSE/ . . . & OF INTENSE FISSIONABLE ENERGIES BLACK & WHITE/ WHICH EITHER JOIN & CREATE OR SEPARATE & DESTROY" (119). Physicists who attempt only to rob the atom of its energy simply add disorder to the universe because their work puts energy in the hands of people who do not know how to use it and bring greater and greater chaos to the world. This was the meaning of Oppenheimer's epiphany at Los Alamos, where, as Ephraim tells Merrill, "THE AIR . . . IS LIKE A BREATH/ SUCKED IN HORROR TOD MORT MUERTE DEATH" (33). Because of its intense contraction of energies and potential for chaos and order, the atom is the visionary focus of Merrill's poem, as it was the focus of his greatest precursor: "IN DANTE THE VISION WAS STARLIKE AS HE LOOKD INTO/ THE ATOM'S EYE HE SAW THE POTENTIAL OF PARADISE" (132).

Visionary literature and prophecy have always viewed paradise as both an advancement toward, and a recovery of, a perfection once enjoyed by human beings. Merrill's poem establishes its own conception of paradise by drawing on pastoral traditions of Arcadia and joining them with its own atomic themes. In the prologue to *Mirabell's Books of Number*, Merrill explains his initial distaste for the task before him but then shows in a remarkable image how his own genius can wed nuclear vocabulary to the pastoral traditions. Objecting that "opaque/ Words like 'quarks'" are scarcely words at all (showing how much more technically conservative his own experimentation is than Joyce's), and preferring words and images like "Wave, Ring, Bond, and Resonance," Merrill writes:

> Proton and Neutron
> Under a plane tree by the stream repeat
> Their eclogue, orbited by twinkling flocks.
> And on the dimmest shore of consciousness
> Polypeptides—in primeval thrall
> To what new moon I wonder—rise and fall.
> (110)

Like shepherds, Proton and Neutron keep their flock of electrons centered on themselves (the nucleus), even while they engage in pastoral eclogues, while polypeptides (the proteins organized by nucleic acids) feel the pull of other forces which will lead to living forms. But once life and human history have emerged (including those earlier civilizations which modern culture considers mythical), it is through the knowledge of such equanimity "WHEREBY SOULS FROM THE R/LAB/ WILL BUILD ARCADIA" (149). And this paradise is not so much an objective goal of evolution and history as a self-evident yet unobserved aspect of existence: "P A R A D I S E ARCADIA SURROUNDS US UNREALIZED/ FILLING EACH OF US FOR THE LENGTH OF A LOVE OR A THOUGHT" (165). Imagination reveals this paradise because, as Mirabell tells them, "IT IS REAL ALL IS REAL THE UNREAL I KNOW NOTHING OF" (174).

The tragic qualities of the second book of Merrill's trilogy reflect the melancholy nature of Mirabell, who rues the ignorance that led him and his fellow creatures to wreck their own world. In *Scripts for the Pageant,* this mournful tone is superceded, as is the melodramatic logic which opposes God Biology and Chaos. The masque of the third book reveals that God Biology's twin is Nature (also known as Psyche and Chaos): all three are aspects of the same creative principle. In the beginning Chaos told God Biology, "LET US DIVIDE THE FORCE OF NATURE, JUST AS WE WILL MAKE/ TWO SIDES TO ALL NATURE,/ FOR IN DUALITY IS DIMENSION, TENSION, ALL THE TRUE GRANDEUR/ WANTING IN A PERFECT THING" (408). Thus Mirabell could only dramatize the tragic and sublime logic of opposition and the Fall, while *Scripts* reveals that the tragedy has always been a comedy, for the twins Biology and Chaos (Negentropy and Entropy), separated at birth, are finally reunited. In an interview, Merrill has spoken about the "secret of Queen Mum" (or Nature) and the findings of chaologists: "They graph 'chaos' like the completely irregular dripping of a faucet, which doesn't recur, and yet on the graph it makes a wondrous pattern." Thus despite Nature's "terrible" and "punitive mask as chaos" one can have an "orderly vision."[33] And yet, just as in the destructive and renewing, the terrifying and comforting icon of the dancing Shiva, it is quite impossible to understand the order without the disorder, the cosmos without the chaos.

The *Changing Light at Sandover* plays upon this continuing reinterpretation of its revelations in order to suggest the limits of any symbolic revelation, however authoritative. Thus having apparently lost his authority, Ephraim disappears when the fallen souls of the second book speak of science. In exactly this way, letters yield to numbers, as art yields to science. But when these spirits of the second book make way for the archangel Michael in *Scripts for the Pageant,* they too lose credibility as the perspective of the four angelic sons of God Biology teach their lessons. When the coda, "The Higher Keys," appears with the collected books and we learn that Michael is Ephraim, the elegant Greek slave is revealed in all his splendor as the messenger of light. The coda concludes with Merrill reciting from the complete work, ending as *Ephraim* begins, "Admittedly, I err. . . . " Besides an implicit acknowledgment of the circular structure of *Finnegans Wake*, these words now echo Dante's, whose erring steps into the dark wood are the necessary prelude to his ascent into paradise and the beatific vision. Merrill's revelations, however, occur in the transposition of keys, letters, numbers, selves, and atoms. In this exchange of figures and myths, the divisive model of reality is replaced by a musical elaboration of relations, so that the baroque and the artificial appear no less substantial than the simple and plain. "By thus celebrating the dead," Peter Sacks writes, "the living come to rehearse their own immortality. The motif of resurrection may, therefore, govern their own experience of an almost alchemical refinement, of stripping to divine intensities."[34]

Lessing's Evolutionary Universe

Doris Lessing's novel sequence *Canopus in Argos: Archives* (1979–83) takes the evolutionary universe as a fundamental premise for its imaginative fusions of quantum physics, modern genetics, non-Western philosophies, and the imperial theme for a novelistic deconstruction of modernity and a visionary prospect of an entirely *other world*. Lessing's five novels assemble a history of Shikasta (Earth) from reports by three extraterrestrial civilizations (Canopus, Sirius, and Shammut) responsible for its life and the development of its civilizations.[35] By working from this extraterrestrial and extratemporal perspective, Lessing is able to *alter* the historical myths and religions of our planet, so that it is only gradually that the reader begins to identify Shikasta as Earth. The "other world" presented in these novels is thus represented through a staple device of science fiction: the alien perspective.

But perhaps the most unsettling aspect of this history of the Colony of Shikasta is that Lessing, who has written acidic commentaries and novels on the effects of colonization on both the exploited and the exploiter, appears to endorse the absolute superiority of a single imperial civilization, Canopus, over the basically modernist Sirians and the early modernists from Shammut.

The Canopeans are superior, simply enough, because they have evolved beyond the demands of the ego. The Canopeans are presented as having realized the "necessity" which dawns on people after they have fully realized the futility of gratifying the ego's constant production of desire. Like the "way" of the Sufi or Taoist or the Dharma of the Buddhist, the Canopean "Necessity" is presented by Lessing as a disinterested and selfless discipline which integrates human life with the process of life. From such a perspective, all relations between bodies, whether inorganic or organic, are subject to forms of "imperialism": gravity, attraction, life, consumption, domination, instruction, and love are all forms of colonization. Not only is all property theft, all life requires the death of another life: parasitism is universal. Since imperialism in this sense cannot be distinguished from the processes of organic and social life, it can only be refined. Canopean imperialism is refined, not because the Canopeans are good, powerful, primary, or white, but because it is guided by the Necessity which calls for the fullest realization of all forms of life.

In this regard, Lessing's work resembles aspects of Mailer's and Merrill's cosmic mythologies. Like the Canopeans, Osiris's divine bureacracy judges souls for admission to the Land of the Dead based on their ability to overcome baser desires. Menenhetet tells his great-grandson: "'It is the passion of Osiris . . . to conquer chaos. That is why in Kher-Neter, He is quick to extinguish the mediocre. It is important that only the Ka of the finest should survive in the Land of the Dead. Otherwise, the human stock that heaven takes into itself would not be rich in courage, pleasure, beauty, and wisdom. Ruthless selection becomes, thereby, the kindness of good husbandry'" (83). And of course the spiritual bureaucracy which directs the cloning of souls in Merrill's world in order to bring life on earth to its fullest realization is no less severe in its judgments. Mirabell tells Merrill: "THIS IS OUR/ CHALLENGE: ELIMINATE HELL MAKE MAN THE CLONE OF GOD" (269). The worlds created by Mailer, Merrill, and Lessing thus not only break with the decorum of modern reality but with the laissez-faire assumptions of liberal culture.

Lessing has discovered that "Space Fiction," as she calls it, makes it possible for her to invent a "new world for myself, a realm where the petty fates of planets, let alone individuals, are only aspects of cosmic evolution expressed in the rivalries and interactions of great galactic empires."[36] By widening her fictional scope to include such vast themes, Lessing has lost some of the readers who saw her fiction as a dependable proponent of anti-imperialism and feminism. Carey Kaplan, for instance, worries that Lessing's interest in decentered states of consciousness indicates a loss of interest in what she imagines are the "real characters" in her earlier fiction.[37] But Lessing is interested in a wider and no less compassionate understanding of human subjectivity, one that requires that she integrate cultural myths according to the dramatic history of our planet. For Lessing, "The sacred literatures of all races and nations have many things in common. Almost as if they can be regarded as the products of a single mind. It is possible we make a mistake when we dismiss them as quaint fossils from a dead past."[38] It is this mistake which Lessing corrects in *Canopus in Argos: Archives* by telling these epic and cosmic tales with the poetic machinery of genetic engineering, nuclear physics, and intergalactic travel.

In what is perhaps the masterpiece of the sequence, *The Making of the Representative for Planet Eight,* these themes are treated with classical restraint and delicacy. The novel concerns death in the broadest sense, the death of a once-fertile planet and the ways in which its people, under the tutelage of Canopus, prepare to meet their end. As the ice consumes the planet of Rohanda, its people gradually begin to recognize that one of them can actually assimilate the complexity and variety of its many minds and carry their legacy into another world. The instruction is given by the Canopean agent Johor, but the medium of the instruction is the very structure of the Rohandans' bodies: "There is a core—of something. Yet that dissolves and dissolves again. . . . I know this solidity I feel is nothing. A shape of mist, I am, a smear of tinted light . . . Can you, Johor, see where the pulses of the atom dissolve into patterns of movement of which you can say: This is envy, this is love?"[39] The Rohandans realize in the structure of matter a living emblem of their integration with each other, their planet, the Canopeans, and the universe: "Now, when we looked back to that huddle of bodies . . . we saw them as webs and veils of light, saw the frail lattice of the atomic structure, saw the vast spaces that had been what we mostly were—though we had not had the eyes to comprehend that, even if our minds knew the truth" (117–118).

For some, insight into one's abysses, into the chaosmos wherein self and world, interiority and exteriority cross, where the word uttered accidentally becomes destiny, may frighten, bore, or appear irrelevant or simply untrue. Certainly the vast majority of Lessing's critics mourned her apparent abandonment of the literature of *political* liberation for the visionary mode of spiritual and sublime liberation—which for many is no liberation at all.

But Lessing, like Mailer and Merrill, has been driven to think beyond the local ambitions of liberal culture and to imagine worlds which make us confront the ultimate purposes and nature of liberation. Mailer's ancient Egypt, unlike the worlds revealed by Merrill and created by Lessing, is a premodern world, not a revealed or purely imagined one. But it clearly shows what is gained and what is lost by the modernist restrictions and techno-logical modifications of natural process and subjectivity. And Merrill, by presenting himself as the scribe of his spiritual muses, takes no personal responsibility for the elitist vision of the universe presented in *The Changing Light at Sandover.* Speaking from the perspective of the spirits, he can make the rather stunning comment: "I think it's more important to save the environment than to save large sections of the population."[40] In different ways, then, these encyclopedic constructions show what a premodern existence could have been like, and how our present and our future could be radically reconceived, how "our" world could be radically other than we think it is. Of course this has turned out to be the case a number of times in recent centuries, but each momentous paradigmatic lurch is followed by the conviction that we have finally arrived at reality.

ᐁ—Conclusion

In the 1920s astrophysicists determined that the universe, far from being the perfectly stable and regular mechanism described in Newtonian theory, was expanding. This discovery was a blow to Einstein and other classically minded physicists who hoped to establish a unified field theory which would integrate atomic and astronomical physics. By the 1960s John Wheeler and others had supposed that the expanding universe had begun as an enormous explosion from which the galaxies of stars and planets had materialized: physicists and poets alike were riding the explosive debris of this original catastrophe/creation.

The glacial and mathematical image of a universe imperturbably observing laws and regularities was supplanted by a thermodynamic drama suggesting a furnace more than a clock. The big bang theory led some scientists to suppose the necessity of a big crunch: at a certain time the field of expanding particles composing the universe would lose its explosive momentum and begin to contract until it eventually formed a minute and inconceivably dense point, which could well explode once again.[1] According to such a scheme, so similar to the Hindu cycles of the creation and destruction of the universe, cosmos and chaos are aspects of a single process. The apocalypse is both destructive and revelatory, creative and obscuring, and thus every moment and utterance and text and body is an expression of both.

This evolutionary universe seems more in keeping with what human beings have learned about the appearance, development, and complexification of organisms. The world-machine, which scientists once could only suppose to be a magnificent artifact assembled and abandoned by a watch-maker God, could now be understood as, if not an organism, at least an evolving, historical system which has, at least this time around, had organic potential. This system and its organic subsystems have thus not only managed, by the invisible hand of natural selection, to produce life, but also the consciousness that can reflect on the entire process. Saying that the world has produced such high-level forms of organization does not mean that there is necessarily anything like intentionality or conscious design at work in the universe, but what can be said is that the evidence of patterning, intentionality, design, and even consciousness is impossible to ignore—if, that is, we can conceive of our own minds, arts, and sciences as inextricably bound with our bodies and the world system out of which they grow. Recently scientists and philosophers have posited a so-called "anthropic principle" to recognize the fact that whatever human beings say about the nature of the universe it must at least implicitly include the fact that human beings and human intelligence have come out of it.[2]

The literary texts treated in this book, while reflecting the evolutionary past, also project the possibility of a future planetary conception of mythology, language, and reference. Following the linguistic and mythological researchs of some decidedly Eurocentric scholars like James Frazer and Max Müller, Joyce, Eliot, and Forster demonstrated in their works how archetypal themes, forms, and rituals could organize works of literature which were no longer contained by the cultural limitations of their origins or languages. To different degrees each of these writers showed how such textual inclusiveness tended to erode the notions of national domains and racial exclusiveness. As an Irishman writing in a "foreign" language, Joyce showed throughout *Ulysses* and *Finnegans Wake* how the individual state constituted individual egos bent on preserving their identities at the expense of other subjects and cultures. The *Wake*, together with *The Waste Land* and *A Passage to India*, thus represent a historic break with the Mediterranean and Atlantic worlds and open onto Pacific and thus global vistas, as well as reflecting a certain redemptive potential within human beings and cultures.[3] Joyce's dream affirms, even in the face of death, the comic, ever-renewing nature of life, while Eliot and Forster indicate the possibilities of transcending or overcoming the ego and the boundaries between cultures.

Mailer, Merrill, and Lessing, like the earlier generation of writers, have a global scope but also open their works to genres long discredited or not yet canonized: historical fiction, occult or visionary poetry, and science fiction. At the same time, *Ancient Evenings, The Changing Light at Sandover,* and *Canopus in Argos: Archives* could be seen to register a marked cultural anxiety in the culture of the later twentieth century, with the fear of nuclear and environmental catastrophes, as they present extraterrestrial or alien or divine bureaucracies which must intervene in worldly affairs to reorient them to the economy of nature or the demands of an evolutionary universe. Indeed since the beginning of the nuclear age countless films, television programs, and novels have dealt with alien redeemers or guides who descend to earth in order to orient or reorient human culture toward universal princi-ples lost sight of in the modern age. The authoritarian aspect of all of these narratives, whether filmed by Steven Spielberg or written by James Merrill, of extraterrestrial and/or divine inter-ventions into human affairs seems less pronounced than the cri-tiques they present of modern culture's aimless pursuit of innovation and distraction, even if these very films and books manage only to innovate and distract.

The chaosmos revealed by theoretical, scientific, or literary discourses in this century is not, then, simply a vision of the world which would complement and satisfy our habitual sense of self and its self-fashioning and self-sustaining desires. This crossing of order with disorder, form and formlessness, requires our own life as well as our own physical death (whatever that may ulti-mately mean), and the death of a certain familiar sense of who we are. The aesthetically satisfying aspects of mythological worlds derive from this recognition that completeness or totality cannot be "tranquillized" with respect to death: it must not only "advance toward death," as Heidegger advises, it must build itself on death. Osiris may wish to conquer chaos and to become the God of renewal, but he can do so only by becoming the God of the Dead. Not simply a vision of "wholeness" which will make us all feel better, the chaosmos requires self-disintegration and dispersion, a real danger and a genuine threat to every value and desire that is derived from thinking of identity in terms of isolation and opposition.

As we have seen, the chaosmos found expression in the twentieth century when the discrepancies between perceived reality and scientific knowledge had become irreconcilable except through a radical reconceptualization of the whole enterprise of representation. Just as the modern novel followed Locke, and romantic poetry followed German idealism, so the literature of the chaosmos followed psychoanalysis, quantum physics, and the beginnings of comparative mythology and religion. Devoted to the discrete and yet moving towards a nonlinear, nonidealized, ragged enactment of holism, the chaosmic text does not so much break with realism as deepen it, make it more capacious, able to play up and down various scales of size and perspective simultaneously, make it less easily satisfied with closure.

This is the core of Bateson's notion that the mind is a necessary aspect of nature—that, in other terms, difference is necessary for relationship. Recall that Bateson defines a story "as a little knot or complex of that species of connectedness which we call relevance."[4] The knot, the crossroads, the X of the chaosmos is a "self-interfering pattern," as Hugh Kenner, after Buckminster Fuller, calls it.[5] The "connectedness" in a knot and a story "involves" the teller and the audience and the reference (however imaginary) within an energetic pattern that cannot be untied or "known" according to linear logic. The chaosmos, like the koan which a Zen student meditates on, is a knot, and such a knot should not be dissolved, cut, or even untied: it is precisely an obstacle to that desire to solve the "problem" of complexity, of our relationship with everything around us. All literature is chaosmic, to some degree, presenting knots in the forms of fictions, metaphors, and symbols which oscillate between poles of reference. The most complex literary texts in the first half of the twentieth century began to find the chaosmos everywhere, while in the second half of the century it has found a contrapuntal philosophical medium in the works of Heidegger, Derrida, Lacan, Deleuze and Guattari, Norman O. Brown, and others.

Most recently, with the emergence of the sciences of chaos, scientists have admitted to rigorous mathematical analysis topics of reflection once attended by poets: rushing streams, changing clouds, the branching of trees, the metamorphoses of weather. Between the microworld of subatomic physics and the macro-world of celestial mechanics, a midworld of fascinating chaos has emerged. And so not only could the dripping of a faucet produce "wondrous patterns," but the stochastic processess of nature could be seen as the obverse side of enormously complex, bilaterally symmetrical, aesthetically pleasing, and self-reflecting life forms.

The literary text is more than the private production of a single mind directed by the deterministic forces of a personal-historical-economic milieu, though it is that too. Before all these much-studied determinants, there were, to cite only a few, other historical events: the puzzling appearance of an egregiously com-plex human cerebral cortex, the evolution of stereoscopic vision which produces depth perception by the brain's synthesis of two different visual fields, the opportune acquisition of the reflexive, appositive thumb which allows a human being to use tools, and the development of speech which allowed someone, who after-ward would be called a poet, to repeat and fulfill the process of the world. Chaosmos includes all of this: the universe, the self-orga-nization of life, the development of our bodies, the emergence of consciousness and language, the invention of writing, and the lit-erary forms which help us to remember them.

ᑫ—Notes

Preface

1. The opposition between the *abyss* of deconstructive analysis and the *ground* of historical analysis is, of course, a recycled form of the fundamental distinctions between nothingness and being, mind and matter, the real and the unreal and has considerable rhetorical effect on those unwilling to be seen as espousing or doing "nothing."

2. Georg Lukács, *Realism in Our Time: Literature and the Class Struggle*, trans. John and Necke Mander (New York: Harper and Row, 1964), 47-92.

3. Thomas Mann, *Joseph and His Brothers*, trans. H. T. Lowe-Porter (New York: Knopf, 1948), 3.

4. Robert Wesson, *Beyond Natural Selection* (Cambridge, MA: MIT Press, 1991), 31–34, 155-56.

5. For an introduction to issues of scientific legitimation, see *Science Observed: Perspectives on the Social Study of Science,* ed. Karin D. Knorr-Cetina and Michael Mulkay (London: Sage Pubs., 1983).

I ᑫ— Towards Chaosmos

1. Paul Valéry, "The Crisis of Mind," in *Paul Valéry: An Anthology,* ed. James R. Lawler (Princeton: Princeton University Press, 1977), 97.

2. Jean-François Lyotard, "Rules and Paradoxes and Svelte Appendix," *Cultural Critique* 5 (Winter 1986–1987), 209.

3. Friedrich Nietzsche, *The Will to Power,* trans. Walter Kaufman and R. J. Hollingdale (New York: Vintage Books, 1968), 7.

4. Jürgen Habermas, *The Philosophical Discourse of Modernity: Twelve Lectures,* trans. Frederick Lawrence (Cambridge, MA: MIT Press, 1987), 159, 182.

5. Todd Gitlin, "Hip-Deep in Post-modernism," *New York Times Book Review* (November 6, 1988), 1.

6. Jürgen Habermas, *The Philosophical Discourse of Modernity*, 140.

7. See Frederic Jameson, "The Failure of Theory: Ideological Positions in the Postmodern Debate," *The Ideologies of Theory: Essays*, vol. 2 (Minneapolis: University of Minnesota Press, 1988), 103–13.

8. William Paulson, "Literature, Complexity, Interdisciplinarity," in *Chaos and Order: Complex Dynamics in Literature and Science*, ed. N. Katherine Hayles (Chicago: University of Chicago Press, 1991), 51.

9. Joseph Needham, *The Grand Titration: Science and Society in East and West* (Toronto: Toronto University Press, 1967), 121.

10. See Joseph Needham, *Science and Civilization in China*, vol. 2 (Cambridge: Cambridge University Press, 1956), 291–93, 496–505.

11. See François Jacob, *The Logic of Life: A History of Heredity*, trans. Betty E. Spillman (New York: Pantheon, 1982), 44–52.

12. Robert Wesson, *Beyond Natural Selection*, 60–63. For an analysis of the ideological foundations of neo-Darwinism, see Philip Kuberski, *The Persistence of Memory: Organism, Myth, Text* (Berkeley: University of California Press, 1992), 94–114.

13. René Descartes, *Discourse on Method and the Meditations*, trans. F. E. Sutcliffe (Harmondsworth: Penguin, 1968), 41.

14. Werner Heisenberg, *Physics and Philosophy* (New York: Harper Torchbook, 1962), 78. Afterwards abbreviated as P&P.

15. Michel Foucault, *Madness and Civilization: A History of Insanity in the Age of Reason*, trans. Richard Howard (New York: Vintage Books, 1972), 38–64.

16. Michel Foucault, *The Order of Things: An Archaeology of the Human Sciences* (New York: Vintage Books, 1973), 54.

17. Samuel Taylor Coleridge, *Biographia Literaria* xiv, in *Critical Theory Since Plato*, ed. Hazard Adams (New York: Harcourt, Brace, Jovanovich, 1971), 471.

18. John Crowe Ransom, "Poetry: A Note in Ontology," in *Critical Theory Since Plato*, 877.

19. See Donald Davie, *The Language of Science and the Language of Literature, 1700–1740* (London: Sheed and Ward, 1963).

20. See Frank Kermode, *The Sense of an Ending* (New York: Galaxy Books, 1967).

21. For a discussion of paranoia in Pynchon's novels, see, for example, Scott Sanders, "Pynchon's Paranoid History," in *Mindful Pleasures: Essays on Thomas Pynchon*, ed. George Levine and David Leverenz (Boston: Little, Brown, 1976) 139–59.

22. See Thomas S. Kuhn, *The Structure of Scientific Revolutions* (Chicago: University of Chicago Press, 1970), 43–51.

23. See, for example, Murray Krieger, *Theory of Criticism: A Tradition and Its System* (Baltimore: Johns Hopkins University Press, 1976), 207–45.

24. William Paulson, "Literature, Complexity, Interdisciplinarity," in *Chaos and Order*, 41.

25. Gregory Bateson, *Mind and Nature: A Necessary Unity* (New York: Dutton, 1979), 19.

26. Stephen Toulmin, *The Return to Cosmology: Postmodern Science and the Theory of Nature* (Berkeley: University of California Press, 1982), 212.

27. Ilya Prigogine and Isabelle Stengers, *Order out of Chaos: Man's New Dialogue with Nature* (New York: Bantam, 1984), 49.

28. Cited in Theodore Roszak, *Where the Waste Land Ends: Politics and Transcendence in Postindustrial Society* (Garden City, NY: Anchor Books, 1973), 179.

29. Karl Marx and Friedrich Engels, *The Communist Manifesto*, ed. Samuel Beer (Arlington Heights, IL: Croft, 1955), 13.

30. Alfred North Whitehead, *Science and the Modern World* (New York: The Free Press, 1953; originally pub. 1925), 16.

31. See Francisco J. Varela and Jean-Pierre Dupuy, *Understanding Origins: Contemporary Views on the Origin of Life, Mind, and Society* (Dordrecht/Boston/London: Kluwer Academic Publishers, 1992), 1–25.

32. Theodor W. Adorno, *Minima Moralia: Reflections from Damaged Life*, trans. E. F. N. Jephcott (London: Verso, 1978), 50.

33. Jan Christian Smuts, *Holism and Evolution* (New York: Macmillan, 1926), 246.

34. Ovid, *Metamorphoses*, trans. Rolfe Humphries (Bloomington: Indiana University Press, 1955), 3.

35. N. J. Girardot, *Myth and Meaning in Early Taoism: The Theme of Chaos* (Berkeley: University of California Press, 1983), 2–6.

36. Zhang Longxi, "The *Tao* and the *Logos*: Notes on Derrida's Critique of Logocentrism," *Critical Inquiry* (March 1985), 391.

37. Michel Serres, *Hermes: Literature, Science, Philosophy*, ed. Josué V. Harari and David F. Bell (Baltimore: Johns Hopkins University Press, 1982), 75.

38. Lancelot Law Whyte, *Essay on Atomism: From Democritus to 1960* (New York: Harper Torchbooks, 1963), 66.

39. Richard P. Feynman, *QED: The Strange Theory of Light and Matter* (Princeton: Princeton University Press, 1985), 55–56.

40. Werner Heisenberg, *Physics and Philosophy*, 202.

41. See Fritjof Capra, *The Tao of Physics*, rev. ed. (New York: Bantam, 1984), 3–71. For a critique of the quantum/ Eastern philosophy linkage, see Ken Wilber, *Eye to Eye: The Quest for the New Paradigm* (New York: Anchor Books, 1983), 162–63.

42. See Benoit B. Mandelbrot, *Fractals: Form, Chance, and Dimension* (San Francisco: W.H. Freeman and Co., 1977), 17.

43. John P. Briggs and F. David Peat, *Looking Glass Universe: The Emerging Science of Wholeness* (New York: Simon and Schuster, 1984), 169.

44. Erich Jantsch, *The Self-Organizing Universe: Scientific and Human Implications of the Emerging Paradigm of Evolution* (Oxford: Pergamon Press, 1980), 291.

45. David Porush, "Fictions as Dissipative Structures: Prigogine's Theory and Postmodernism's Roadshow," in *Chaos and Order*, 75–76.

46. William Paulson, "Literature, Complexity, Interdisciplinarity," in *Chaos and Order*, 42, 44.

47. See Richard Ellmann, *James Joyce*, rev. ed. (New York: Oxford University Press, 1982), 591–92.

II ᭞— Joycean Chaosmos and the Self-Organizing World

1. Cited in Gary Zukav, *The Dancing Wu Li Masters: An Overview of the New Physics* (New York: Bantam, 1979), 50.

2. A number of literary critics have pointed out links between modern science and literature. See, for example, N. Katherine Hayles, *Chaos Bound: Orderly Disorder in Contemporary Literature and Science* (Ithaca: Cornell University Press, 1990), and William Paulson, *The Noise of Culture: Literature in a World of Information* (Ithaca: Cornell University Press, 1989).

3. Lancelot Law Whyte, *Essay on Atomism: From Democritus to 1960* (New York: Harper Torchbooks, 1963),100.

4. Edmund Husserl, "Philosophy and the Crisis of European Man," trans. Quentin Lauer, in *Phenomenology and the Crisis of Philosophy* (New York: Harper Torchbooks, 1965), 178.

5. Martin Heidegger, *Being and Time*, trans. John Maquarrie and Edward Robinson (New York: Harper and Row, 1962), 27.

6. James Joyce, *Finnegans Wake* (New York: Viking, 1972), 612.12.

7. Ian Watt, *The Rise of the Novel* (Berkeley: University of California Press, 1957), 28, 30.

8. Michel Foucault, *The Order of Things: An Archaeologyof the Human Sciences* (New York: Vintage Books, 1973), 42.

9. Philippe Sollers, "Joyce and Co.," *TriQuarterly*, 38 (Winter 1977), 109.

10. James Joyce, *A Portrait of the Artist as a Young Man* (New York: Viking, 1964), 189.

11. Daniel Defoe, *Robinson Crusoe: A Norton Critical Edition*, ed. Michael Shinagel (New York: W. W. Norton, 1975), 356.

12. Jacques Derrida, *Edmund Husserl's The Origin of Geometry: An Introduction*, trans. John P. Leavey, Jr. (London: Nicholas Hay, 1978), 102.

13. Margot Norris, *The Decentered Universe of Finnegans Wake* (Baltimore: Johns Hopkins University Press, 1977), 61, 127.

14. Colin MacCabe, *James Joyce and the Revolution of the Word* (New York: Barnes and Noble, 1978), 153.

15. S. P. Purdy, "Let's Hear What Science Has to Say: *Finnegans Wake* and the Gnosis of Science" in *The Seventh of Joyce*, ed. Bernard Benstock (Bloomington: Indiana University Press, 1982), 216.

16. Cited in Norman Feather, *Lord Rutherford* (London: Priory Press, 1940), 144–45.

17. Heinz Pagels, *The Cosmic Code: Quantum Physics as the Language of Nature* (New York: Bantam, 1983), 51–52.

18. A. S. Eve, *Rutherford: Being the Life and Letters of the Rt. Honorable Lord Rutherford, O.M.* (Cambridge: Cambridge University Press, 1939), 360–63.

19. Werner Heisenberg, *Physics and Beyond: Encounters and Conversations*, trans. Arnold J. Pomerans (New York: Harper Torchbooks, 1971), 41. Afterwards abbreviated as PB.

20. See John Horgan, "Profile: Karl R. Popper," *Scientific American*, vol. 267, no. 5 (November 1992): 41–42.

21. See William York Tindall, *James Joyce: His Way of Interpreting the Modern World* (New York: Scribners, 1950), 91; and Clive Hart, *Structure and Motif in Finnegans Wake* (Chicago: Northwestern University Press, 1962), 65–66.

22. David Overstreet, "Oxymoronic Language and Logic in Quantum Mechanics and James Joyce," *SubStance* 28 (1980): 43.

23. Richard Ellmann, *James Joyce,* rev. ed. (New York: Oxford University Press, 1982), 543.

24. Wallace Stevens, *Collected Poems* (New York: Knopf, 1982), 383.

25. See Nino Frank, "The Shadow That Had Lost its Man" in *Portraits of the Artist in Exile: Recollections of James Joyce by Europeans,* ed. Willard Potts (Seattle: University of Washington Press, 1979), 97.

26. *The Letters of James Joyce,* ed. Stuart Gilbert (New York: Viking, 1957), 213.

27. For an analysis of the family romances in *Finnegans Wake,* see Philip Kuberski, "The Joycean Gaze: Lucia in the I of the Father," *Substance* 46 (Spring 1985): 49–66.

28. Roland McHugh, *The Sigla of Finnegans Wake* (London: Edwin Arnold, 1976), 10.

29. Jacques Lacan, *The Four Fundamentals of Psychoanalysis,* trans. Alan Sheridan (New York: Norton, 1979), 68.

30. M. M. Bakhtin, *The Dialogic Imagination: Four Essays,* trans. Caryl Emerson and Michael Holquist (Austin: University of Texas Press, 1981), 47.

31. Samuel Johnson, "Preface to Shakespeare" in *Critical Theory Since Plato,* ed. Hazard Adams (New York: Harcourt, Brace, Jovanovich, 1971), 334.

32. *Magill's Survey of Science,* ed. Frank N. Magill (Pasadena: Salem Press, 1992), 2777. See also Hugh Kenner, *The Pound Era,* 126: "Writing is largely quotation, quotation newly energized, as a cyclotron augments the energies of common particles circulating."

33. Richard Ellmann, *James Joyce,* 397.

34. Hugh Kenner, *The Pound Era* (Berkeley: University of California Press, 1971), 274.

35. Gregory Bateson, *Mind and Nature: A Necessary Unity* (New York: Dutton, 1979), 14.

36. Richard Ellmann, *James Joyce,* 546.

37. Michel Serres, *Hermes: Literature, Science, Philosophy,* ed. Josué V. Harari and David F. Bell (Baltimore: Johns Hopkins University Press, 1982), 61.

38. See Kenneth Clark, *The Nude: A Study in Ideal Form* (Garden City, NY: Anchor, 1959), 35–38.

39. *The Koran,* trans. N. J. Dawood (Baltimore: Penguin, 1966), Chapters 82 and 99.

40. Carl Gustav Jung, *Symbols of Transformation*, trans. R. F. C. Hull (Princeton: Princeton University Press, 1976), 368.

41. Werner Heisenberg, *Physics and Beyond*, 79.

42. Richard Ellmann, *James Joyce*, 546.

43. Ibid., 544.

44. Ibid., 546.

45. T. S. Eliot, "*Ulysses:* Order and Myth," in *Selected Prose of T. S. Eliot*, ed. Frank Kermode (London: Faber, 1975), 175–178. Derek Attridge and Daniel Ferrer show how Eliot and Pound emphasized Joyce's "control," "mastery," and "technique" and underplayed the indeterminacy and slippage of language in *Ulysses*. See *Poststructuralist Joyce: Essays from the French*, ed. Derek Attridge and Daniel Ferrer (Cambridge: Cambridge University Press, 1984), 4.

46. Claude Lévi-Strauss, *The Savage Mind* (Chicago: Chicago University Press, 1966), 3.

47. Benjamin Lee Whorf, *Language, Thought, and Reality* (Cambridge, MA: MIT Press, 1956), 240.

48. Eugene Jolas, *Transition* (April and May, 1938).

49. Umberto Eco, *The Aesthethics of Chaosmos: The Middle Ages of James Joyce*, trans. Ellen Escrock (Cambridge, MA: Harvard University Press, 1989), 84–85.

50. William Irwin Thompson, *The Time Falling Bodies Take to Light: Mythology, Sexuality, and the Origin of Culture* (New York: St. Martin's Press, 1981), 214.

51. R. T. Rundle Clark, *Myth and Symbol in Ancient Egypt* (London: Thames and Hudson, 1978), 266.

52. Giambattista Vico, *The New Science*, trans. Thomas Goddard Bergin and Max Harold Fisch (Ithaca: Cornell University Press, 1948), 375.

53. John Bishop, *Joyce's Book of the Dark* (Madison: University of Wisconsin Press, 1986), 177.

54. Jacques Derrida, *Speech and Phenomena and Other Essays on Husserl's Theory of Signs*, trans. David B. Allison (Evanston: Northwestern University Press, 1973), 137.

55. William Paulson, "Literature, Complexity, Interdisciplinarity," in *Chaos and Order: Complex Dynamics in Literature and Science*, ed. N. Katherine Hayles (Chicago: University of Chicago Press, 1991), 40, 46.

56. See Murray Gell-Mann, Yuval Ne'eman, *The Eight-Fold Way* (New York, Amsterdam: W.A. Benjamin, 1964), a collection of technical papers.

57. Interview with John Bell in *The Ghost in the Atom*, eds. P. C. W. Davies and J. R. Brown (Cambridge: Cambridge University Press, 1986), 48.

58. David Bohm, *Wholeness and the Implicate Order* (London: Ark Paperbacks, 1980), 3. See Philip Kuberski, *The Persistence of Memory: Organism, Myth, Text* (Berkeley: University of California Press, 1992),115–30, for the holographic aspects of Proust's *Remembrance of Things Past.*

59. P. C. W. Davies and J. R. Brown, *The Ghost in the Atom*, 46.

60. See Winston E. Kock, *Laser and Holography: An Introduction to Coherent Optics* (New York: Dover, 1981).

61. Werner Heisenberg, *Physics and Beyond*, 101.

62. *A Buddhist Bible*, ed. Dwight Goddard (Boston: Beacon Press, 1970), 296.

63. James Lovelock, *Gaia: A New Look at Life on Earth* (Oxford: Oxford University Press, 1979), vii.

III ᠀— The Chaosmic Self

1. Peter Goodchild, *J. Robert Oppenheimer: Shatterer of Worlds* (New York: Fromm, 1985), 162.

2. The *Brihadaranyaka Upanishad*, with commentary by Shankaracharya, trans. Swami Madhvananda (Calcutta: Advaita Ashrama, 1965), VII.1–3. All subsequent citations of this *Upanishad* will follow Chapter, Section, and Verse, as noted here.

3. Jacques Lacan, *Ecrits: A Selection*, trans. Alan Sheridan (New York: Norton, 1977), 107. Unless otherwise indicated, all Lacan citations are taken from this volume.

4. Sigmund Freud, *Beyond the Pleasure Principle*, trans. James Strachey (New York: Norton, 1961), 9.

5. T.S. Eliot, *Collected Poems: 1909–1962* (New York: Harcourt Brace, 1963).

6. Hugh Kenner, *The Pound Era* (Berkeley: University of California Press, 1971), 110.

7. Martin Heidegger, *Being and Time*, trans. John Maquarrie and Edward Robinson (New York: Harper and Row, 1962), 27.

8. Jacques Derrida, *The Post Card: From Socrates to Freud and Beyond*, trans. Alan Bass (Chicago: University of Chicago Press, 1987), 358.

9. See Roger-Pol Droit, *L'amnesie philosophique* (Paris: Presses Universitaires de France, 1989).

10. Henry David Thoreau, *Walden* (Harmondsworth: Penguin, 1986), 396.

11. For deconstructive readings, see Harriet Davidson, *T. S. Eliot and Hermeneutics* (Baton Rouge: Louisiana State University Press, 1981), and Gregory Jay, *T. S. Eliot and the Poetics of Literary History* (Baton Rouge: Louisiana State University Press, 1983).

12. See Harold Bloom's introduction to Harold Bloom and David Rosenberg, *The Book of J* (New York: Vintage, 1991), 9–55.

13. David Trotter, "Modernism and Empire: Reading *The Waste Land*," *Critical Quarterly*, 28, nos. 1 & 2 (1987), 146.

14. See T.S. Eliot, *The Idea of a Christian Society* (New York: Harcourt, 1940), and *Notes Toward a Definition of Culture* (New York: Harcourt, 1948).

15. See I.A. Richards, "Mr Eliot's Poem," *New Statesman* 26 (1926): 548–85; and F.R. Leavis, *New Bearings in English Poetry* (Ann Arbor: University of Michigan Press, 1960).

16. *The Sacred Books of the East*, translated by various Oriental scholars, was first published by the Clarendon Press, Oxford University, beginning with F. Max Müller's translation of *The Upanishads* in 1884, and continued into the twentieth century. *The Harvard Oriental Series*, including Henry Clarke Warren's *Buddhism: In Translations* and supported by his bequest, was begun in the last years of the nineteenth century and continues to publish translations.

17. See *The Works of Sir William Jones*, vol. 3 (London: 1807), 85–204.

18. Murray B. Emeneau, *Language and Linguistic Area*, ed. Anwar S. Dil (Stanford, CA: Stanford University Press, 1980), 26.

19. Paul Deussen, *The Philosophy of the Upanishads*, trans. A. S. Geden (New York: Dover, 1966), 41.

20. Henry Clarke Warren, *Buddhism: In Translations* (New York: Atheneum, 1963; originally published, 1896), 134.

21. For a discussion of the Indian aspects of *The Waste Land*, see Eloise Knapp Hay, *T. S. Eliot's Negative Way* (Cambridge, MA: Harvard University Press, 1982).

22. T. S. Eliot, *Selected Essays* (New York: Harcourt, Brace, 1952), 10.

23. *The Brihadaranyaka Upanishad*, 4.

24. James N. Powell, *The Tao of Symbols* (New York: Quill, 1982), 42.

25. Raimundo Pannikar, *The Vedic Experience* (Berkeley: University of California, Press, 1980), 101.

26. Jacques Lacan, *Ecrits: A Selection*, 7.

27. See John P. Muller and William J. Robinson, *Lacan and Language: A Reader's Guide to Ecrits* (New York: International University Press, 1982).

28. Aldous Huxley, *The Perennial Philosophy* (New York: Harper and Brothers, 1945), 1–21.

29. F. Max Müller, *The Upanishads*, 135.

30. G. W. F. Hegel, *The Phenomenology of Spirit*, trans. A. V. Miller (Oxford: Oxford University Press, 1977), 49–52.

31. *A Buddhist Bible*, ed. Dwight Goddard, 282.

32. Jacques Lacan, *The Four Fundamentals of Psychoanalysis*, trans. Alan Sheridan (New York: Norton, 1979), 10. Afterwards abbreviated as FF.

33. Jacques Lacan and the *école freudienne, Feminine Sexuality*, ed. Juliet Mitchell and Jacqueline Rose; trans. Jacqueline Rose (New York: Norton, 1982). All citations in the text are from 146–47.

34. Jacques Lacan, *Ecrits: A Selection*, 122.

35. John Drew, *India and the Romantic Imagination* (Dehli: Oxford University Press, 1987), 122–23.

36. Edward W. Said, *Orientalism* (New York: Vintage Books, 1979).

37. Krishna Chaitanya, *Sanskrit Poetics* (London: Asia Publishing House, 1965), 120.

38. E. M. Forster, *A Passage to India* (New York: Harcourt, Brace, 1924), 124.

39. Paul Armstrong, "Reading India: E. M. Forster and the Politics of Interpretation," *Twentieth Century Literature* vol. 38, no. 4 (Winter 1992), 367.

40. Jacques Lacan, *Feminine Sexuality*, 146–47.

41. See V. A. Shahane, "Mrs. Moore's Experience in the Marabar Caves: A Zen Buddhist Perspective," *Twentieth Century Literature*, vol. 31. nos. 2 & 3 (Summer/Fall 1985): 279–86.

42. See *Language: An Inquiry into Meaning and Function*, ed. Ruth Nanda Ansen (New York: Harpers, 1957), 81.

43. See the introduction to *The Upanishads*, trans. Swami Prabhavananda and Frederick Manchester 1948).

44. Lionel Trilling, "A Passage to India," in *Modern Critical Interpretations: A Passage to India*, ed. Harold Bloom (New York: Chelsea, 1987), 23.

45. Edward W. Said, *Orientalism*, 244.

46. Rustom Bharucha, "Forster's Friends," in *Modern Critical Interpretations: A Passage to India*, 103.

47. Frederick von Schlegel, *The Philosophy of Life and the Philosophy of Language*, trans. A. J. W. Morrison (London: Henry G. Bohn, 1847), 392.

48. Paul de Man, *Blindness and Insight*, rev. ed. (Minneapolis: University of Minnesota Press, 1983), 218, 219.

49. John Drew, *India and the Romantic Imagination*, 38.

IV ᴗ— *Chaosmoi*

1. Michel Foucault, *The Order of Things: An Archaeology of the Human Sciences* (New York: Vintage Books, 1973), 387.

2. Jacques Derrida, *Of Grammatology*, trans. Gayatri Chakravorty Spivak (Baltimore: Johns Hopkins University Press, 1976), 5; *Writing and Difference*, trans. Alan Bass (Chicago: University of Chicago Press, 1978), 293.

3. Theodor W. Adorno, *Negative Dialectics*, trans. E. B. Ashton (New York: Continuum, 1973), 3.

4. For an analysis of the organic, and more specifically, the botanical aspects of Derrida's work, see Claudette Sartiliot, *Herbarium/Verbarium: The Discourse of Flowers* (Lincoln: University of Nebraska Press, 1993).

5. Cited in Gary Zukav, *The Dancing Wu Li Masters: An Overview of the New Physics* (New York: Bantam, 1979), 39.

6. Werner Heisenberg, *Physics and Philosophy* (New York: Harper Torchbooks, 1962), 41.

7. Ibid., 71–72.

8. G. W. F. Hegel, *The Phenomenology of Spirit*, trans. A. V. Miller (Oxford: Oxford University Press, 1977), 5.

9. Martin Heidegger, *Being and Time*, trans. John Maquarrie and Edward Robinson (New York: Harper and Row, 1962), 297.

10. Jacques Derrida, "Les morts de Roland Barthes," *Psyché: Inventions de l'autre* (Paris: Galilée, 1987), 280 (my translation).

11. Jacques Derrida, *Schibboleth* (Paris: Galilée, 1986), 96 (my translation).

12. Jacques Derrida, *Speech and Phenomena and Other Essays on Husserl's Theory of Signs*, trans. David B. Allison (Evanston: Northwestern University Press, 1973), 96–97.

13. Ibid., 102.

14. William Paulson, "Literature, Complexity, Interdisciplinarity," in *Chaos and Order: Complex Dynamics in Literature and Science*, ed. N. Katherine Hayles (Chicago: University of Chicago Press, 1991), 47.

15. See Gregory Ulmer, *Applied Grammatology* (Baltimore: Johns Hopkins University Press, 1985), and Claudette Sartiliot, *Citation and Modernity: Derrida, Joyce, Brecht* (Norman: Oklahoma University Press, 1993).

16. Martin Heidegger, *The Question Concerning Technology and Other Essays*, trans. William Lovitt (New York: Harper Torchbooks, 1977), 34.

17. E. H. Gombrich, *The Story of Art* (Oxford: Phaidon, 1984), 34.

18. E. A. Wallis Budge, *The Gods of the Egyptians: Or Studies in Egyptian Mythology*, vol. 1 (New York: Dover, 1969; originally pub. 1904), 301.

19. Norman Mailer, *Ancient Evenings* (Boston: Little, Brown, 1983); *Advertisements for Myself* (New York: Putnam, 1959), 107.

20. Harold Bloom, "Norman in Egypt," *New York Review of Books* (April 28, 1983), 4.

21. Richard Poirier, "In Pyramid and Palace," reprinted in *Critical Essays on Norman Mailer*, ed. J. Michael Lennon (Boston: G.K. Hall & Co., 1986), 84.

22. John T. Irwin, *American Hieroglyphics: The Symbol of the Egyptian Hieroglyphics in the American Renaissance* (Baltimore: Johns Hopkins University Press, 1980).

23. Jacques Derrida, "Scribble (Writing-Power)," *Yale French Studies*, vol. 58 (1979), 138.

24. Jean-Paul Sartre, *Being and Nothingness*, trans. Hazel Barnes (New York: Philosophical Library, 1953), 338–39.

25. Julia Kristeva, *Powers of Horror: An Essay on Abjection*, trans. Leon S. Roudiez (New York: Columbia University Press, 1982), 2.

26. Jacques Derrida, *Glas*, trans. John P. Leavey, Jr., and Richard Rand (Lincoln: University of Nebraska Press, 1986), 87b.

27. James Merrill, *The Changing Light at Sandover* (New York: Atheneum, 1982), 446.

28. Peter Sacks, "The Divine Translation: Elegiac Aspects of *The Changing Light at Sandover*," in *James Merrill: Essays in Criticism*, ed. David Lehman and Charles Berger (Ithaca: Cornell University Press, 1983), 159.

29. Harold Bloom, *The Anxiety of Influence* (New York: Oxford University Press, 1973), 140–41.

30. C. A. Buckley, "Exploring *The Changing Light at Sandover:* An Interview with James Merrill," *Twentieth Century Literature*, vol. 38, no. 4 (Winter 1992): 420.

31. Henry Pierce Stapp, cited in Gary Zukav, *The Dancing Wu Li Masters: An Overview of the New Physics*, 72.

32. Lancelot Law Whyte, *Essay On Atomism: From Democritus to 1960* (New York: Harper Torchbooks, 1963), 16.

33. C. A. Buckley, "Exploring *The Changing Light at Sandover:* An Interview with James Merrill," 432.

34. Peter Sacks, "The Divine Translation: Elegiac Aspects of *The Changing Light at Sandover*," in *James Merrill: Essays in Criticism*.

35. Doris Lessing, *Canopus in Argos: Archives* (New York: Knopf, 1979–83).

36. Doris Lessing, *Shikasta* (New York: Knopf, 1979), "Introduction," ix.

37. Carey Kaplan, "Britain's Imperial Past in Lessing's Futurist Fiction," in *Doris Lessing: The Alchemy of Survival*, ed. Carey Kaplan and Ellen Cronan Rose (Columbia, OH: Ohio State University Press, 1988), 149–58.

38. Doris Lessing, *Shikasta*, "Introduction," x.

39. Doris Lessing, *The Making of the Representative for Planet 8*, (New York: Knopf, 1982), 66, 68.

40. C. A. Buckley, "Exploring *The Changing Light at Sandover:* An Interview with James Merrill," 421.

Conclusion

1. Paul Davies, *God and the New Physics* (New York: Simon and Schuster, 1983), 171, 205.

2. See John Gribbin and Martin Rees, *Cosmic Coincidences: Dark Matter, Mankind, and Anthropic Cosmology* (New York: Bantam Books, 1989), 11.

3. See William Irwin Thompson, *Pacific Shift* (San Francisco: Sierra Books, 1986).

4. Gregory Bateson, *Mind and Nature: A Necessary Unity* (New York: Dutton, 1979), 14.

5. Hugh Kenner, *The Pound Era* (Berkeley: University of California Press, 1971), 145–146.

℃—Index